Learning Swift
Second Edition

Develop the skills required to create compelling,
maintainable, and robust iOS and OS X apps with Swift

Andrew J Wagner

BIRMINGHAM - MUMBAI

Learning Swift
Second Edition

First published: June 2015

Second edition: March 2016

Production reference: 1170316

Published by Packt Publishing Ltd.
Livery Place
35 Livery Street
Birmingham B3 2PB, UK.

ISBN 978-1-78588-751-2

www.packtpub.com

Credits

Author
Andrew J Wagner

Reviewer
Guan Gui

Commissioning Editor
Kartikey Pandey

Acquisition Editors
Vivek Anantharaman

Chaitanya Nair

Content Development Editor
Viranchi Shetty

Technical Editor
Saurabh Malhotra

Copy Editors
Kevin McGowan

Sneha Singh

Project Coordinator
Izzat Contractor

Proofreader
Safis Editing

Indexer
Hemangini Bari

Production Coordinator
Shantanu N. Zagade

Cover Work
Shantanu N. Zagade

About the Author

Andrew J Wagner is a software developer who concentrates on iOS development and backend web services. He has a degree in computer engineering from Rensselaer Polytechnic Institute, New York. Currently, he works for a development shop named Chronos Interactive based in Denver, CO. He has experience of working with and for large-scale and small-scale companies, as well as running his own contracting and app companies. He is passionate about using computers as a creative outlet and writing software that is beautiful in implementation, functionality, and experience.

When he isn't working or spending time with friends and family, he writes for his blog at `http://drewag.me`.

I would like to thank my friends and family for being there for me as support for both my troubles and triumphs. Without their encouragement, I would not have finished this book or achieved any of the other things in my life that make me proud. An especially big thanks to my parents, Fern and Joe, for continually providing me with the tools I need to do the things I love.

About the Reviewer

Guan Gui graduated from the University of Melbourne. He implemented the first system of its kind for beekeepers using satellite sensory data to help them deploy their honeybees better. He is also a big fan of Apple. He started his own open source project—Uni Call (`unicall.guiguan.net`) for OS X. While his research focus is on machine learning, he enjoys the more practical side of CS: developing apps using Swift and JavaScript. Currently, he is trying to set his own start-up. Big ideas to change the world always spin in his head!

www.PacktPub.com

eBooks, discount offers, and more

Did you know that Packt offers eBook versions of every book published, with PDF and ePub files available? You can upgrade to the eBook version at www.PacktPub.com and as a print book customer, you are entitled to a discount on the eBook copy. Get in touch with us at customercare@packtpub.com for more details.

At www.PacktPub.com, you can also read a collection of free technical articles, sign up for a range of free newsletters and receive exclusive discounts and offers on Packt books and eBooks.

https://www2.packtpub.com/books/subscription/packtlib

Do you need instant solutions to your IT questions? PacktLib is Packt's online digital book library. Here, you can search, access, and read Packt's entire library of books.

Why subscribe?

- Fully searchable across every book published by Packt
- Copy and paste, print, and bookmark content
- On demand and accessible via a web browser

Table of Contents

Preface

This book will help you to get started with Swift in no time. It helps you understand the nuances of iOS programming not only from a conceptual but also from an implementation perspective. This book is an invaluable resource if you are looking forward to exploring the world of iOS application programming.

What this book covers

Chapter 1, *Introducing Swift*, will take the reader through the process of installing Swift and running their first Swift program, in order to expose its power right away.

Chapter 2, *Building Blocks - Variables, Collections, and Flow Control*, introduces you to the various built-in mechanisms Swift has for representing complex information in expressive and accessible ways, with the help of a real-world example.

Chapter 3, *One Piece at a Time - Types, Scopes, and Projects*, introduces the tools necessary to closely model the real world with code. It will teach you how to define your own custom types using structures, classes, and enumerations. It also explores the concept of scope and access control.

Chapter 4, *To Be or Not To Be - Optionals*, focuses on a special and critical type in Swift, called optionals. It includes a detailed explanation of how optionals work and how they can be used, which turns a seemingly complex topic into a very intuitive concept.

Chapter 5, *A Modern Paradigm - Closures and Functional Programming*, introduces you to a new way of thinking about code called functional programming. We learn how Swift supports this technique and how we can apply it to our programs to make it even more understandable and expressive.

Chapter 6, *Make Swift Work For You - Protocols and Generics*, describes what generics and protocols are and how they can provide power and safety at the same time.

Chapter 7, Everything Is Connected - Memory Management, dives deeper into the inner-workings of Swift. We discuss how a computer stores information and how we can use that knowledge in combination with some new tools in Swift, to ensure that our code remains responsive and minimizes its effect on battery life.

Chapter 8, Paths Less Traveled – Error Handling, goes into gracefully handling error situations in Swift with error throwing and catching.

Chapter 9, Writing Code the Swift Way - Design Patterns and Techniques, introduces the reader to the art of programming by taking them through a number of specific design patterns that help reduce the complexity of code.

Chapter 10, Harnessing the Past - Understanding and Translating Objective-C, develops a basic understanding of Objective-C with a focus on how it compares to Swift. This allows the reader to make use of the vast resources that exist in Objective-C to help with their Swift development.

Chapter 11, A Whole New World - Developing an App, focuses on explaining the process of creating a real world iOS application, with the help of an example.

Chapter 12, What's Next? - Resources, Advice, and the Next Steps, discusses how to move forward to become the best app developer you possibly can. It provides a list of resources and advice the reader can use to continue their Swift and app development learning process.

What you need for this book

To run the code in this book, you will need Xcode 7.2.

Who this book is for

If you want to build iOS or OS X apps using the most modern technology, this book is ideal for you. *Learning Swift* will place you into a small developer community that will explode in demand when all the development for Apple's platforms transitions to it. You will find this book especially useful if you are new to programming or if you have yet to develop for iOS or OS X.

Conventions

In this book, you will find a number of text styles that distinguish between different kinds of information. Here are some examples of these styles and an explanation of their meaning.

When mentioning pieces of code in text we will use the style as follows: "You can see that "Hello, playground" was indeed stored in the variable.

If the code is longer it will presented as a block as follows:

```
if invitees.count > 20 {
    println("Too many people invited")
}
else if invitees.count <= 3 {
    println("Not really a party")
}
else {
    println("Just right")
}
```

New terms and **important words** are shown in bold. Words that you see on the screen, for example, in menus or dialog boxes, appear in the text like this: "Now, click on **Connect** on the **Remote Desktop Viewer**". Keyboard shortcuts will be displayed using the *key* style.

Reader feedback

Feedback from our readers is always welcome. Let us know what you think about this book—what you liked or disliked. Reader feedback is important for us as it helps us develop titles that you will really get the most out of.

To send us general feedback, simply e-mail feedback@packtpub.com, and mention the book's title in the subject of your message.

If there is a topic that you have expertise in and you are interested in either writing or contributing to a book, see our author guide at www.packtpub.com/authors.

Customer support

Now that you are the proud owner of a Packt book, we have a number of things to help you to get the most from your purchase.

Downloading the example code

You can download the example code files for this book from your account at http://www.packtpub.com. If you purchased this book elsewhere, you can visit http://www.packtpub.com/support and register to have the files e-mailed directly to you.

You can download the code files by following these steps:

1. Log in or register to our website using your e-mail address and password.
2. Hover the mouse pointer on the **SUPPORT** tab at the top.
3. Click on **Code Downloads & Errata**.
4. Enter the name of the book in the **Search** box.
5. Select the book for which you're looking to download the code files.
6. Choose from the drop-down menu where you purchased this book from.
7. Click on **Code Download**.

Once the file is downloaded, please make sure that you unzip or extract the folder using the latest version of:

* WinRAR/7-Zip for Windows
* Zipeg/iZip/UnRarX for Mac
* 7-Zip/PeaZip for Linux

Downloading the color images of this book

We also provide you with a PDF file that has color images of the screenshots/ diagrams used in this book. The color images will help you better understand the changes in the output. You can download this file from `http://www.packtpub.com/sites/default/files/downloads/LearningSwiftSecondEdition_ColorImages.pdf`.

Errata

Although we have taken every care to ensure the accuracy of our content, mistakes do happen. If you find a mistake in one of our books—maybe a mistake in the text or the code—we would be grateful if you could report this to us. By doing so, you can save other readers from frustration and help us improve subsequent versions of this book. If you find any errata, please report them by visiting `http://www.packtpub.com/submit-errata`, selecting your book, clicking on the **Errata Submission Form** link, and entering the details of your errata. Once your errata are verified, your submission will be accepted and the errata will be uploaded to our website or added to any list of existing errata under the Errata section of that title.

To view the previously submitted errata, go to `https://www.packtpub.com/books/content/support` and enter the name of the book in the search field. The required information will appear under the **Errata** section.

Piracy

Piracy of copyrighted material on the Internet is an ongoing problem across all media. At Packt, we take the protection of our copyright and licenses very seriously. If you come across any illegal copies of our works in any form on the Internet, please provide us with the location address or website name immediately so that we can pursue a remedy.

Please contact us at `copyright@packtpub.com` with a link to the suspected pirated material.

We appreciate your help in protecting our authors and our ability to bring you valuable content.

Questions

If you have a problem with any aspect of this book, you can contact us at `questions@packtpub.com`, and we will do our best to address the problem.

1
Introducing Swift

What are you trying to achieve by reading this book? Learning Swift can be fun, but most of us are trying to achieve something bigger. There is something we want to create, a career we want to follow, or maybe something else entirely. Whatever that goal is, I encourage you to keep it in mind as you read this book. It will be much easier for you to learn, from this or any other resource, if you can always relate it to your goal.

With that in mind, before we dive into learning Swift, we have to understand what it really is and how it will help us in achieving our goals. We also need to move forward with an effective learning technique and get a taste of what is to come. To do all of that, we will cover the following topics in this chapter:

- Defining our goals for this book
- Setting up the development environment
- Running our first Swift code
- Understanding playgrounds
- Learning with this book

Defining our goals for this book

Swift is a programming language developed by Apple primarily to allow developers to continue to push their platforms forward. It is their attempt to make iOS, OS X, watchOS, and tvOS app development more modern, safe, and powerful.

However, Apple has also released Swift as Open Source and begun an effort to add support for Linux with the intent to make Swift even better and a general purpose programming language available everywhere. Some developers have already begun using it to create command-line scripts as a replacement/supplement of the existing scripting languages, such as Python or Ruby and many can't wait to be able to share some of their app code with Web backend code. Apple's priority, at least for now, is to make it the best language possible, to facilitate app development. However, the most important thing to remember is that modern app development almost always requires pulling together multiple platforms into a single-user experience. If a language could bridge those gaps and stay enjoyable to write, safe, and performant, we would have a much easier time making amazing products. Swift is well on its way to reach that goal.

Now, it is important to note that learning Swift is only the first step towards developing. To develop for a device, you must learn the programming language and the frameworks the device maker provides. Being skilled with a programming language is the foundation of getting better at using frameworks and ultimately building apps.

Developing software is like building a table. You can learn the basics of woodworking and nail a few pieces of wood together to make a functional table, but you are very limited in what you can do because you lack advanced woodworking skills. If you want to make a truly great table, you need to step away from the table and focus first on developing your skill set. The better you are at using the tools, the greater the number of possibilities that open up to you to create a more advanced and higher quality piece of furniture. Similarly, with a very limited knowledge of Swift, you can start to piece together a functional app from the code you find online. However, to really make something great, you have to put the time and effort into refining your skill set with the language. Every language feature or technique that you learn opens up more possibilities for your app.

That being said, most developers are driven by a passion to create things and solve problems. We learn best when we can channel our passions into truly improving ourselves and the world around us. We don't want to get stuck learning the minutia of a language with no practical purpose.

The goal of this book is to develop your skills and confidence to dive passionately into creating compelling, maintainable, and elegant apps in Swift. To do that, we will introduce the syntax and features of Swift in a practical way. You will build a rich toolset, while seeing that toolset put to real world usage. So, without further ado, let's jump right into setting up our development environment.

Setting up the development environment

In order to use Swift, you will need to run OS X, the operating system that comes with all Macs. The only piece of software that you will need is called **Xcode** (version 7 and higher). This is the environment that Apple provides, which facilitates development for its platforms. You can download Xcode for free from the Mac App Store at www.appstore.com/mac/Xcode.

Once downloaded and installed, you can open the app and it will install the rest of Apple's developer tool components. It is as simple as that! We are now ready to run our first piece of Swift code.

Running our first swift code

We will start by creating a new Swift playground. As the name suggests, a playground is a place where you can play around with code. With Xcode open, navigate to **File | New | Playground...** from the menu bar, as shown in the following screenshot:

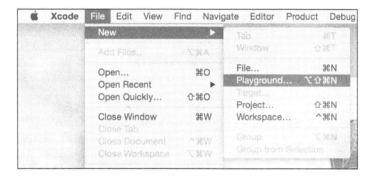

Name it MyFirstPlayground, leave the platform as **iOS**, and save it wherever you wish.

Once created, a playground window will appear with some code already populated inside it for you:

You have already run your first Swift code. A playground in Xcode runs your code every time you make a change and shows you the code results in the sidebar, on the right-hand side of the screen.

Let's break down what this code is doing. The first line is a comment that is ignored while being run. It can be really useful in adding extra information about your code inline with it. In Swift, there are two types of comments: single-line and multi-line. Single-line comments, such as the preceding one, always start with a //. You can also write comments that span multiple lines by surrounding them with /* and */. For example:

```
/*
   This is a multi-line comment
   that takes up more than one line
   of code
*/
```

As you can see in the preceding screenshot, the second line, `import UIKit`, imports a framework called UIKit. UIKit is the name of Apple's framework for iOS development. For this example, we are not actually making use of the UIKit framework so it is safe to completely remove that line of code.

Finally, on the last line, the code defines a variable called `str` that is being assigned to the text `"Hello, playground"`. In the results sidebar, next to that line, you can see that `"Hello, playground"` was indeed stored in the variable. As your code becomes more complex, this will become incredibly useful to help you track and watch the state of your code, as it is run. Every time you make a change to the code, the results will update, showing you the consequences of the change.

If you are familiar with other programming languages, many of them require some sort of line terminator. In Swift, you do not need anything like that.

The other great thing about Xcode playgrounds is that they will show you errors as you type them in. Let's add a third line to the playground:

```
var str = "Something Else"
```

On its own, this is completely valid Swift code. It stores the text `"Something Else"` into a new variable called `str`. However, when we add this to the playground, we are shown an error in the form of a red exclamation mark next to the line number. If you click on the exclamation mark, you will be shown the full error:

This line is highlighted in red and we are shown the **Invalid redeclaration of 'str'** error. This is because you cannot declare two different variables with the exact same name. Also, notice that the results along the right turned gray instead of black. This indicates that the result being shown is not from the latest code, but the last successful run of the code. The code cannot be successfully run to create a new result because of the error. If we change the second variable to strTwo, the error goes away:

Downloading the example code

You can download the example code files for this book from your account at http://www.packtpub.com. If you purchased this book elsewhere, you can visit http://www.packtpub.com/support and register to have the files e-mailed directly to you.

You can download the code files by following these steps:

- Log in or register to our website using your e-mail address and password.
- Hover the mouse pointer on the SUPPORT tab at the top.
- Click on Code Downloads & Errata.
- Enter the name of the book in the Search box.
- Select the book for which you're looking to download the code files.
- Choose from the drop-down menu where you purchased this book from.
- Click on Code Download.

Once the file is downloaded, please make sure that you unzip or extract the folder using the latest version of:

- WinRAR/7-Zip for Windows
- Zipeg/iZip/UnRarX for Mac
- 7-Zip/PeaZip for Linux

Now the results are shown in black again, and we can see that they have been updated according to the latest code. Especially if you have experience with other programming environments, the reactiveness of the playground may be surprising to you. Let's take a peek under the hood to get a better understanding of what is happening and how Swift works.

Understanding playgrounds

A playground is not truly a program. While it does execute code like a program, it is not really useful outside of the development environment. Before we can understand what the playground is doing for us, we must first understand how Swift works.

Swift is a compiled language, which means that for Swift code to be run, it must first be converted into a form that the computer can actually execute. The tool that does this conversion is called a **compiler**. A compiler is actually a program and it is also a way to define a programming language.

The Swift compiler takes the Swift code as input and, if it can properly parse and understand the code, outputs machine code. Apple developed the Swift compiler to understand the code according to a series of rules. Those rules are what define the Swift programming language and those rules are what we are trying to learn, when we say we are learning Swift.

Once the machine code is generated, Xcode can wrap the machine code up inside an app that users can run. However, we are running Swift code inside our playground, so clearly building an app is not the only way to run code; something else is going on here.

Every time you make a change to a playground, it automatically tries to compile your code. If it is successful, instead of wrapping up the machine code in an app to be run later, it runs the code immediately and shows you the results. If you had to do this process yourself, you would first have to consciously make the decision to build the code into an app and then run it when you wanted to test something. This would be a huge waste of time; especially, if you write an error that you don't catch until the moment you decide to actually run it. The quicker you can see the result of a code change, the faster you will be at developing the code and the fewer mistakes you will make.

For now, we will be developing all of our code inside a playground because it is a fantastic learning environment. Playgrounds are even more powerful than what we have seen so far and we will see that as we explore deeper into the Swift language.

We are just about ready to get to the meat of learning Swift, but first let's take a moment to make sure that you can get the most out of this book.

Learning with this book

The learning process of this book follows very closely to the philosophy behind playgrounds. You will get the most out of this book if you play around with the code and ideas that we discuss. Instead of just passively reading through this, glancing at the code, put the code into a playground, and observe how it really works. Make changes to the code, try to break it, try to extend it, and you will learn far more. If you have a question, don't default to looking up the answer, try it out.

At its core, programming is a creative exercise. Yes, it requires the ability to think logically through a problem, but nine times out of ten there is no *right way* there is no correct answer. Technology is pushed by those of us who won't settle for the accepted solution, who aren't OK with following a fixed set of instructions, who want to push the boundaries. As we move forward in learning Swift, make this book and Swift work for you by not taking everything at face value.

Summary

We're off to a good start. We've gone over how Swift is a language designed primarily for app development, which often includes multiple different platforms. We already ran our first code and learned a little bit about how a computer runs it indirectly by first compiling it into a form it understands how to run. Most importantly, we've learned that you will learn best from this book by having a goal to work towards and by playing around with the concepts as you read along. So let's get started!

Next, we will start breaking down the basics of Swift and then put them together to make our first program.

2
Building Blocks – Variables, Collections, and Flow Control

One of the coolest things about programming is the way that concepts build on each other. If you've never programmed anything before, even the most basic app can seem very complex. The reality is that, if you analyze everything going on in an app down to the ones and zeros flowing through the processor, it is incredibly complex. However, every aspect of using a computer is an abstraction. When you use an app, the complexity of the programming is being abstracted away for you. Learning to program is just going one level deeper in making a computer work for you.

As you learn the basic concepts behind programming, they will become second nature and this will free your mind to grasp even more complex concepts. When you first learn to read, sounding out each word is challenging. However, eventually, you reach a level where you glance at a word and you know the meaning instantaneously. This frees you up to start looking for deeper meaning from the text.

In this chapter, we will build up your knowledge of the building blocks of programming in Swift. Each of these building blocks is exciting on its own and they will become even more exciting as we start to see the possibilities they open up. No matter how complex programming might seem to you now, I guarantee that one day you will look back and marvel at how all of these concepts have become second nature.

In this chapter, we will cover:

- Core Swift types
- Swift's type system
- Printing to the console
- Controlling the flow of your program
- A comprehensive example of all concepts covered

Core Swift types

Every programming language needs to name a piece of information so that it can be referenced later. This is the fundamental way in which code remains readable after it is written. Swift provides a number of core types that help you represent your information in a very comprehensible way.

Constants and variables

Swift provides two types of information: a **constant** and a **variable**:

```
// Constant
let pi = 3.14

// Variable
var name = "Sarah"
```

All constants are defined using the `let` keyword followed by a name, and all variables are defined using the `var` keyword. Both constants and variables in Swift must contain a value before they are used. This means that, when you define a new one, you will most likely give it an initial value. You do so by using the assignment operator (=) followed by a value.

The only difference between the two is that a constant can never be changed, whereas a variable can be. In the preceding example, the code defines a constant called `pi` that stores the information `3.14` and a variable called `name` that stores the information `"Sarah"`. It makes sense to make `pi` a constant because `pi` will always be `3.14`. However, we need to change the value of `name` in the future so we defined it as a variable.

One of the hardest parts of managing a program is the state of all the variables. As a programmer, it is often impossible to calculate all the different possible values a variable might have, even in relatively small programs. Since variables can often be changed by distant, seemingly unrelated code, more states will cause more bugs that are harder to track down. It is always best to default to using constants until you run into a practical scenario in which you need to modify the value of the information.

Containers

It is often helpful to give a name to more complex information. We often have to deal with a collection of related information or a series of similar information like lists. Swift provides three main collection types called **tuples**, **arrays**, and **dictionaries**.

Tuples

A tuple is a fixed sized collection of two or more pieces of information. For example, a card in a deck of playing cards has three properties: color, suit, and value. We could use three separate variables to fully describe a card, but it would be better to express it in one:

```
var card = (color: "Red", suit: "Hearts", value: 7)
```

Each piece of information consists of a name and a value separated by a colon (:) and each is separated by a comma (,). Finally, the whole thing is surrounded by parentheses (()).

Each part of a tuple can be accessed separately by name using a period (.), otherwise referred to as a dot:

```
card.color // "Red"
card.suit // "Hearts"
card.value // 7
```

You are also able to create a tuple with no names for each part of it. You can then access them based on where they are in the list, starting with zero as the first element:

```
var diceRoll = (4, 6)
diceRoll.0 // 4
diceRoll.1 // 6
```

Another way to access specific values in a tuple is to capture each of them in a separate variable:

```
let (first, second) = diceRoll
first // 4
second // 6
```

If you want to change a value in a tuple, you can assign every value at once or you can update a single value, using the same reference as in the preceding code:

```
diceRoll = (4, 5)
diceRoll.0 = 2
```

Arrays

An array is essentially a list of information of variable length. For example, we could create a list of people we want to invite to a party, as follows:

```
var invitees = ["Sarah", "Jamison", "Marcos", "Roana"]
```

An array always starts and ends with a square bracket and each element is separated by a comma. You can even declare an empty array with open and closing brackets: `[]`.

You can then add values to an array by adding another array to it, like this:

```
invitees += ["Kai", "Naya"]
```

Note that `+=` is the shorthand for the following:

```
invitees = invitees + ["Kai", "Naya"]
```

You can access values in an array based on their position, usually referred to as their index, as shown:

```
invitees[2] // Marcos
```

The index is specified using square brackets (`[]`) immediately after the name of the array. Indexes start at `0` and go up from there like tuples. So, in the preceding example, index `2` returned the third element in the array, `Marcos`. There is additional information you can retrieve about an array, like the number of elements that you can see as we move forward.

Dictionaries

A dictionary is a collection of **keys** and **values**. Keys are used to store and look up specific values in the container. This container type is named after a word dictionary in which you can look up the definition of a word. In that real life example, the word would be the key and the definition would be the value. As an example, we can define a dictionary of television shows organized by their genre:

```
var showsByGenre = [
    "Comedy": "Modern Family",
    "Drama": "Breaking Bad",
]
```

A dictionary looks similar to an array but each key and value is separated by a colon (`:`). Note that Swift is pretty forgiving with how whitespace is used. The array could be defined with each element on its own line and the dictionary could be defined with every element on a single line. It is up to you to use whitespace to make your code as readable as possible.

With the dictionary defined as shown above, you would get the value `Modern Family` if you looked up the key `Comedy`. You access a value in code similar to how you would in an array but, instead of providing an index in the square brackets, you provide the key:

```
showsByGenre["Comedy"] // Modern Family
```

You can define an empty dictionary in a similar way to an empty array but with a dictionary you must also include a colon between the brackets: `[:]`.

Adding a value to a dictionary is similar to retrieving a value but you use the assignment operator (=):

```
showsByGenre["Variety"] = "The Colbert Report"
```

As a bonus, this can also be used to change the value for an existing key.

You might have noticed that all of my variable and constant names begin with a lower case letter and each subsequent word starts with a capital letter. This is called camel case and it is the widely accepted way of writing variable and constant names. Following this convention makes it easier for other programmers to understand your code.

Now that we know about Swift's basic containers, let's explore what they are in a little more detail.

Swift's type system

Swift is a strongly typed language, which means that every constant and variable is defined with a specific **type**. Only values of matching types can be assigned to them. So far, we have taken advantage of a feature of Swift called **Type Inference.** This means that the code does not have to explicitly declare a type if it can be inferred from the value being assigned to it during the declaration.

Without Type Inference, the `name` variable declaration from before would be written as follows:

```
var name: String = "Sarah"
```

This code is explicitly declaring `name` as the type `String` with the value `Sarah`. A constant or variable's type can be specified by adding a colon (`:`) and a type after its name.

A string is defined by a series of characters. This is perfect for storing text, as in our name example. The reason that we don't need to specify the type is that `Sarah` is a **string literal**. Text surrounded by quotation marks is a string literal and can be inferred to be of the type `String`. That means that `name` must be of the type `String` if you make its initial value `Sarah`.

Similarly, if we had not used type inference for our other variable declarations, they would look like this:

```
let pi: Double = 3.14

var invitees: [String] = ["Sarah", "Jamison", "Roana"]

let showsByGenre: [String:String] = [
    "Comedy": "Modern Family",
    "Drama": "Breaking Bad",
]
```

`Double` is a numeric type that can store decimal numbers. An array's type is declared by putting the type of element it stores in square brackets. Finally, a dictionary's type is defined in the form `[KeyType:ValueType]`. All of these types can be inferred because each of them is assigned to a value that has an inferable type.

The code is much cleaner and easier to understand if we leave the types out as the original examples showed. Just keep in mind that these types are always implied to be there, even if they are not written explicitly. If we tried to assign a number to the `name` variable, we would get an error, as shown:

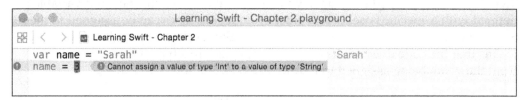

Here, we are trying to assign a number, specifically an `Int`, to a variable that was inferred to be a `String`. Swift does not allow that.

When dealing with inferred types, it is extremely useful to ask Xcode what type a variable is inferred to be. You can do this by holding down the *Option* key on your keyboard and clicking on the variable name. This will display a pop-up that looks like this:

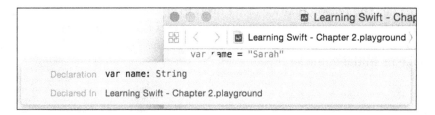

As was expected, the variable was indeed inferred to be of the type `String`.

Types are an integral part of Swift. They are one of the major reasons that Swift is so safe as a programming language. They help the compiler learn more about your code and, because of that, the compiler can warn you about bugs automatically without even running your code.

Printing to the console

It is very useful to write output to a log so that you can trace the behavior of code. As a codebase grows in complexity, it gets hard to follow the order in which things happen and exactly what the data looks like as it flows through the code. Playgrounds help a lot with this but it is not always enough.

In Swift, this process is called printing to the console. To do this, you use something called `print`. It is used by writing `print` followed by text surrounded by parentheses. For example, to print `Hello World!` to the console, the code would look like this:

```
print("Hello World!")
```

If you put that code in a playground, you would see `Hello World!` written in the results pane. However, this is not truly the console. To view the console, you can go to **View | Debug Area | Show Debug Area**. A new view will appear at the bottom of the window and it will contain all text the code has printed to the console:

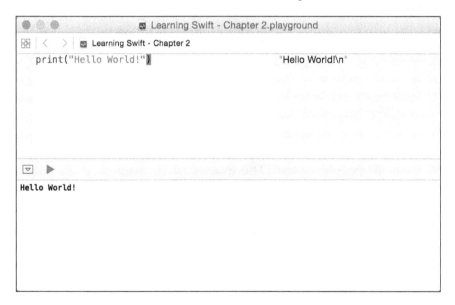

Not only can you print static text to the console, you can also print out any variable. For example, if you wanted to print out the name variable, you would write:

```
print(name)
```

You can even use a feature of Swift called **string interpolation** to insert variables into a string, like this:

```
print("Hello \(name)!")
```

At any point in a string literal, even when not printing, you can insert the results of the code by surrounding the code with \(and). Normally this would be the name of a variable but it could be any code that returns a value.

Printing to the console is even more useful when we start using more complex code.

Control flow

A program wouldn't be very useful if it were a single fixed list of commands that always did the same thing. With a single code path, a calculator app would only be able to perform one operation. There are a number of things we can do to make an app more powerful and collect the data to make decisions as to what to do next.

Conditionals

The most basic way to control the flow of a program is to specify code that should only be executed if a certain condition is met. In Swift, we do that with an if statement. Let's look at an example:

```
if invitees.count > 20 {
    print("Too many people invited")
}
```

Semantically, the preceding code reads; if the number of invitees is greater then 20, print 'Too many people invited". This example only executes one line of code if the condition is true, but you can put as much code as you like inside the curly brackets ({}).

Anything that can be evaluated as either true or false can be used in an if statement. You can then chain multiple conditions together using an else if and/or an else:

```
if invitees.count > 20 {
    print("Too many people invited")
}
else if invitees.count <= 3 {
```

```
        print("Not really a party")
    }
    else {
        print("Just right")
    }
```

Each condition is checked from top to bottom until a condition is satisfied. At that point, the code block is executed and the remaining conditions are skipped, including the final `else` block.

As an exercise, I recommend adding an additional scenario to the preceding code in which, if there were exactly zero invitees, it would print "One is the loneliest number". You can test out your code by adjusting how many invitees you add to the `invitees` declaration. Remember that the order of the conditions is very important.

As useful as conditionals are, they can become very verbose if you have a lot of them chained together. To solve this type of problem, there is another control structure called a **switch.**

Switches

A switch is a more expressive way of writing a series of `if` statements. A direct translation of the example from the conditionals section would look like this:

```
switch invitees.count {
    case let x where x > 20:
        print("Too many people invited")
    case let x where x <= 3:
        print("Not really a party")
    default:
        print("Just right")
}
```

A switch consists of a value and a list of conditions for that value with the code to execute if the condition is true. The value to be tested is written immediately after the `switch` command and all of the conditions are contained in curly brackets (`{}`). Each condition is called a **case**. Using that terminology, the semantics of the preceding code is "Considering the number of invitees, in the case that it is greater than 20, print "`Too many people invited`", otherwise, in the case that it is less than or equal to three, print "`Too many people invited`", otherwise, by default print "`Just right`".

This works by creating a temporary constant x that is given the value that the switch is testing. It then performs a test on x. If the condition passes, it executes the code for that case and then exits the switch.

Just like in conditionals, each case is only considered if all of the previous cases are not satisfied. Unlike conditionals, all the cases need to be exhaustive. That means that you need to have a case for every possible value that the variable being passed in could be. For example, `invitees.count` is an integer, so it could theoretically be any value from negative infinity to positive infinity.

The most common way to handle that is by using a default case as designated by the `default` keyword. Sometimes, you don't actually want to do anything in the default case, or possibly even in a specific case. For that, you can use the `break` keyword, as shown here:

```
switch invitees.count {
    case let x where x > 20:
        print("Too many people invited")
    case let x where x <= 3:
        print("Not really a party")
    default:
        break
}
```

Note that the default case must always be the last one.

We have seen so far that switches are nice because they enforce the condition of being exhaustive. This is great for letting the compiler catch bugs for you. However, switches can also be much more concise. We can rewrite the preceding code like this:

```
switch invitees.count {
    case 0...3:
        print("Not really a party")
    case 4...20:
        print("Just right")
    default:
        print("Too many people invited")
}
```

Here, we have described each case as a range of possible values. The first case includes all of the values between and including 0 and 3. This is way more expressive than using a `where` clause. This example also shows a rethinking of the logic. Instead of having a case specific for values over 20, we have cases for the closed ranges that we know and then capture everything for the case above 20 in the default case. Note that this version of the code does not properly handle the situation in which the count might be negative, whereas the original version did. In this version, if the count were -1, it would fall all the way through to the default case and print out `"Too many people invited"`. For this use case, it is fine because the count of an array can never be negative.

Switches don't only work with numbers. They are great for performing any type of test:

```
switch name {
    case "Marcos", "Amy":
        print("\(name) is an honored guest")
    case let x where x.hasPrefix("A"):
        print("\(name) will be invited first")
        fallthrough
    default:
        print("\(name) is someone else")
}
```

This code shows some other interesting features of switches. The first case is actually made up of two separate conditions. Each case can have any number of conditions separated by commas (,). This is useful when you have multiple cases that you want to use the same code for.

The second case uses a custom test on the name to see if it starts with the letter A. This is great for demonstrating the way in which switches are executed. Even though the string Amy would satisfy the second condition, this code would only print, Amy is an honored guest because the other cases are not evaluated once the first case is satisfied. For now, don't worry if you don't understand completely how hasPrefix works.

Lastly, the second case uses the fallthrough keyword. This tells the program to execute the code in the following case. Importantly, this bypasses the next case's condition; it does not matter if the value passes the condition, the code is still executed.

To make sure that you understand how a switch is executed, put the following code into a playground and try to predict what will be printed out with various names:

```
let testName = "Andrew"
switch testName {
    case "Marcos", "Amy":
        print("\(testName) is an honored guest")
    case let x where x.hasPrefix("A"):
        print("\(testName) will be invited first")
        fallthrough
    case "Jamison":
        print("\(testName) will help arrange food")
    default:
        print("\(testName) is someone else")
}
```

Some good names to try are `Andrew`, `Amy`, and `Jamison`.

Now we have full control over which code we want executed in which circumstances. However, a program often requires that we execute the same code more than once. For example, if we want to perform an operation on every element in an array, it would not be viable to copy and paste a bunch of code. Instead, we can use control structures called **loops**.

Loops

There are many different types of loops but all of them execute the same code repeatedly until a condition is no longer true. The most basic type of loop is called a `while` loop:

```
var index = 0
while index < invitees.count {
    print("\(invitees[index]) is invited")

    index+=1
}
```

A `while` loop consists of a condition to test and code to be run until that condition fails. In the preceding example, we have looped through every element in the `invitees` array. We used the variable `index` to track which invitee we were currently on. To move to the next index, we used a new operator `+=` which added one to the existing value. This is the same as writing `index = index + 1`.

There are two important things to note about this loop. Firstly, our index starts at `0`, not `1`, and it goes on until it is less than the number of invitees, not less than or equal to them. This is because, if you remember, array indexes start at `0`. If we started at `1` we would miss the first element and, if we included `invitees.count`, the code would crash because it would try to access an element beyond the end of the array. Always remember: *the last element of an array is at the index one less than the count.*

The other thing to note is that, if we were to forget to include `index+=1` in the loop, we would have an infinite loop. The loop would continue to run forever because `index` would never go beyond `invitees.count`.

This pattern of wanting to loop through a list is so common that there is a more concise and safe loop called a **for-in** loop:

```
for invitee in invitees {
    print("\(invitee) is invited")
}
```

Now this is getting pretty cool. We no longer have to worry about indexes. There is no risk of accidentally starting at 1 or going past the end. Also, we get to give our own name to the specific element as we go through the array. One thing to note is that we did not declare the `invitee` variable with `let` or `var`. This is particular to a `for-in` loop because the constant used there is newly declared each time through the loop.

`for-in` loops are great for looping through different types of containers. They can also be used to loop through a dictionary, as shown:

```
for (genre, show) in showsByGenre {
    print("\(show) is a great \(genre) series")
}
```

In this case, we get access to both the key and the value of the dictionary. This should look familiar because `(genre, show)` is actually a tuple used for each iteration through the loop. It may be confusing to determine whether or not you have a single value from a `for-in` loop like arrays or a tuple like dictionaries. At this point, it would be best for you to remember just these two common cases. The underlying reasons will become clear when we start talking about **sequences** in *Chapter 6, Make Swift Work For You – Protocols and Generics.*

Another feature of `for-in` loops is the ability to only loop through elements that pass a given test. You could achieve this with an `if` statement but Swift provides a more concise way of writing it using the `where` keyword:

```
for invitee in invitees where invitee.hasPrefix("A") {
    print("\(invitee) is invited")
}
```

Now, the loop will only be run for each of the invitees that start with the letter A.

These loops are great but sometimes we need access to the index we are currently on and, at other times, we may want to loop through a set of numbers without an array. To do this, we can use a range similar to a `Switch`, as shown:

```
for index in 0 ..< invitees.count {
    print("\(index): \(invitees[index])")
}
```

This code runs the loop using the variable `index` from the value 0 up to but not including `invitees.count`. There are actually two types of ranges. This one is called a **half open range** because it does not include the last value. The other type of range, which we saw with switches, is called a **closed range**:

```
print("Counting to 10:")
for number in 1 ... 10 {
    print(number)
}
```

The closed range includes the last value so that the loop will print out every number starting with 1 and ending with 10.

All loops have two special keywords that let you modify their behavior, which are called `continue` and `break`. `continue` is used to skip the rest of the loop and move back to the condition to see whether or not the loop should be run again. For example, if we didn't want to print out invitees whose name began with A, we would use the following:

```
for invitee in invitees {
    if invitee.hasPrefix("A") {
        continue
    }
    print("\(invitee) is invited")
}
```

If the condition `invitee.hasPrefix("A")` were satisfied, the continue command would be run and it would skip the rest of the loop, moving onto the next invitee. Because of this, only invitees not starting with A would be printed.

The `break` keyword is used to immediately exit a loop:

```
for invitee in invitees {
    print("\(invitee) is invited")

    if invitee == "Tim" {
        print("Oh wait, Tim can't come")
        break
    }
}
print("Jumps here")
```

As soon as a break is encountered, the execution jumps to after the loop. In this case, it jumps to the final line.

Loops are great for dealing with variable amounts of data, like our list of invitees. When writing your code, you probably won't know how many people will be in that list. Using a loop gives you the flexibility to handle a list of any length.

As an exercise, I recommend you try writing a loop to find the sum of all the multiples of 3 under 10,000. You should get 16,668,333.

Loops are also a great way of reusing code without duplicating it but they are just the first step towards quality code reuse. Next, we will talk about functions, which opens up a whole new world of writing understandable and reusable code.

Functions

All of the code we have explored so far is very linear down the file. Each line is processed one at a time and then the program moves onto the next. This is one of the great things about programming: everything the program does can be predicted by stepping through the program yourself mentally, one line at a time.

However, as your program gets larger, you will notice that there are places that reuse very similar or identical code that you cannot reuse by using loops. Moreover, the more code you write, the harder it becomes to know exactly what it is doing. Code comments can help with that but there is an even better solution to both of these problems and they're called **functions**. A function is essentially a named collection of code that can be executed and reused by using that name.

There are various different types of functions but each builds on the previous type.

Basic functions

The most basic type of function simply has a name with some static code to be executed later. Let's look at a simple example. The following code defines a function named sayHello:

```
func sayHello() {
    print("Hello World!")
}
```

Functions are defined using the keyword func followed by a name and parentheses (()). The code to be run in the function is surrounded by curly brackets ({}). Just like in loops, a function can consist of any number of lines of code.

From our knowledge of printing, we know that this function will print out the text Hello World!. However, when will it do that? The terminology used for telling a function to execute is "calling a function." You call a function by using its name followed by parentheses (()):

```
sayHello() // Prints "Hello World!"
```

This is a very simple function that is not that useful but we can already see some pretty great benefits of functions. In reality, what happens when you call this function is that the execution moves into the function and, when it has finished executing every line of the function, it exits out and continues on from where the function was called. However, as programmers, we are often not concerned with what is happening inside a function unless something has gone wrong. If functions are named well, they tell you what they will do and that is all you need to know to follow the rest of the code. In fact, well-named functions can almost always take the place of comments in your code. This really reduces clutter without harming the legibility of your code.

The other advantage this function has over using `print` directly is that the code becomes more maintainable. If you use `print` in multiple places in your code and then change your mind about how you want to say `Hello`, you have to change a lot of code. However, if you use a function like the one above, you can easily change how it says `Hello` by changing the function and it will then be changed in each place you use that function.

You may have noticed some similarity in how we have named our `sayHello` function and how we used `print`. This is because `print` is a function that is built into Swift itself. There is complex code in the `print` function that makes printing to the console possible and accessible to all programmers. But hey, `print` is able to take in a value and do something with it, how do we write a function like that? The answer is: parameters.

Parameterized functions

A function can take zero or more parameters, which are input values. Let's modify our `sayHello` function to be able to say `Hello` to an arbitrary name using string interpolation:

```
func sayHelloToName(name: String) {
    print("Hello \(name)!")
}
```

Now our function takes in an arbitrary parameter called `name` of the type `String` and prints `hello` to it. The name of this function is now `sayHelloToName:`. We didn't include the parameter name because, when you call the method, you don't use the first parameter's name by default:

```
sayHelloToName("World") // Prints "Hello World!"
```

We included a colon (:) at the end of the name to indicate that it takes a parameter there. This makes it different from a function named `sayHelloToName` that does not take a parameter. The naming may seem unimportant and arbitrary but it is very important that we are all able to communicate about our code using common and precise terminology, so that we can more effectively learn from and collaborate with each other.

As mentioned before, a function can take more than one parameter. A parameter list looks a lot like a tuple. Each parameter is given a name and a type separated by a colon (:), and these are then separated by commas (,). On top of that, functions can not only take in values but can also return values to the calling code.

Functions that return values

The type of value to be returned from a function is defined after the end of all of the parameters separated by an arrow ->. Let's write a function that takes a list of invitees and one other person to add to the list. If there are spots available, the function adds the person to the list and returns the new version. If there are no spots available, it just returns the original list, as shown here:

```
func addInviteeToListIfSpotAvailable
    (
    invitees: [String],
    newInvitee: String
    )
    -> [String]
{
    if invitees.count >= 20 {
        return invitees
    }
    return invitees + [newInvitee]
}
```

In this function, we tested the number of names on the invitee list and, if it was greater than 20, we returned the same list as was passed in to the `invitees` parameter. Note that `return` is used in a function in a similar way to `break` in a loop. As soon as the program executes a line that returns, it exits the function and provides that value to the calling code. So, the final `return` line is only run if the `if` statement does not pass. It then adds the `newinvitee` parameter to the list and returns that to the calling code.

You would call this function like so:

```
var list = ["Sarah", "Jamison", "Marcos"]
var newInvite = "Roana"
list = addInviteeToListIfSpotAvailable(list, newInvite: newInvitee)
```

It is important to note that we must assign `list` to the value returned from our function because it is possible that the new value will be changed by the function. If we did not do this, nothing would happen to the list.

If you try typing this code into a playground, you will notice something very cool. As you begin typing the name of the function, you will see a small pop-up that suggests the name of the function you might want to type, as shown:

You can use the arrow keys to move up and down the list to select the function you want to type and then press the *Tab* key to make Xcode finish typing the function for you. Not only that, but it highlights the first parameter so that you can immediately start typing what you want to pass in. When you are done defining the first parameter, you can press *Tab* again to move on to the next parameter. This greatly increases the speed with which you can write your code.

This is a pretty well-named function because it is clear what it does. However, we can give it a more natural and expressive name by making it read more like a sentence:

```
func addInvitee
    (
    invitee: String,
    ifPossibleToList invitees: [String]
    )
    -> [String]
{
    if invitees.count >= 20 {
        return invitees
    }
    return invitees + [invitee]
}
list = addInvitee(newInvite, ifPossibleToList: list)
```

This is a great feature of Swift that allows you to have a function called with **named parameters**. We can do this by giving the second parameter two names, separated by a space. The first name is the one to be used when calling the function, otherwise referred to as the **external name**. The second name is the one to be used when referring to the constant being passed in from within the function, otherwise referred to as the **internal name**. As an exercise, try to change the function so that it uses the same external and internal names and see what Xcode suggests. For more of a challenge, write a function that takes a list of invitees and an index for a specific invitee to write a message to ask them to just bring themselves. For example, it would print `Sarah, just bring yourself` for the index `0` in the preceding list.

Functions with default arguments

Sometimes we write functions where there is a parameter that commonly has the same value. It would be great if we could provide a value for a parameter to be used if the caller did not override that value. Swift has a feature for this called **default arguments**. To define a default value for an argument, you simply add an equal sign after the argument, followed by the value. We can add a default argument to the `sayHelloToName:` function, as follows:

```
func sayHelloToName(name: String = "World") {
    print("Hello \(name)!")
}
```

This means that we can now call this function with or without specifying a name:

```
sayHelloToName("World") // Prints "Hello World!"
sayHelloToName() // Also Print "Hello World!"
```

When using default arguments, the order of the arguments becomes unimportant. We can add default arguments to our `addInvitee:ifPossibleToList:` function and then call it with any combination or order of arguments:

```
func addInvitee
    (
    invitee: String = "Default Invitee",
    ifPossibleToList invitees: [String] = []
    )
    -> [String]
{
    // ...
}
list = addInvitee(ifPossibleToList: list, newInvite)
list = addInvitee(newInvite, ifPossibleToList: list)
list = addInvitee(ifPossibleToList: list)
list = addInvitee(newInvite)
list = addInvitee()
```

Clearly, the call still reads much better when it is written in the same order but not all functions are designed in that way. The most important part of this feature is that you can specify only the arguments that you want to be different from the defaults.

Guard statement

The last feature of functions that we are going to discuss is another type of conditional called a **guard statement**. We have not discussed it until now because it doesn't make much sense unless it is used in a function or loop. A guard statement acts in a similar way to an `if` statement but the compiler forces you to provide an `else` condition that must exit from the function, loop, or switch case. Let's rework our `addInvitee:ifPossibleToList:` function to see what it looks like:

```
func addInvitee
    (
    invitee: String,
    ifPossibleToList invitees: [String]
    )
    -> [String]
{
```

```
    guard invitees.count < 20 else {
        return invitees
    }
    return invitees + [newInvitee]
}
```

Semantically, the guard statement instructs us to ensure that the number of invitees is less than 20 or else return the original list. This is a reversal of the logic we used before, when we returned the original list if there were 20 or more invitees. This logic actually makes more sense because we are stipulating a prerequisite and providing a failure path. The other nice thing about using the guard statement is that we can't forget to return out of the `else` condition. If we do, the compiler will give us an error.

It is important to note that guard statements do not have a block of code that is executed if it passes. Only an `else` condition can be specified with the assumption that any code you want to run for the passing condition will simply come after the statement. This is safe only because the compiler forces the `else` condition to exit the function and, in turn, ensures that the code after the statement will not run.

Overall, guard statements are a great way of defining preconditions to a function or loop without having to indent your code for the passing case. This is not a big deal for us yet but, if you have lots of preconditions, it often becomes cumbersome to indent the code far enough to handle them.

Bringing it all together

At this point, we have learned a lot about the basic workings of Swift. Let's take a moment to bring many of these concepts together in a single program. We will also see some new variations on what we have learned.

The goal of the program is to take a list of invitees and a list of television shows and ask random people to bring a show from each genre. It should also ask the rest to just bring themselves.

Before we look at the code, I will mention the three small new features that I will use:

- Generating a random number
- Using a variable to store only true or false
- Repeat-while loops

The most important feature is the ability to generate a random number. To do this, we have to import the `Foundation` framework. This is the most basic framework made available by Apple. As the name suggests, it forms the basis of the framework for both OS X and iOS.

`Foundation` includes a function called `rand` that returns a random number. Computers are actually not capable of generating truly random numbers and, by default, `rand` always returns the same values in the same order. To make it return different values each time the program is run, we use a function called `srand` that stands for seed random. Seeding random means that we provide a value for `rand` on which to base its first value. A common way of seeding the random number is using the current time. We will use a method called `clock` that is also from `Foundation`.

Lastly, `rand` returns a number anywhere from 0 to a very large number but, as you will see, we want to restrict the random number to between 0 and the number of invitees. To do this, we use the remainder operator (`%`). This operator gives you the remainder after dividing the first number by the second number. For example, 14 % 4 returns 2 because 4 goes into 14, 3 times with 2 left over. The great feature of this operator is that it forces a number of any size to always be between 0 and 1 less than the number you are dividing by. This is perfect for changing all of the possible random values.

The full code for generating a random number looks like this:

```
// Import Foundation so that "rand" can be used
import Foundation

// Seed the random number generator
srand(UInt32(clock()))

// Random number between 0 and 9
var randomNumber = Int(rand()) % 10
```

You may notice one other thing about this code. We are using new syntax `UInt32()` and `Int()`. This is a way of changing one type into another. For example, the `clock` function returns a value of the type `clock_t` but `srand` takes a parameter of the type `UInt32`. Remember, just like with variables, you can hold the option key and click on a function to see what types it takes and returns.

The second feature we will use a variable that can store only true or false. This is called a `Bool`, which is short for Boolean. We have used this type many times before as it is used in all conditionals and loops but this is the first time that we will store a `Bool` directly in a variable. At its most basic level, a Boolean variable is defined and used like this:

```
var someBool = false
if someBool {
    print("Do This")
}
```

Note that we can use the Boolean directly in a conditional. This is because a Boolean is the exact type a conditional is expecting. All of our other tests like `<=` actually result in a `Bool`.

Lastly, the third feature we will use is a variation of the `while` loop called a **repeat-while** loop. The only difference with a `repeat-while` loop is that the condition is checked at the end of the loop instead of at the beginning. This is significant because, unlike with a `while` loop, a `repeat-while` loop will always be executed at least once, as shown:

```
var inviteeIndex: Int
repeat {
    inviteeIndex = Int(rand()) % 5
} while inviteeIndex != 3
```

With this loop, we will continue to generate a random number between 0 and 4 until we get a number that does not equal 3.

Everything else in the code builds off the concepts we already know. I recommend that you read through the code and try to understand it. Try to not only understand it from the perspective of how it works but why I wrote it in that way. I included comments to help explain both what the code is doing and why it is written in that way:

```
// Import Foundation so that "rand" can be used
import Foundation

// Seed the random number generator
srand(UInt32(clock()))
```

```
// ----------------------------
// Input Data
// ----------------------------

// invitees
//
// Each element is a tuple which contains a name
// that is a String and a Bool for if they have been
// invited yet. It is a variable because we will be
// tracking if each invitee has been invited yet.

var invitees = [
    (name: "Sarah", alreadyInvited: false),
    (name: "Jamison", alreadyInvited: false),
    (name: "Marcos", alreadyInvited: false),
    (name: "Roana", alreadyInvited: false),
    (name: "Neena", alreadyInvited: false),
]


// showsByGenre
//
// Constant because we will not need to modify
// the show list at all
let showsByGenre = [
    "Comedy": "Modern Family",
    "Drama": "Breaking Bad",
    "Variety": "The Colbert Report",
]
```

This first section of code gives us a localized place in which to put all of our data. We can easily come back to the program and change the data if we want and we don't have to go searching through the rest of the program to update it:

```
// ----------------------------
// Helper functions
// ----------------------------

// inviteAtIndex:toBringShow:
//
// Another function to help make future code
// more comprehensible and maintainable
func inviteAtIndex
    (
```

```
        index: Int,
        toBringShow show: (genre: String, name: String)
        )
    {
        let name = invitees[index].name
        print("\(name), bring a \(show.genre) show")
        print("\(show.name) is a great \(show.genre)")

        invitees[index].alreadyInvited = true
    }

    // inviteToBringThemselvesAtIndex:
    //
    // Similar to the previous function but this time for
    // the remaining invitees
    func inviteToBringThemselvesAtIndex(index: Int) {
        let invitee = invitees[index]
        print("\(invitee.name), just bring yourself")

        invitees[index].alreadyInvited = true
    }
```

Here, I have provided a number of functions that simplify more complex code later on in the program. Each one is given a meaningful name so that, when they are used, we do not have to go and look at their code to understand what they are doing:

```
    // ----------------------------
    // Now the core logic
    // ----------------------------

    // First, we want to make sure each genre is assigned
    // to an invitee
    for show in showsByGenre {
        // We need to pick a random invitee that has not
        // already been invited. With the following loop
        // we will continue to pick an invitee until we
        // find one that has not already been invited
        var inviteeIndex: Int
        repeat {
            inviteeIndex = Int(rand()) % invitees.count
        } while invitees[inviteeIndex].alreadyInvited
```

```
        // Now that we have found an invitee that has not
        // been invited, we will invite them
        inviteAtIndex(inviteeIndex, toBringShow: (show))
    }

    // Now that we have assigned each genre, we
    // will ask the remaining people to just bring
    // themselves
    for index in 0 ..< invitees.count {
        let invitee = invitees[index]
        if !invitee.alreadyInvited {
            inviteToBringThemselvesAtIndex(index)
        }
    }
}
```

This last section contains the real logic of the program, which is commonly referred to as the **business logic**. The functions from the previous section are just details and the final section is the logic that really defines what the program does.

This is far from the only way to organize a program. This will become even clearer as we learn more advanced organization techniques. However, this breakdown shows you the general philosophy behind how you should organize your code. You should strive to write every piece of code as if it were going to be published in a book. Many of the comments in this example will become excessive as you get better with Swift but, when in doubt, explain what you are doing using either a comment or a well-named function. Not only will it help others understand your code, it will also help you understand it when you come back to it in six months and you are a stranger to the code again. Not only that, if you force yourself to formalize your thoughts as you write the code, you will find yourself creating a lot less bugs.

Let's also look at an interesting limitation of this implementation. This program is going to run into a major problem if the number of invitees is less than the number of shows. The repeat-while loop will continue forever, never finding an invitee that was not invited. Your program doesn't have to handle every possible input but you should at least be aware of its limitations.

Summary

In this chapter, we have developed a great basis for Swift knowledge. We have learned about the various built-in mechanisms Swift has for representing complex information in expressive and accessible ways. We know that, by default, we should declare information as a constant until we find a practical need to change it, and then we should make it a variable. We have explored how every piece of information in Swift has a type associated with it by the compiler, whether it is through type inference or declared explicitly. We are familiar with many of the built-in types, including simple types like `String`, `Int`, and `Bool` as well as containers like tuples, arrays, and dictionaries. We can use the console output to better investigate our programs, especially by using string interpolation for dynamic output. We recognize the power of controlling the flow of our programs with `if` statements, conditionals, switches, and loops. We have functions in our skill set to write more legible, maintainable, and reusable code. Finally, we have seen an example of how all of these concepts can be combined to write a full program.

As a challenge to you, I suggest you fix the final program so that it stops trying to assign shows if there are not enough invitees. When you can do that, you are more than ready to move on to the next topic, which is **types**, **scopes**, and **projects**.

These are all tools that we can use to write even more organized code and they will become more critical as we write larger and larger projects.

3
One Piece at a Time – Types, Scopes, and Projects

In *Chapter 2, Building Blocks – Variables, Collections, and Flow Control*, we developed a very simple program that helped organize a party. Even though we separated parts of the code in a logical way, everything was written in a single file and our functions were all lumped together. As projects grow in complexity, this way of organizing code is not sustainable. In the same way we use functions to separate out logical components in our code at scale, we also need to be able to separate out the logical components of our functions and data. To do this, we can define code in different files and we can also create our own types that contain custom data and functionality. These types are commonly referred to as **objects**, as a part of the programming technique called **object-oriented programming**. In this chapter we will cover the following:

- Structs
- Classes and inheritance
- Enumerations
- Projects
- Extensions
- Scope
- Access control

Structs

The most basic way that we can group together data and functionality into a logical unit or object is to define something called a **structure**. Essentially, a structure is a named collection of data and functions. Actually, we have already seen several different structures because all of the types such as string, array, and dictionary that we have seen so far are structures. Now we will learn how to create our own.

Types versus instances

Let's jump straight into defining our first structure to represent a contact:

```
struct Contact {
    var firstName: String = "First"
    var lastName: String = "Last"
}
```

Here we have created a structure by using the `struct` keyword followed by a name and curly brackets ({}) with code inside them. Just like with a function, everything about a structure is defined inside its curly brackets. However, code in a structure is not run directly, it is all part of defining what the structure is. Think of a structure as a specification for future behavior instead of code to be run, in the same way that blueprints are the specification for building a house.

Here, we have defined two variables for the first and last name. This code does not create any actual variables nor does it remember any data. As with a function, this code is not truly used until another piece of code uses it. Just like with a string, we have to define a new variable or constant of this type. However, in the past we have always used literals like `Sarah` or `10`. With our own structures, we will have to *initialize* our own *instances*, which is just like building a house based on the specifications.

An instance is a specific incarnation of a type. This could be when we create a `String` variable and assign it the value `Sarah`. We have created an instance of a `String` variable that has the value `Sarah`. The string itself is not a piece of data; it simply defines the nature of instances of String that actually contain data.

Initializing is the formal name for creating a new instance. We initialize a new `Contact` like this:

```
let someone = Contact()
```

You may have noticed that this looks a lot like calling a function and that is because it is very similar. Every type must have at least one special function called an **initializer**. As the name implies, this is a function that initializes a new instance of the type. All initializers are named after their type and they may or may not have parameters, just like a function. In our case, we have not provided any parameters so the first and last names will be left with the default values that we provided in our specification: First and Last.

You can see this in a playground by clicking on the plus sign next to **Contact** to the right of that line. This inserts a result pane after the line where it displays the value of firstName and lastName. We have just initialized our first custom type!

If we define a second contact structure that does not provide default values, it changes how we call the initializer. Since there are no default values, we must provide the values when initializing it:

```
struct Contact2 {
    var firstName: String
    var lastName: String
}

let someone2 = Contact2(firstName: "Sarah", lastName: "Smith")
```

Again, this looks just like calling a function that happens to be named after the type that we defined. Now, someone2 is an instance of Contact2 with firstName equal to Sarah and lastName equal to Smith.

Properties

The two variables, firstName and lastName, are called **member variables** and, if we change them to be constants, they are then called **member constants**. This is because they are pieces of information associated with a specific instance of the type. You can access member constants and variables on any instance of a structure:

```
print("\(someone.firstName) \(someone.lastName)")
```

This is in contrast to a **static constant**. We could add a static constant to our type by adding the following line to its definition:

```
struct Contact {
    static let UnitedStatesPhonePrefix = "+1" // "First Last"
}
```

Note the `static` keyword before the constant declaration. A static constant is accessed directly from the type and is independent of any instance:

```
print(Contact.UnitedStatesPhonePrefix) // "+1"
```

Note that we will be adding code to existing code every so often like this. If you are following along in a playground, you should have added the `static let` line to the existing `Contact` structure.

Member and static constants and variables all fall under the category of **properties**. A property is simply a piece of information associated with an instance or a type. This helps reinforce the idea that every type is an object. A ball, for example, is an object that has many properties including its radius, color, and elasticity. We can represent a ball in code in an object-oriented way by creating a ball structure that has each of those properties:

```
struct Ball {
    var radius: Double
    var color: String
    var elasticity: Double
}
```

Note that this `Ball` type does not define default values for its properties. If default values are not provided in the declaration, they are required when initializing an instance of the type. This means that an empty initializer is not available for that type. If you try to use one, you will get an error:

```
Ball() // Missing argument for parameter 'radius' in call
```

Just like with normal variables and constants, all properties must have a value once initialized.

Member and static methods

Just as you can define constants and variables within a structure, you can also define **member** and static functions. These functions are referred to as **methods** to distinguish them from global functions that are not associated with any type. You declare member methods in a similar way to functions but you do so inside the type declaration, as shown:

```
struct Contact {
    var firstName: String = "First"
    var lastName: String = "Last"
```

```swift
    func printFullName() {
        print("\(self.firstName) \(self.lastName)")
    }
}
```

Member methods always act on a specific instance of the type they are defined in. To access that instance within the method, you use the `self` keyword. `Self` acts in a similar way to any other variable in that you can access properties and methods on it. The preceding code prints out the `firstName` and `lastName` properties. You call this method in the same way we called methods on any other type:

```swift
someone.printFullName()
```

Within a normal structure method, `self` is constant, which means you can't modify any of its properties. If you tried, you would get an error like this:

```swift
struct Ball {
    var radius: Double
    var color: String
    var elasticity: Double

    func growByAmount(amount: Double) {
        // Error: Left side of mutating operator
        // isn't mutable: 'self' is immutable
        self.radius += amount
    }
}
```

In order for a method to modify `self`, it must be declared as a **mutating method** using the `mutating` keyword:

```swift
mutating func growByAmount(amount: Double) {
    self.radius += amount
}
```

We can define static properties that apply to the type itself but we can also define **static methods** that operate on the type by using the `static` keyword. We can add a static method to our `Contact` structure that prints the available phone prefixes, as shown here:

```swift
struct Contact {
    static let UnitedStatesPhonePrefix = "+1"

    static func printAvailablePhonePrefixes() {
```

```
        print(self.UnitedStatesPhonePrefix)
    }
}
```

```
Contact.printAvailablePhonePrefixes() // "+1"
```

In a static method, `self` refers to the type instead of an instance of the type. In the preceding code, we have used the `UnitedStatesPhonePrefix` static property through `self` instead of writing out the type name.

In both static and instance methods, Swift allows you to access properties without using `self`, for brevity. `self` is simply implied:

```
func printFullName() {
    print("\(firstName) \(lastName)")
}
```

```
static func printAvailablePhonePrefixes() {
    print(UnitedStatesPhonePrefix)
}
```

However, if you create a variable in the method with the same name, you will have to use `self` to distinguish which one you want:

```
func printFirstName() {
    let firstName = "Fake"
    print("\(self.firstName) \(firstName)") // "First Fake"
}
```

I recommend avoiding this feature of Swift. I want to make you aware of it so you are not confused when looking at other people's code but I feel that always using `self` greatly increases the readability of your code. `self` makes it instantly clear that the variable is attached to the instance instead of only defined in the function. You could also create bugs if you add code that creates a variable that hides a member variable. For example, you would create a bug if you introduced the `firstName` variable to the `printFullName` method in the preceding code without realizing you were using `firstName` to access the member variable later in the code. Instead of accessing the member variable, the later code would start to only access the local variable.

Computed properties

So far, it seems that properties are used to store information and methods are used to perform calculations. While this is generally true, Swift has a feature called **computed properties**. These are properties that are calculated every time they are accessed. To do this, you define a property and then provide a method called a **getter** that returns the calculated value, as shown:

```
struct Ball {
    var radius: Double
    var diameter: Double {
        get {
            return self.radius * 2
        }
    }
}

var ball = Ball(radius: 2)
print(ball.diameter) // 4.0
```

This is a great way to avoid storing data that could potentially conflict with other data. If, instead, `diameter` were just another property, it would be possible for it to be different to the `radius`. Every time you changed the radius you would have to remember to change the diameter. Using a computed property eliminates this concern.

You can even provide a second function called a **setter** that allows you to assign a value to this property like normal properties:

```
var diameter: Double {
    get {
        return self.radius * 2
    }
    set {
        self.radius = diameter / 2
    }
}

var ball = Ball(radius: 2)
ball.diameter = 16
print(ball.radius) // 8.0
```

If you provide a setter then you must also explicitly provide a getter. If you don't, Swift allows you to leave out the `get` syntax:

```swift
var volume: Double {
    return self.radius * self.radius * self.radius * 4/3 * 4.13
}
```

This provides a nice concise way of defining read-only computed properties.

Reacting to property changes

It is pretty common to need to perform an action whenever a property is changed. One way to achieve this is to define a computed property with a setter that performs the necessary action. However, Swift provides a better way of doing this. You can define a `willSet` function or a `didSet` function on any stored property. `willSet` is called just *before* the property is changed and it is provided with a variable `newValue`. `didSet` is called just *after* the property is changed and it is provided with a variable `oldValue`, as you can see here:

```swift
var radius: Double {
    willSet {
        print("changing from \(self.radius) to \(newValue)")
    }
    didSet {
        print("changed from \(oldValue) to \(self.radius)")
    }
}
```

Be careful to avoid creating an infinite loop when using `didSet` and `willSet` with multiple properties. For example, if you tried to use this technique to keep `diameter` and `radius` synchronized instead of using a computed property, it would look like this:

```swift
struct Ball {
    var radius: Double {
        didSet {
            self.diameter = self.radius * 2
        }
    }
    var diameter: Double {
        didSet {
            self.radius = self.diameter / 2
        }
    }
}
```

In this scenario, if you set the `radius`, it triggers a change on the `diameter` which triggers another change on the `radius` and that then continues on forever.

Subscripts

You may also have realized that there is another way that we have interacted with a structure in the past. We have used square brackets ([]) with both arrays and dictionaries to access elements. These are called **subscripts** and we can use them on our custom types as well. The syntax for them is similar to the computed properties that we saw before except that you define it more like a method with parameters and a return type, as you can see here:

```
struct MovieAssignment {
    var movies: [String:String]

    subscript(invitee: String) -> String? {
        get {
            return self.movies[invitee]
        }

        set {
            self.movies[invitee] = newValue
        }
    }
}
```

You declare the arguments you want to use as the parameters to the subscript method in the square brackets. The return type for the subscript function is the type that will be returned when used to access a value. It is also the type for any value you assign to the subscript:

```
var assignment = MovieAssignment(movies: [:])
assignment["Sarah"] = "Modern Family"
print(assignment["Sarah"]) // "Modern Family"
```

You may have noticed a question mark (?) in the return type. This is called an **optional** and we will discuss this more in the next chapter. For now, you only need to know that this is the type that is returned when accessing a dictionary by key because a value does not exist for every possible key.

Just like with computed properties, you can define a subscript as read-only without using the get syntax:

```
struct MovieAssignment {
    var movies: [String:String]

    subscript(invitee: String) -> String? {
        return self.movies[invitee]
    }
}
```

subscript can have as many arguments as you want if you add additional parameters to the subscript declaration. You would then separate each parameter with a comma in the square brackets when using the subscript, as shown:

```
struct MovieAssignment {
    subscript(param1: String, param2: Int) -> Int {
        return 0
    }
}

print(assignment["Sarah", 2])
```

Subscripts are a good way to shorten your code but you should always be careful to avoid sacrificing clarity for brevity. Writing clear code is a balance between being too wordy and not wordy enough. If your code is too short, it will be hard to understand because meanings will become ambiguous. It is much better to have a method called movieForInvitee: rather than using a subscript. However, if all of your code is too long, there will be too much noise around and you will lose clarity in that way. Use subscripts sparingly and only when they would appear intuitive to another programmer based on the type of structure you are creating.

Custom initialization

If you are not satisfied with the default initializers provided to you, you can define your own. This is done using the init keyword, as shown:

```
init(contact: Contact) {
    self.firstName = contact.firstName
    self.lastName = contact.lastName
}
```

Just like with a method, an initializer can take any number of parameters including none at all. However, initializers have other restrictions. One rule is that every member variable and constant must have a value by the end of the initializer. If we were to omit a value for `lastName` in our initializer, we would get an error like this:

```
struct Contact4 {
    var firstName: String
    var lastName: String

    init(contact: Contact4) {
        self.firstName = contact.firstName
    }// Error: Return from initializer without
     // initializing all stored properties
}
```

Note that this code did not provide default values for `firstName` and `lastName`. If we add that back, we no longer get an error because a value is then provided:

```
struct Contact4 {
    var firstName: String
    var lastName: String = "Last"

    init(contact: Contact4) {
        self.firstName = contact.firstName
    }
}
```

Once you provide your own initializer, Swift no longer provides any default initializers. In the preceding example, `Contact` can no longer be initialized with the `firstName` and `lastName` parameters. If we want both, we have to add our own version of that initializer, as shown:

```
struct Contact3 {
    var firstName: String
    var lastName: String

    init(contact: Contact3) {
        self.firstName = contact.firstName
        self.lastName = contact.lastName
    }

    init(firstName: String, lastName: String) {
        self.firstName = firstName
        self.lastName = lastName
    }
}
```

```
    }
    var sarah = Contact3(firstName: "Sarah", lastName: "Smith")
    var sarahCopy = Contact3(contact: sarah)
    var other = Contact3(firstName: "First", lastName: "Last")
```

Another option for setting up the initial values in an initializer is to call a different initializer:

```
init(contact: Contact4) {
    self.init(
        firstName: sarah.firstName,
        lastName: sarah.lastName
    )
}
```

This is a great tool for reducing duplicate code in multiple initializers. However, when using this, there is an extra rule that you must follow. You cannot access `self` before calling the other initializer:

```
init(contact: Contact4) {
    self.print()
    // Use of 'self' in delegating initializer
    // before self.init is called
    self.init(
        firstName: contact.firstName,
        lastName: contact.lastName
    )
}
```

This is a great example of why the requirement exists. If we were to call `print` before calling the other initializer, `firstName` and `lastName` would not have a value. What would be printed in that case? Instead, you can only access `self` after calling the other initializer, like this:

```
init(contact: Contact4) {
    self.init(
        firstName: contact.firstName,
        lastName: contact.lastName
    )
    self.print()
}
```

This guarantees that all the properties have a valid value before any method is called.

You may have noticed that initializers follow a different pattern for parameter naming. By default, initializers require a label for all parameters. However, remember that this is only the default behavior. You can change the behavior by either providing an internal and external name or by using an underscore (_) as the external name.

Structures are an incredibly powerful tool in programming. They are an important way that we, as programmers, can abstract away more complicated concepts. As we discussed in *Chapter 2, Building Blocks – Variables, Collections, and Flow Control*, this is the way we get better at using computers. Other people can provide these abstractions to us for concepts that we don't understand yet or in circumstances where it isn't worth our time to start from scratch. We can also use these abstractions for ourselves so that we can better understand the high-level logic going on in our app. This will greatly increase the reliability of our code. Structures make our code more understandable both for other people and for ourselves in the future.

However, structures are limited in one important way, they don't provide a good way to express parent-child relationships between types. For example, a dog and a cat are both animals and share a lot of properties and actions. It would be great if we only had to implement the common attributes once. We could then split those types into different species. For this, Swift has a different system of types called **classes**.

Classes

A class can do everything that a structure can do except that a class can use something called **inheritance**. A class can inherit the functionality from another class and then extend or customize its behavior. Let's jump right into some code.

Inheriting from another class

Firstly, let's define a class called `Building` that we can inherit from later:

```
class Building {
    let squareFootage: Int

    init(squareFootage: Int) {
        self.squareFootage = squareFootage
    }
}
var aBuilding = Building(squareFootage: 1000)
```

Predictably, a class is defined using the `class` keyword instead of `struct`. Otherwise, a class looks extremely similar to a structure. However, we can also see one difference. With a structure, the initializer we created before would not be necessary because it would have been created for us. With classes, initializers are not automatically created unless all of the properties have default values.

Now let's look at how to inherit from this building class:

```
class House: Building {
    let numberOfBedrooms: Int
    let numberOfBathrooms: Double

    init(
        squareFootage: Int,
        numberOfBedrooms: Int,
        numberOfBathrooms: Double
        )
    {
        self.numberOfBedrooms = numberOfBedrooms
        self.numberOfBathrooms = numberOfBathrooms

        super.init(squareFootage: squareFootage)
    }
}
```

Here, we have created a new class called `House` that inherits from our `Building` class. This is denoted by the colon (`:`) followed by `Building` in the class declaration. Formally, we would say that `House` is a **subclass** of `Building` and `Building` is a **superclass** of `House`.

If we initialize a variable of the type `House`, we can then access both the properties of `House` and those of `Building`, as shown:

```
var aHouse = House(
    squareFootage: 800,
    numberOfBedrooms: 2,
    numberOfBathrooms: 1
)
print(aHouse.squareFootage)
print(aHouse.numberOfBedrooms)
```

This is the beginning of what makes classes powerful. If we need to define ten different types of buildings, we don't have to add a separate `squareFootage` property to each one. This is true for properties as well as methods.

Beyond a simple *superclass* and *subclass* relationship, we can define an entire hierarchy of classes with subclasses of subclasses of subclasses, and so on. It is often helpful to think of a class hierarchy as an upside down tree:

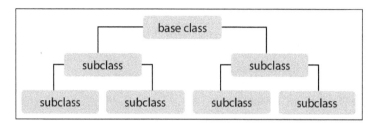

The trunk of the tree is the topmost superclass and each subclass is a separate branch off of that. The topmost superclass is commonly referred to as the base class as it forms the foundation for all the other classes.

Initialization

Because of the hierarchical nature of classes, the rules for their initializers are more complex. The following additional rules are applied:

- All initializers in a subclass must call the initializer of its superclass
- All properties of a subclass must be initialized before calling the superclass initializer

The second rule enables us to use `self` before calling the initializer. However, you cannot use `self` for any reason other than to initialize its properties.

You may have noticed the use of the keyword `super` in our `house` initializer. `super` is used to reference the current instance as if it were its superclass. This is how we call the superclass initializer. We will see more uses of `super` when we explore inheritance further later in the chapter.

Inheritance also creates four types of initializers shown here:

- Overriding initializer
- Required initializer
- Designated initializer
- Convenience initializer

Overriding initializer

An **overriding initializer** is used to replace the initializer in a superclass:

```
class House: Building {
    let numberOfBedrooms: Int
    let numberOfBathrooms: Double

    override init(squareFootage: Int) {
        self.numberOfBedrooms = 0
        self.numberOfBathrooms = 0
        super.init(squareFootage: squareFootage)
    }
}
```

An initializer that takes only `squareFootage` as a parameter already exists in `Building`. This initializer replaces that initializer so if you try to initialize `House` using only `squareFootage`, this initializer will be called. It will then call the `Building` version of the initializer because we asked it to with the `super.init` call.

This ability is especially important if you want to initialize subclasses using their superclass initializer. By default, if you don't specify a new initializer in a subclass, it inherits all of the initializers from its superclass. However, as soon as you declare an initializer in a subclass, it hides all of the superclass initializers. By using an overriding initializer, you can expose the superclass version of the initializer again.

Required initializer

A **required initializer** is a type of initializer for superclasses. If you mark an initializer as required, it forces all of the subclasses to also define that initializer. For example, we could make the `Building` initializer required, as shown:

```
class Building {
    let squareFootage: Int

    required init(squareFootage: Int) {
        self.squareFootage = squareFootage
    }
}
```

Then, if we implemented our own initializer in House, we would get an error like this:

```
class House: Building {
    let numberOfBedrooms: Int
    let numberOfBathrooms: Double

    init(
        squareFootage: Int,
        numberOfBedrooms: Int,
        numberOfBathrooms: Double
        )
    {
        self.numberOfBedrooms = numberOfBedrooms
        self.numberOfBathrooms = numberOfBathrooms

        super.init(squareFootage: squareFootage)
    }

    // 'required' initializer 'init(squareFootage:)' must be
    // provided by subclass of 'Building'
}
```

This time, when declaring this initializer, we repeat the required keyword instead of using override:

```
required init(squareFootage: Int) {
    self.numberOfBedrooms = 0
    self.numberOfBathrooms = 0
    super.init(squareFootage: squareFootage)
}
```

This is an important tool when your superclass has multiple initializers that do different things. For example, you could have one initializer that creates an instance of your class from a data file and another one that sets its properties from code. Essentially, you have two paths for initialization and you can use the required initializers to make sure that all subclasses take both paths into account. A subclass should still be able to be initialized from both a file and in code. Marking both of the superclass initializers as required makes sure that this is the case.

Designated and convenience initializers

To discuss **designated initializers,** we first have to talk about **convenience initializers**. The normal initializer that we started with is really called a designated initializer. This means that they are core ways to initialize the class. You can also create convenience initializers which, as the name suggests, are there for convenience and are not a core way to initialize the class.

All convenience initializers must call a designated initializer and they do not have the ability to manually initialize properties like a designated initializer does. For example, we can define a convenience initializer on our `Building` class that takes another building and makes a copy:

```
class Building {
    // ...

    convenience init(otherBuilding: Building) {
        self.init(squareFootage: otherBuilding.squareFootage)
    }
}
var aBuilding = Building(squareFootage: 1000)
var defaultBuilding = Building(otherBuilding: aBuilding)
```

Now, as a convenience, you can create a new building using the properties from an existing building. The other rule about convenience initializers is that they cannot be used by a subclass. If you try to do that, you will get an error like this:

```
class House: Building {

    // ...

    init() {
        self.numberOfBedrooms = 0
        self.numberOfBathrooms = 0
        super.init() // Missing argument for parameter 'squareFootage'
in call
    }
}
```

This is one of the main reasons that convenience initializers exist. Ideally, every class should only have one designated initializer. The fewer designated initializers you have, the easier it is to maintain your class hierarchy. This is because you will often add additional properties and other things that need to be initialized. Every time you add something like that, you will have to make sure that every designated initializer sets things up properly and consistently. Using a convenience initializer instead of a designated initializer ensures that everything is consistent because it must call a designated initializer that, in turn, is required to set everything up properly. Basically, you want to funnel all of your initialization through as few designated initializers as possible.

Generally, your designated initializer is the one with the most arguments, possibly with all of the possible arguments. In that way, you can call that from all of your other initializers and mark them as convenience initializers.

Overriding methods and computed properties

Just as with initializers, subclasses can **override** methods and computed properties. However, you have to be more careful with these. The compiler has fewer protections.

Methods

Even though it is possible, there is no requirement that an **overriding method** calls its superclass implementation. For example, let's add clean methods to our `Building` and `House` classes:

```
class Building {
    // ...

    func clean() {
        print(
            "Scrub \(self.squareFootage) square feet of floors"
        )
    }
}

class House: Building {
    // ...
```

```
        override func clean() {
            print("Make \(self.numberOfBedrooms) beds")
            print("Clean \(self.numberOfBathrooms) bathrooms")
        }
    }
```

In our `Building` superclass, the only thing that we have to clean is the floors. However, in our `House` subclass, we also have to make the beds and clean the bathrooms. As it has been implemented above, when we call `clean` on `House`, it will not clean the floors because we overrode that behavior with the `clean` method on `House`. In this case, we also need to have our `Building` superclass do any necessary cleaning, so we must call the superclass version, as shown:

```
    override func clean() {
        super.clean()

        print("Make \(self.numberOfBedrooms) beds")
        print("Clean \(self.numberOfBathrooms) bathrooms")
    }
```

Now, before doing any cleaning based on the house definition, it will first clean based on the building definition. You can control the order in which things happen by changing the place in which you call the super version.

This is a great example of the need to override methods. We can provide common functionality in a superclass that can be extended in each of its subclasses instead of rewriting the same functionality in multiple classes.

Computed properties

It is also useful to override computed properties using the `override` keyword again:

```
    class Building {
        // ...

        var estimatedEnergyCost: Int {
            return squareFootage / 10
        }
    }

    class House: Building {
        // ...

        override var estimatedEnergyCost: Int {
            return 100 + super.estimatedEnergyCost
        }
    }
```

In our `Building` superclass, we have provided an estimate for energy costs based on $100 per 1000 square feet. That estimate still applies to the house but there are additional costs related to someone else living in the building. We must therefore override the `estimatedEnergyCost` computed property to return the `Building` calculation plus $100.

Again, using the super version of an overriding computed property is not required. A subclass could have a completely different implementation disregarding what is implemented in its superclass, or it could make use of its superclass implementation.

Casting

We have already talked about how classes are great for sharing functionality between a hierarchy of types. Another thing that makes classes powerful is that they allow code to interact with multiple types in a more general way. Any subclass can be used in code that treats it as if it were its superclass. For example, we might want to write a function that calculates the total square footage of an array of buildings. For this function, we don't care what specific type of building it is, we just need to have access to the `squareFootage` property that is defined in the superclass. We can define our function to take an array of buildings and the actual array can contain `House` instances:

```
func totalSquareFootageOfBuildings(buildings: [Building]) -> Int {
    var sum = 0
    for building in buildings {
        sum += building.squareFootage
    }
    return sum
}

var buildings = [
    House(squareFootage: 1000),
    Building(squareFootage: 1200),
    House(squareFootage: 900)
]
print(totalSquareFootageOfBuildings(buildings)) // 3100
```

Even though this function thinks we are dealing with classes of the type `Building`, the program will execute the `House` implementation of `squareFootage`. If we had also created an office subclass of `Building`, instances of that would also be included in the array as well with its own implementation.

We can also assign an instance of a subclass to a variable that is defined to be one of its superclasses:

```
var someBuilding: Building = House(squareFootage: 1000)
```

This provides us with an even more powerful abstraction tool than the one we had when using structures. For example, let's consider a hypothetical class hierarchy of images. We might have a base class called `Image` with subclasses for the different types of encodings like `JPGImage` and `PNGImage`. It is great to have the subclasses so that we can cleanly support multiple types of images but, once the image is loaded, we no longer need to be concerned with the type of encoding the image is saved in. Every other class that wants to manipulate or display the image can do so with a well-defined image superclass; the encoding of the image has been abstracted away from the rest of the code. Not only does this create easier to understand code but it also makes maintenance much easier. If we need to add another image encoding like **GIF**, we can create another subclass and all the existing manipulation and display code can get GIF support with no changes to that code.

There are actually two different types of casting. So far, we have only seen the type of casting called **upcasting**. Predictably, the other type of casting is called **downcasting**.

Upcasting

What we have seen so far is called upcasting because we are going up the class tree that we visualized earlier by treating a subclass as its superclass. Previously, we upcasted by assigning a subclass instance to a variable that was defined as its superclass. We could do the same thing using the `as` operator instead, like this:

```
var someBuilding2 = House(squareFootage: 1000) as Building
```

It is really personal preference as to which you should use.

Downcasting

Downcasting means that we treat a superclass as one of its subclasses.

While upcasting can be done implicitly by using it in a function declared to use its superclass or by assigning it to a variable with its superclass type, downcasting must be done explicitly. This is because upcasting cannot fail based on the nature of its inheritance, but downcasting can. You can always treat a subclass as its superclass but you cannot guarantee that a superclass is, in fact, one of its specific subclasses. You can only downcast an instance that is, in fact, an instance of that class or one of its subclasses.

We can force downcast by using the `as!` Operator, like this:

```
var house = someBuilding as! House
print(house.numberOfBathrooms)
```

The `as!` operator has an exclamation point added to it because it is an operation that can fail. The exclamation point serves as a warning and ensures that you realize that it can fail. If the forced downcasting fails, for example, if `someBuilding` were not actually `House`, the program would crash as so:

```
var anotherHouse = aBuilding as! House // Execution was interrupted
```

A safer way to perform downcasting is using the `as?` operator in a special `if` statement called an optional binding. We will discuss this in detail in the next chapter, which concerns optionals but, for now, you can just remember the syntax:

```
if let house = someBuilding as? House {
    // someBuilding is of type House
    print(house.numberOfBathrooms)
}
else {
    print("someBuilding is not a house")
}
```

This code prints out `numberOfBathrooms` in the building only if it is of the type `House`. The `House` constant is used as a temporary view of `someBuilding` with its type explicitly set to `House`. With this temporary view, you can access `someBuilding` as if it were `House` instead of just `Building`.

Enumerations

So far, we have covered two of the three types of classification in Swift: structure and class. The third classification is called **enumeration**. Enumerations are used to define a group of related values for an instance. For example, if we want values to represent one of the three primary colors, an enumeration is a great tool.

Basic declaration

An enumeration is made up of **cases** much like a switch and uses the keyword `enum` instead of `struct` or `class`. An enumeration for primary colors should look like this:

```
enum PrimaryColor {
    case Red
    case Green
    case Blue
}
```

You can then define a variable with this type and assign it one of the cases:

```
var color = PrimaryColor.Green
```

Note that, to use one of the values, we must use the name of the type followed by a dot (.) and then the specific case. If the type of the variable can be inferred, you can even leave out the enumeration name and just start with a dot:

```
var color = PrimaryColor.Green
color = .Red
```

During the assignment to .Red, the compiler already knows that the color variable is of the type PrimaryColor so it doesn't need us to specify that again. This is a great way of making your code more concise but make sure you don't sacrifice legibility. If you leave out the type name, it should still be obvious from the context of the code.

Testing enumeration values

Enumeration instances can be tested for a specific value as with any other type, using the equality operator (==):

```
if color == PrimaryColor.Red {
}
else if color == .Blue {
}
```

Note that, in the second if statement, where color is checked for if it is blue, the code takes advantage of type inference and doesn't bother specifying PrimaryColor.

This method of comparison is familiar and useful for one or two possible values. However, there is a better way to test an enumeration for different values. Instead of using an if statement, you can use a switch. This is a logical solution considering that enumerations are made up of cases and switches test for cases:

```
switch color {
    case .Red:
        print("color is red")
    case .Green:
        print("color is green")
    case .Blue:
        print("color is blue")
}
```

This is great for all the same reasons that switches themselves are great. In fact, switches work even better with enumerations because the possible values for an enumeration are always finite, unlike other basic types. You may remember that switches require that you have a case for every possible value. This means that, if you don't have a test case for every case of the enumeration, the compiler will produce an error. This is usually great protection and that is why I recommend using switches rather than simple `if` statements in most circumstances. If you ever add additional cases to an enumeration, it is great to get an error everywhere in your code that doesn't consider that new case so that you make sure you address it.

Raw values

Enumerations are great because they provide the ability to store information that is not based on the basic types provided by Swift such as strings, integers, and doubles. There are many abstract concepts like our color example, that are not at all related to a basic type. However, you often want each enumeration case to have a **raw value** that is another type. For example, if we wanted to represent all of the coins in United States currency along with their monetary value, we could make our enumeration have an integer raw value type, like this:

```
enum USCoins: Int {
    case Quarter = 25
    case Dime = 10
    case Nickel = 5
    case Penny = 1
}
```

The raw value type is specified in the same way that inheritance is specified with classes and then each case is individually assigned a specific value of that type.

You can access the raw value of a case at any time by using the `rawValue` property:

```
print("A Quarter is worth \(USCoins.Quarter.rawValue) cents.")
```

Keep in mind that an enumeration can only have raw value types that can be defined with literals like `10`, or `String`. You cannot define an enumeration with your own custom type as its raw value.

Associated values

Raw values are great for when every case in your enumeration has the same type of value associated with it and its value never changes. However, there are also scenarios where each case has different values associated with it and those values are different for each instance of the enumeration. You may even want a case that has multiple values associated with it. To do this, we use a feature of enumerations called **associated values**.

You can specify zero or several types to be associated separately with each case with associated values. Then, when creating an instance of the enumeration, you can give it any value you want, as shown:

```
enum Height {
    case Imperial(feet: Int, inches: Double)
    case Metric(meters: Double)
    case Other(String)
}
var height1 = Height.Imperial(feet: 6, inches: 2)
var height2 = Height.Metric(meters: 1.72)
var height3 = Height.Other("1.9 × 10-16 light years")
```

Here, we have defined an enumeration to store a height measurement using various measurement systems. There is a case for the imperial system that uses feet and inches and a case for the metric system that is in just meters. Both of these cases have labels for their associated values which are similar to a tuple. The last case is there to illustrate that you don't have to provide a label if you don't want to. It simply takes a string.

Comparing and accessing values of enumerations with associated values is a little bit more complex than for regular enumerations. We can no longer use the equality operator (==). Instead, we must always use a case. Within a case, there are multiple ways that you can handle the associated values. The easiest thing to do is to access the specific associated value. To do that, you can assign it to a temporary variable:

```
switch height1 {
    case .Imperial(let feet, var inches):
        print("\(feet)ft \(inches)in")
    case let .Metric(meters):
        print("\(meters) meters")
    case var .Other(text):
        print(text)
}
```

In the imperial case, the preceding code assigned `feet` to a temporary constant and `inches` to a temporary variable. The names match the labels used for the associated values but that is not necessary. The metric case shows that, if you want all of the temporary values to be constant, you can declare `let` before the enumeration case. No matter how many associated values there are, `let` only has to be written once instead of once for every value. The other case is the same as the metric case except that it creates a temporary variable instead of a constant.

If you wanted to create separate cases for conditions on the associated values, you could use the `where` syntax that we saw in the previous chapter:

```
switch height1 {
    case .Imperial(let feet, var inches) where feet > 1:
        print("\(feet)ft \(inches)in")
    case let .Metric(meters) where meters > 0.3:
        print("\(meters) meters")
    case var .Other(text):
        print(text)
    default:
        print("Too Small")
}
```

Note that we had to add a default case because our restrictions on the other cases were no longer exhaustive.

Lastly, if you don't actually care about the associated value, you can use an underscore (_) to ignore it, as shown:

```
switch height1 {
    case .Imperial(_, _):
        print("Imperial")
    case .Metric(_):
        print("Metric")
    case .Other(_):
        print("Other")
}
```

This shows you that, with enumerations, switches have even more power than we saw previously.

Now that you understand how to use associated values, you might have noticed that they can change the conceptual nature of enumerations. Without associated values, an enumeration represents a list of abstract and constant possible values. An enumeration with associated values is different because two instances with the same case are not necessarily equal; each case could have different associated values. This means that the conceptual nature of enumerations is really a list of ways to look at a certain type of information. This is not a concrete rule but it is common and it gives you a better idea of the different types of information that can best be represented by enumerations. It will also help you make your own enumerations more understandable. Each case could theoretically represent a completely unrelated concept from the rest of the cases using associated values but that should be a sign that an enumeration may not be the best tool for that particular job.

Methods and properties

Enumerations are actually very similar to structures. As with structures, enumerations can have methods and properties. To improve the `Height` enumeration, we could add methods to access the height in any measurement system we wanted. As an example, let's implement a `meters` method, as follows:

```
enum Distance {
    case Imperial(feet: Int, inches: Double)
    case Metric(meters: Double)

    func meters() -> Double {
        switch self {
            case let .Imperial(feet, inches):
                return Double(feet)*0.3048+inches*0.3048/12
            case let .Metric(meters):
                return meters
        }
    }
}
var distance1 = Distance.Imperial(feet: 6, inches: 2)
distance1.meters() // 1.8796
```

In this method, we have switched on `self` which tells us which unit of measurement this instance was created with. If it is in meters we can just return that but, if it is in feet and inches, we must do the conversion. As an exercise, I recommend you try to implement a `feetAndInches` method that returns a tuple with the two values. The biggest challenge is in handling the mathematical operations using the correct types. You cannot perform operations with mismatching types mathematically. If you need to convert from one number type to another, you can do so by initializing a copy as shown in the code above: `Double(feet)`. Unlike the casting that we discussed earlier, this process simply creates a new copy of the `feet` variable that is now `Double` instead of `Int`. This is only possible because the `Double` type happens to define an initializer that takes `Int`. Most number types can be initialized with any of the other ones.

You now have a great overview of all of the different ways in which we can organize Swift code in a single file to make the code more understandable and maintainable. It is now time to discuss how we can separate our code into multiple files to improve it even more.

Projects

If we want to move away from developing with a single file, we need to move away from playgrounds and create our first project. In order to simplify the project, we are going to create a **command-line tool**. This is a program without a graphical interface. As an exercise, we will redevelop our example program from *Chapter 2, Building Blocks – Variables, Collections, and Flow Control* which managed invitees to a party. We will develop an app with a graphical interface in *Chapter 11, A Whole New World – Developing an App*.

Setting up a command-line Xcode project

To create a new command-line tool project, open Xcode and from the menu bar on the top, select **File | New | Project...**. A window will appear allowing you to select a template for the project. You should choose **Command Line Tool** from the **OS X | Application** menu:

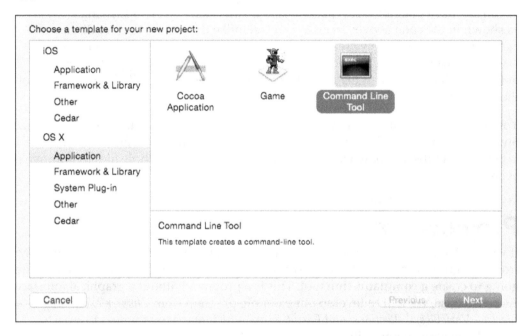

From there, click **Next** and then give the project a name like `Learning Swift Command Line`. Any **Organization Name** and **Identifier** are fine. Finally, make sure that **Swift** is selected from the **Language** dropdown and click **Next** again. Now, save the project somewhere that you can find later and click **Create**.

Xcode will then present you with the project development window. Select the `main.swift` file on the left and you should see the `Hello, World!` code that Xcode has generated for you:

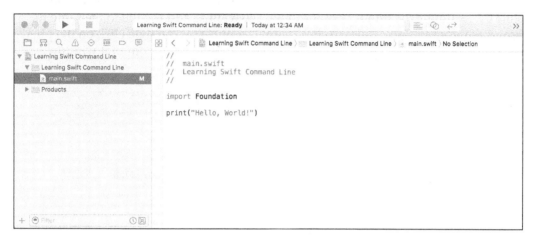

This should feel pretty similar to a playground except that we can no longer see the output of the code on the right. In a regular project like this, the code is not run automatically for you. The code will still be analyzed for errors as you write it, but you must run it yourself whenever you want to test it. To run the code, you can click the run button on the toolbar, which looks like a play button.

The program will then build and run. Once it does, Xcode shows the console on the bottom where you will see the text `Hello, World!` which is the result of running this program. This is the same console as we saw in playgrounds.

Unlike a playground, we have the Project Navigator along the left. This is where we organize all of the source files that go into making the application work.

Creating and using an external file

Now that we have successfully created our command-line project, let's create our first new file. It is common to create a separate file for each type that you create. Let's start by creating a file for an `invitee` class. We want to add the file to the same file group as the `main.swift` file, so click on that group. You can then click on the plus sign (**+**) in the lower left of the window and select **New File**. From that window, select **OS X | Source | Swift File** and click **Next**:

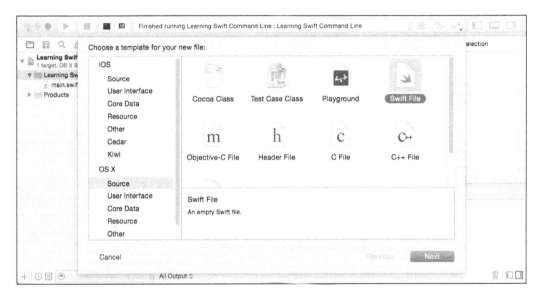

The new file will be placed in whatever folder was selected before entering the dialog. You can always drag a file around to organize it however you want. A great place for this file is next to `main.swift`. Name your new file `Invitee.swift` and click **Create**. Let's add a simple `Invitee` structure to this file. We want `Invitee` to have a name and to be able to ask them to the party with or without a show:

```swift
// Invitee.swift
struct Invitee {
    let name: String

    func askToBringShowFromGenre(genre: ShowGenre) {
        print("\(self.name), bring a \(genre.name) show")
        print("\(genre.example) is a great \(genre.name)")
    }

    func askToBringThemselves() {
        print("\(self.name), just bring yourself")
    }
}
```

This is a very simple type and does not require inheritance, so there is no reason to use a class. Note that inheritance is not the only reason to use a class, as we will see in later chapters but, for now, a structure will work great for us. This code provides simple, well-named methods to print out the two types of invites.

We are already making use of a structure that we have not created yet called ShowGenre. We would expect it to have a name and example property. Let's implement that structure now. Create another file called ShowGenre.swift and add the following code to it:

```
// ShowGenre.swift
struct ShowGenre {
    let name: String
    let example: String
}
```

This is an even simpler structure. This is just a small improvement over using a tuple because it is given a name instead of just properties and it also gives us finer control over what is constant or not. It may seem like a waste to have an entire file for just this but this is great for maintainability in the future. It is easier to find the structure because it is in a well-named file and we may want to add more code to it later.

An important principle in code design is called **separation of concerns**. The idea is that every file and every type should have a clear and well-defined concern. You should avoid having two files or types responsible for the same thing and you want it to be clear why each file and type exists.

Interfacing with code from other files

Now that we have our basic data structures, we can use a smarter container for our list of invitees. This list contains the logic for assigning a random invitee a genre. Let's start by defining the structure with some properties:

```
// InviteList.swift
struct InviteList {
    var invited: [Invitee] = []
    var pendingInvitees: [Invitee]

    init(invitees: [Invitee]) {
        srand(UInt32(clock()))
        self.pendingInvitees = invitees
    }
}
```

Instead of storing a single list of both invited and pending invitees, we can store them in two separate arrays. This makes selecting a pending invitee much easier. This code also provides a custom initializer, so that all we need to provide from other classes is an invitee list without worrying whether or not it is a list of pending invitees. We could have just used the default initializer but the parameter would then have been named `pendingInvitees`. We also seed the random number generator for later use.

Note that we did not need to provide a value for `invited` in our initializer because we gave it the default value of an empty array.

Note also that we are using our `Invitee` structure freely in this code. Swift automatically finds code from other files in the same project and allows you to use it. Interfacing with code from other files is as simple as that.

Now, let's add a helper function to move an invitee from the `pendingInvitee` list to the `invited` list:

```
// InviteList.swift
struct InviteList {

    // ...

    // Move invitee from pendingInvitees to invited
    //
    // Must be mutating because we are changing the contents of
    // our array properties
    mutating func invitedPendingInviteeAtIndex(index: Int) {
        // Removing an item from an array returns that item
        let invitee = self.pendingInvitees.removeAtIndex(index)
        self.invited.append(invitee)
    }
}
```

This makes our other methods cleaner and easier to understand. The first thing we want to allow is the inviting of a random invitee and then asking them to bring a show from a specific genre:

```
// InviteList.swift
struct InviteList {

    // ...
```

```
    // Must be mutating because it calls another mutating method
    mutating func askRandomInviteeToBringGenre(genre: ShowGenre) {
        if self.pendingInvitees.count > 0 {
            let randomIndex = Int(rand()) % self.pendingInvitees.count
            let invitee = self.pendingInvitees[randomIndex]
            invitee.askToBringShowFromGenre(genre)
            self.invitedPendingInviteeAtIndex(randomIndex)
        }
    }
}
```

The picking of a random invitee is much cleaner than in our previous implementation. We can create a random number between 0 and the number of pending invitees instead of having to keep trying a random invitee until we find one that hasn't been invited yet. However, before we can pick that random number, we have to make sure that the number of pending invitees is greater than zero. If there were no remaining invitees we would have to divide the random number by 0 in `Int(rand()) % self.pendingInvitees.count`. This would cause a crash. It has the extra benefit of allowing us to handle the scenarios where there are more genres than invitees.

Lastly, we want to be able to invite everyone else to just bring themselves:

```
// InviteList.swift
struct InviteList {

    // ...

    // Must be mutating because it calls another mutating method
    mutating func inviteeRemainingInvitees() {
        while self.pendingInvitees.count > 0 {
            let invitee = self.pendingInvitees[0]
            invitee.askToBringThemselves()
            self.invitedPendingInviteeAtIndex(0)
        }
    }
}
```

Here, we have simply repeatedly invited and removed the first pending invitee from the `pendingInvitees` array until there are none left.

We now have all of our custom types and we can return to the `main.swift` file to finish the logic of the program. To switch back, you can just click on the file again in Project Navigator (the list of files on the left). Here, all we want to do is to create our invitee list and a list of genres with example shows. Then, we can loop through our genres and ask our invitee list to do the inviting:

```swift
var inviteeList = InviteList(invitees: [
    Invitee(name: "Sarah"),
    Invitee(name: "Jamison"),
    Invitee(name: "Marcos"),
    Invitee(name: "Roana"),
    Invitee(name: "Neena"),
])

let genres = [
    ShowGenre(name: "Comedy", example: "Modern Family"),
    ShowGenre(name: "Drama", example: "Breaking Bad"),
    ShowGenre(name: "Variety", example: "The Colbert Report"),
]

for genre in genres {
    inviteeList.askRandomInviteeToBringGenre(genre)
}
inviteeList.inviteeRemainingInvitees()
```

That is our complete program. You can now run the program by clicking the **Run** button and examine the output. You have just completed your first real Swift project!

File organization and navigation

As your project gets larger, it can be cumbersome to have just one single list of files. It helps to organize your files into folders to help differentiate which role they are playing in your app. In Project Navigator, folders are called groups. You can create a new group by selecting the group you would like to add the new group to, and going to **File | New | Group**. It isn't terribly important exactly how you group your files; the important thing is that you should be able to come up with a relatively simple system that makes sense. If you are having trouble doing that, you should consider how you could improve the way you are breaking up your code. If you are having trouble categorizing your files, then your code is probably not being broken up in a maintainable way.

I would recommend using lots of files and groups to better separate your code. However, the drawback of that is that Project Navigator can fill up pretty quickly and become hard to navigate around. A great trick in Xcode to navigate to files more quickly is to use the keyboard shortcut *Command* + *Shift* + *O*. This displays the Open Quickly search. Here, you can start to type the name of the file you want to open and Xcode shows you all of the matching files. Use the arrow keys to navigate up and down and press *Enter* to open the file you want.

Extensions

Up until this point, we had to define our entire custom type in a single file. However, it is sometimes useful to separate out part of our custom types into different files, or even just in the same file. To achieve this, Swift provides a feature called extensions. Extensions allow us to add additional functionality to existing types from anywhere.

This functionality is limited to additional functions and additional computed properties:

```swift
extension Building {
    var report: String {
        return "This building is \(self.squareFootage) sq ft"
    }

    func isLargerThanOtherBuilding(building: Building) -> Bool {
        return self.squareFootage > building.squareFootage
    }
}
```

Note that, to define an extension, we use the `extension` keyword, followed by the type that we would like to extend. Extensions can also be used on an existing class, struct, or enumeration, even those defined within Swift like String. Let's add an extension to String that allows us to repeat a string any number of times:

```swift
extension String {
    func repeatNTimes(nTimes: Int) -> String {
        var output = ""
        for _ in 0..<nTimes {
            output += self
        }
        return output
    }
}
"-".repeatNTimes(4) // ----
```

This is just one simple idea, but it is often incredibly useful to extend the built-in types.

Now that we have a good overview of what tools we have at our disposal for organizing our code, it is time to discuss an important concept in programming called **scope**.

Scope

Scope is all about which code has access to which other pieces of code. Swift makes it relatively easy to understand because all scope is defined by curly brackets ({ }). Essentially, code in curly brackets can only access other code in the same curly brackets.

How scope is defined

To illustrate scope, let's look at some simple code:

```
var outer = "Hello"
if outer == "Hello" {
    var inner = "World"
    print(outer)
    print(inner)
}
print(outer)
print(inner) // Error: Use of unresolved identifier 'inner'
```

As you can see, `outer` can be accessed from both in and out of the `if` statement. However, since `inner` was defined in the curly brackets of the `if` statement, it cannot be accessed from outside of them. This is true of structs, classes, loops, functions, and any other structure that involves curly brackets. Everything that is not in curly brackets is considered to be at **global scope**, meaning that anything can access it.

Nested types

Sometimes, it is useful to control scope yourself. To do this, you can define types within other types:

```
class OuterClass {
    struct InnerStruct {
    }
}
```

In this scenario, `InnerStruct` is only directly visible from within `OuterClass`. This, however, provides a special scenario that is not there for other control structures like `if` statements and loops. If code at the global scope wanted to access `InnerStruct`, it could only do so through `OuterClass` which it does have direct access to, as shown:

```
var inner = OuterClass.InnerStruct()
```

This can be useful to better segment your code but it is also great for hiding code that is not useful to any code outside other code. As you program in bigger projects, you will start to rely on Xcode's autocomplete feature more and more. In big code bases, autocomplete offers a lot of options, and nesting types into other types is a great way to reduce unnecessary clutter in the autocomplete list.

Access control

Swift provides another set of tools that helps to control what code other code has access to called **access controls**. All code is actually given three levels of access control:

- **Private**: Only accessible from within the same file
- **Internal**: Only accessible from within the same module or app
- **Public**: Accessible by any code that imports the module

Before we can really discuss this further, you should understand completely what a module is. It is beyond the scope of this book to talk about implementing a module but a module is a collection of code that can be used in other modules and apps. So far, we have used the `Foundation` module provided by Apple. A module is anything that you use when using the `import` keyword.

All code, by default, is defined to be at the internal level. That means that any given piece of code in your program can access any piece of code defined in any other file that is also included in your program as long as it follows the scoping rules we have already discussed.

As described previously, code declared as private is only accessible from the same file. This is an even better way to protect outside code from seeing code you don't want it to see. You can declare any variable or type as private by writing the `private` keyword before it, like this:

```
private var mySecretString = "Hello World"
private struct MyPrivateStruct {
    private var privateProperty: String
    private func privateMethod() {
    }
}
```

Note that access control is independent of the curly bracket scope. It is built on top of it. All of the existing scope rules apply, with access controls acting as an additional filter.

This is a fantastic way of improving the idea of abstractions. The simpler the outside view of your code, the easier it is to understand and use your abstraction. You should look at every file and every type as a small abstraction. In any abstraction, you want the outside world to have as little knowledge of the inner workings of it as possible. You should always keep in mind how you want your abstraction to be used and hide any code that does not serve that purpose. This is because code becomes harder and harder to understand and maintain as the walls between different parts of the code break down. You will end up with code that resembles a bowl of pasta. In the same way that it can be difficult to find where one noodle starts and ends, code with lots of interdependencies and minimal barriers between code components is very hard to make sense of. An abstraction that provides too much knowledge or access about its internal workings is often called a **leaky abstraction**.

Public code is defined in the same way, except that you would use the `public` keyword instead of `private`. However, since we will not study designing your own modules, this is not useful to us. It is good to know it exists for future learning but the default **internal** access level is enough for our apps.

Summary

This was a very dense chapter. We have covered a lot of ground. We have delved deep into defining our own custom types using structures, classes, and enumerations. Structures are great for simple types, while classes are great for types that require a hierarchy of related types. Enumerations provide a way to group related things together and express more abstract concepts through associated values.

We have also created our first project, which made use of multiple source files improving the maintainability of our code bases, especially at scale. Extensions can be used across and within those files to add additional functionality to existing types, including those not defined by us.

Finally, we developed a good understanding of what scope is and how we can control it to our advantage, especially with the help of access controls to give us an even more fine grained filter on what code can interact with other code.

Now that you have made it this far, you are well on your way to becoming a quality Swift programmer. I definitely recommend that you take a breather and experiment with everything that you have learned so far. We have only a few more concepts left to learn until we have all the tools necessary for creating a great app.

Once you are ready to move on, we can talk about **optionals**, which I have already hinted at. Optionals are somewhat complex but are an integral part of using the Swift language effectively. In the next chapter, we will dive deep into what they are and then how to take advantage of them in the most effective ways possible.

4
To Be or Not To Be – Optionals

As we discussed in *Chapter 2, Building Blocks – Variables, Collections, and Flow Control*, all variables and constants must always have a value before they are used. This is a great safety feature because it prevents you from creating a scenario where you forget to give a variable an initial value. It may make sense for some number variables, such as the number of sandwiches ordered to start at zero, but it doesn't make sense for all variables. For example, the number of bowling pins standing should start at 10, not zero. In Swift, the compiler forces you to decide what the variable should start at, instead of providing a default value that could be incorrect.

However, there are other scenarios where you will have to represent the complete absence of a value. A great example is if you have a dictionary of word definitions and you try to lookup a word that isn't in the dictionary. Normally, this will return a String, so you could potentially return an empty String, but what if you also need to represent the idea that a word exists without a definition? Also, for another programmer who is using your dictionary, it will not be immediately obvious what will happen when they look up a word that doesn't exist. To satisfy this need to represent the absence of a value, Swift has a special type called an **optional**.

In this chapter, we will cover the following topics:

- Defining an optional
- Unwrapping an optional
- Optional chaining
- Implicitly unwrapped optionals
- Debugging optionals
- The underlying implementation

Defining an optional

So we know that the purpose of optionals in Swift is to allow the representation of the absence of a value, but what does that look like and how does it work? An optional is a special type that can "wrap" any other type. This means that you can make an optional String, optional Array, and so on. You can do this by adding a question mark (?) to the type name, as shown:

```
var possibleString: String?
var possibleArray: [Int]?
```

Note that this code does not specify any initial values. This is because all optionals, by default, are set to no value at all. If we want to provide an initial value we can do so similar to any other variable:

```
var possibleInt: Int? = 10
```

Also, note that if we left out the type specification (: Int?), possibleInt would be inferred to be of type Int instead of an optional Int.

Now, it is pretty verbose to say that a variable lacks a value. Instead, if an optional lacks a variable, we say it is nil. So both possibleString and possibleArray are nil, while possibleInt is 10. However, possibleInt is not truly 10. It is still wrapped in an optional.

You can see all the forms a variable can take by putting the following code into a playground:

```
var actualInt = 10
var possibleInt: Int? = 10
var nilInt: Int?
print(actualInt) // 10
print(possibleInt) // Optional(10)
print(nilInt) // nil
```

As you can see, actualInt prints out just as we expected, but possibleInt prints out as an optional that contains the value 10 instead of just 10. This is a very important distinction because an optional cannot be used as the value it is wrapping. nilInt just reports that it is nil. At any point, you can update the value within an optional; this includes assigning it a value for the first time, using the assignment operator (=):

```
nilInt = 2
print(nilInt) // Optional(2)
```

You can even remove the value within an optional by assigning it to `nil`:

```
nilInt = nil
print(nilInt) // nil
```

So we have this wrapped form of a variable that may or may not contain a value. What do we do if we need to access the value within an optional? The answer is that we must unwrap it.

Unwrapping an optional

There are multiple ways to unwrap an optional. All of them essentially assert that there is truly a value within the optional. This is a wonderful safety feature of Swift. The compiler forces you to consider the possibility that an optional lacks any value at all. In other languages, this is a very commonly overlooked scenario that can cause obscure bugs.

Optional binding

The safest way to unwrap an optional is to use something called **optional binding**. With this technique, you can assign a temporary constant or variable to the value contained within the optional. This process is contained within an `if` statement, so that you can use an else statement when there is no value. Optional binding looks similar to the following code:

```
if let string = possibleString {
    print("possibleString has a value: \(string)")
}
else {
    print("possibleString has no value")
}
```

An optional binding is distinguished from an `if` statement primarily by the `if let` syntax. Semantically, this code is saying, "if you can let the constant `string` be equal to the value within `possibleString`, print out its value; otherwise, print that it has no value." The primary purpose of an optional binding is to create a temporary constant that is the normal (non-optional) version of the optional.

We can also use a temporary variable in an optional binding:

```
possibleInt = 10
if var actualInt = possibleInt {
    actualInt *= 2
    print(actualInt) // 20
}
print(possibleInt) // Optional(10)
```

Note that an asterisk (*) is used for multiplication in Swift. You should also notice something important about this code. If you put it into a playground, even though we multiplied the `actualInt` by 2, the value within the optional does not change. When we print out `possibleInt` later, the value is still `Optional(10)`. This is because even though we made `actualInt` a variable (otherwise known as mutable), it is simply a temporary copy of the value within `possibleInt`. No matter what we do with `actualInt`, nothing will get changed about the value within `possibleInt`. If we have to update the actual value stored within `possibleInt`, we simply assign `possibleInt` to `actualInt` after we are done modifying it:

```
possibleInt = 10
if var actualInt = possibleInt {
    actualInt *= 2
    possibleInt = actualInt
}
print(possibleInt) // Optional(20)
```

Now, the value wrapped inside `possibleInt` has actually been updated.

A common scenario that you will probably come across is the need to unwrap multiple optional values. One option is to simply nest the optional bindings:

```
if let actualString = possibleString {
    if let actualArray = possibleArray {
        if let actualInt = possibleInt {
            print(actualString)
            print(actualArray)
            print(actualInt)
        }
    }
}
```

However, this can be a pain, as it increases the indentation level each time to keep the code organized. Instead, you can actually list multiple optional bindings into a single statement separated by commas:

```
if let actualString = possibleString,
    let actualArray = possibleArray,
    let actualInt = possibleInt
{
    print(actualString)
    print(actualArray)
    print(actualInt)
}
```

This generally produces more readable code.

Another great way to do a concise optional binding within functions is to use the guard statement. This way, you can do a series of unwrapping without increasing the indent level of the code at all:

```
func someFunc2() {
    guard let actualString = possibleString,
        let actualArray = possibleArray,
        let actualInt = possibleInt
    else {
        return
    }

    print(actualString)
    print(actualArray)
    print(actualInt)
}
```

This construct allows us to access the unwrapped values after the guard statement, because the guard statement guarantees that we would have exited the function before reaching that code, if the optional value was nil.

This way of unwrapping is great, but saying that optional binding is the safest way to access the value within an optional, implies that there is an unsafe way to unwrap an optional. This way is called **forced unwrapping**.

Forced unwrapping

The shortest way to unwrap an optional is to use forced unwrapping. It is done using an exclamation mark (!) after the variable name when being used:

```
possibleInt = 10
possibleInt! *= 2
print(possibleInt) // "Optional(20)"
```

However, the reason it is considered unsafe is that your entire program will crash if you try to unwrap an optional that is currently nil:

```
nilInt! *= 2 // fatal error
```

The complete error you get is **unexpectedly found nil while unwrapping an optional value**. This is because the forced unwrapping is essentially your personal guarantee that the optional truly does hold a value. That is why it is called "forced".

Therefore, forced unwrapping should be used in limited circumstances. It should never be used just to shorten up the code. Instead, it should only be used when you can guarantee from the structure of the code that it cannot be nil, even though it is defined as an optional. Even in that case, you should see if it is possible to use a non-optional variable instead. The only other place you may use it is if your program truly could not recover from an optional being nil. In those circumstances, you should at least consider presenting an error to the user, which is always better than simply having your program crash.

An example of a scenario where it may be used effectively is with lazily calculated values. A lazily calculated value is the one that is not created until the first time it is accessed. To illustrate this, let's consider a hypothetical class that represents a file system directory. It will have a property listing its contents that is lazily calculated. The code will look similar to the following code:

```
class FileSystemItem {}
class File: FileSystemItem {}
class Directory: FileSystemItem {
    private var realContents: [FileSystemItem]?
    var contents: [FileSystemItem] {
        if self.realContents == nil {
            self.realContents = self.loadContents()
        }
        return self.realContents!
    }

    private func loadContents() -> [FileSystemItem] {
        // Do some loading
        return []
    }
}
```

Here, we have defined a superclass called `FileSystemItem` that both `File` and `Directory` inherit from. The content of a directory is a list of `FileSystemItem`. We define `contents` as a calculated variable and store the real value within the `realContents` property. The calculated property checks if there is a value loaded for `realContents`; if there isn't, it loads the contents and puts them into the `realContents` property. Based on this logic, we know for 100% certainty that there will be a value within `realContents` by the time we get to the return statement, so it is perfectly safe to use forced unwrapping.

Nil coalescing

In addition to optional binding and forced unwrapping, Swift also provides an operator called the **nil coalescing operator** to unwrap an optional. This is represented by a double question mark (??). Basically, this operator lets us provide a default value for a variable or operation result, in case it is nil. This is a safe way to turn an optional value into a non-optional value and it would look similar to the following code:

```
var possibleString: String? = "An actual string"
print(possibleString ?? "Default String") // "An Actual String"
```

Here, we are asking the program to print out `possibleString` unless it is nil; in which case, it will just print `"Default String"`. Since we did give it a value, it printed out that value and it is important to note that it printed out as a regular variable, not an optional. This is because one way or another, an actual value was going to be printed.

This is a great tool for concisely and safely unwrapping an optional when a default value makes sense.

Optional chaining

A common scenario in Swift is to have an optional that you must calculate something from. If the optional has a value, you will want to store the result of the calculation on it, but if it is nil, the result should just be set to nil:

```
var invitee: String? = "Sarah"
var uppercaseInvitee: String?
if let actualInvitee = invitee {
    uppercaseInvitee = actualInvitee.uppercaseString
}
```

This is pretty verbose. To shorten this up in an unsafe way, we could use forced unwrapping:

```
uppercaseInvitee = invitee!.uppercaseString
```

However, optional chaining will allow us to do this safely. Essentially, it allows optional operations on an optional. When the operation is called, if the optional is nil, it immediately returns nil; otherwise, it returns the result of performing the operation on the value within the optional:

```
uppercaseInvitee = invitee?.uppercaseString
```

So in this call, `invitee` is an optional. Instead of unwrapping it, we use optional chaining by placing a question mark (?) after it, followed by the optional operation. In this case, we are asking for the `uppercaseInvitee` property on it. If `invitee` is nil, `uppercaseInvitee` is immediately set to nil without even trying to access `uppercaseString`. If it actually does contain a value, `uppercaseInvitee` gets set to the `uppercaseString` property of the contained value. Note that all optional chains return an optional result.

You can chain as many calls as you want, both optional and non-optional, together in this way:

```
var invitees: [String]? = ["Sarah", "Jamison", "Marcos", "Roana"]
invitees?.first?.uppercaseString.hasPrefix("A")
```

This code checks if the first element of the invitees-list starts with the letter A, even if it is a lowercase A. First, it uses an optional chain in case `invitees` is nil. Then the call to `first` uses an additional optional chain because that method returns an optional `String`. We then call `uppercaseString`, which does not return an optional, allowing us to access `hasPrefix` on the result without having to use another optional chain. If at any point any of the optionals are nil, the result will be nil. This can happen for two different reasons:

- `invitees` is `nil`
- `first` returns `nil` because the array is empty

If the chain makes it all the way to `uppercaseString`, there is no longer a failure path and it will definitely return an actual value. You will notice that there are exactly two question marks being used in this chain and there are two possible failure reasons.

At first, it can be hard to understand when you should and should not use a question mark to create a chain of calls; the rule is to always use a question mark if the previous element in the chain returns an optional. However, so you are prepared, let's take a look at what happens if you use an optional chain improperly:

```
invitees.first // Error
```

In this case, we try to call a method directly on an optional without a chain, so we get an error that says **Value of optional type '[String]?' not unwrapped; did you mean to use '!' or '?'?**. Not only does it tell us that the value is not unwrapped, it even suggests two common ways of dealing with the problem: forced unwrapping or optional chaining.

We also have the case where we try to use an optional chain inappropriately:

```
var otherInvitees = ["Kai", "Naya"]
otherInvitees?.first // Error
```

Here, we get an error that says **Cannot use optional chaining on non-optional value of type '[String]'**. It is great to have a good sense of the errors you might see when you make mistakes; so that you can correct them quickly because we all make silly mistakes from time-to-time.

Another great feature of optional chaining is that it can be used for method calls on an optional that does not actually return a value:

```
invitees?.removeAll()
```

In this case, we only want to call `removeAll` if there is truly a value within the optional array. So with this code, if there is a value, all the elements are removed from it; otherwise, it remains nil.

In the end, option chaining is a great choice for writing a concise code that still remains expressive and understandable.

Implicitly unwrapped optionals

There is a second type of optional called an **implicitly unwrapped optional**. There are really two ways to look at what an implicitly unwrapped optional is; one way is to say that it is a normal variable that can also be nil; the other way is to say that it is an optional that you don't have to unwrap to use. The important thing to understand about them is that, similar to optionals, they can be nil, but you do not have to unwrap them like a normal variable.

You can define an implicitly unwrapped optional with an exclamation mark (!) instead of a question mark (?) after the type name:

```
var name: String!
```

Similar to regular optionals, implicitly unwrapped optionals do not need to be given an initial value because they are nil by default.

At first it may sound like it is the best of both worlds, but in reality it is more like the worst of both worlds. Even though an implicitly unwrapped optional does not have to be unwrapped, it will crash your entire program if it is nil when used:

```
name.uppercaseString // Crash
```

A great way to think about them is that every time it is used, it is implicitly doing a forced unwrapping. The exclamation mark is placed in its type declaration, instead of each time it is used. This can be problematic because it appears the same as any other variable except for how it is declared. That means it is very unsafe to use, unlike a normal optional.

So if the implicitly unwrapped optionals are the worst of both worlds and are so unsafe, why do they even exist? The reality is that in rare circumstances, they are necessary. They are used in circumstances where a variable is not truly optional, but you also cannot give an initial value to it. This is almost always the case for custom types that have a member variable that is non-optional but cannot be set during initialization.

A rare example of this is with a view in iOS. UIKit, as we discussed before, is the framework Apple provides for iOS development. In it, Apple has a class called UIView that is used to display content on the screen. Apple also provides a tool in Xcode called Interface Builder that lets you design these views in a visual editor instead of in code. Many views designed in this way will need references to other views that can be accessed later, programmatically. When one of these views is loaded, it is initialized without anything connected and then all the connections are made. Once all of the connections are made, a function called awakeFromNib is called on the view. This means that these connections are not available to be used during initialization but are available once awakeFromNib is called. This order of operations also ensures that awakeFromNib is always called before anything actually uses the view. This is a circumstance where it is necessary to use an implicitly unwrapped optional. A member variable may not be able to be defined until after the view is initialized, when it is completely loaded:

```
Import UIKit
class MyView: UIView {
    @IBOutlet var button: UIButton!
    var buttonOriginalWidth: CGFloat!

    override func awakeFromNib() {
        self.buttonOriginalWidth = self.button.frame.size.width
    }
}
```

Notice that we have actually declared two implicitly unwrapped optionals. The first is a connection to a button. We know that this is a connection because it is preceded by `@IBOutlet`. This is declared as an implicitly unwrapped optional because connections are not set up until after initialization, but they are still guaranteed to be set up before any other methods are called on the view.

This then leads us to unwrapping our second variable, `buttonOriginalWidth`, implicitly because we need to wait until the connection is made before we can determine the width of the button. After `awakeFromNib` is called, it is safe to treat both `button` and `buttonOriginalWidth` as non-optional.

You may have noticed that we had to dive pretty deep into app development to find a valid use case for implicitly unwrapped optionals and this is arguably only because UIKit is implemented in Objective-C, as we will learn more about in *Chapter 10, Harnessing the Past – Understanding and Translating Objective-C*. This is another testament to the fact that they should be used sparingly.

Debugging optionals

We have already seen a couple of the compiler errors we will commonly see because of optionals. If we try to call a method on an optional that we intended to call on the wrapped value, we will get an error. If we try to unwrap a value that is not actually optional, we will also get an error. We also need to be prepared for the runtime errors that optionals can cause.

As we have discussed, optionals cause runtime errors that are also referred to as crashes, if you try to forcefully unwrap one that is nil. This can happen with both explicit and implicitly forced unwrapping. If you have followed my advice so far in this chapter, this should be a rare occurrence. However, we all end up working with a third party code and maybe they were lazy or maybe they use forced unwrapping to enforce their expectations about how their code should be used.

Also, we all suffer from being lazy from time to time. It can be exhausting or discouraging to worry about all the edge cases when you are excited about programming the core functionality of your app. We may use forced unwrapping temporarily while we worry about that main functionality and plan to come back to handle it later. After all, during development it is better to have a forced unwrapping crash the development version of your app than it is for it to fail silently if you have not yet handled that edge case. We may even decide that an edge case is not worth the development effort of handling because everything about developing an app is a trade off. Either way, we need to recognize a crash from forced unwrapping quickly so we don't waste extra time trying to figure out what went wrong.

When an app tries to unwrap a nil value, if you are currently debugging the app, Xcode will show you the line that is trying to do the unwrapping. The line will report that there was an **EXC_BAD_INSTRUCTION** error and you will also get a message in the console saying **fatal error: unexpectedly found nil while unwrapping an Optional value**:

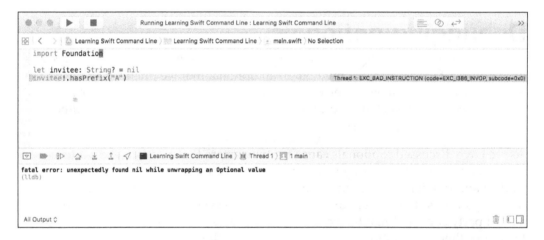

You will also sometimes have to look at what code is currently calling the code that failed. To do that, you can use the call stack in Xcode. The call stack is the full path of all function calls that got to this location. So, if you have `function1` call `function2`, which then calls `function3`, `function3` will be at the top and `function1` will be at the bottom. Once the execution exits `function3`, it will be removed from the stack so you will just have `function2` on top of `function1`.

When your program crashes, Xcode will automatically display the call stack, but you can also manually show it by navigating to **View | Navigators | Show Debug Navigator**. It will look similar to the following screenshot:

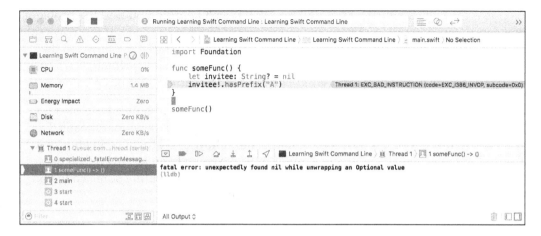

Here, you can click around different levels of code to see the state of things. This will become even more important if the program is crashing within one of Apple's framework, where you do not have access to the code. In that case, you will want to move up the call stack to the point where your code called into the framework. You may also be able to look at the names of the functions to help you figure out what may have gone wrong.

Anywhere on the call stack, you can look at the state of the variables in the debugger, as shown:

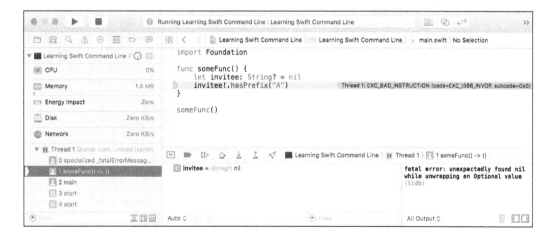

If you do not see this variable's view, you can display it by clicking on the button in the bottom-right corner of the screen, second from the right that will be grayed out. Here, you can see that `invitee` is indeed nil, which is what caused the crash.

As powerful as the debugger is, if you find that it isn't helping you find the problem, you can always put `print` statements in important parts of the code. It is always safe to print out an optional, as long as you don't forcefully unwrap it as shown in the preceding example. As we have seen before, when an optional is printed, it will print **nil** if it doesn't have a value, or it will print **Optional(<value>)** if it has a value.

Debugging is an extremely important part of becoming a productive developer because we all make mistakes and create bugs. Being a great developer means that you can identify problems quickly and understand how to fix them soon after that. This will largely come from practice, but it will also come from having a firm grasp of what is really happening with your code versus simply adapting some code you find online to fit your needs through trial and error.

The underlying implementation

At this point, you should have a pretty strong grasp of what an optional is and how to use and debug it, but it will be valuable to look a little deeper at optionals to see how they actually work.

In reality, the question mark syntax for optionals is just special shorthand. Writing `String?` is equivalent to writing `Optional<String>`. Writing `String!` is equivalent to writing `ImplicitlyUnwrappedOptional<String>`. The Swift compiler has the shorthand versions because they are so commonly used. This allows the code to be more concise and readable.

If you declare an optional using the long form, you can see Swift's implementation by holding *Command* and clicking on the word **Optional**. Here, you can see that `Optional` is implemented as an enumeration. Simplifying the code a little, we have:

```
enum Optional<T> {
    case None
    case Some(T)
}
```

So we can see that an optional really has two cases: `None` and `Some`. `None` stands for the nil case, while the `Some` case has an associated value, which is the value wrapped inside the optional. Unwrapping is the process of retrieving the associated value out of the `Some` case.

The one part of this that you have not seen yet is the angled bracket syntax (`<T>`). This is called a **generic** and it essentially allows the enumeration to have an associated value of any type. We will cover generics in-depth in *Chapter 6, Make Swift Work For You – Protocols and Generics*.

Realizing that optionals are simply enumerations will help you understand how to use them. It also gives you some insight into how concepts are built on top of other concepts. Optionals seem really complex until you realize that they are just a two case enumeration. Once you understand enumerations, you can pretty easily understand optionals as well.

Summary

We have only covered a single concept, optionals, in this chapter, but we have seen that this is a pretty dense topic. We have seen that at the surface level, optionals are pretty straightforward. They are a way to represent a variable that has no value. However, there are multiple ways to get access to the value wrapped within an optional that have very specific use cases. Optional binding is always preferred, as it is the safest method, but we can also use forced unwrapping if we are confident that an optional is not nil. We also have a type called implicitly unwrapped optional, to delay the assigning of a variable that is not intended to be optional; however, we should use it sparingly because there is almost always a better alternative.

Now that we have a firm understanding of optionals, we can begin to look at something else that may appear minor on the surface but actually opens up a whole world of possibilities. All functions in Swift are actually variables or constants themselves. We will explore what this means in the next chapter.

5
A Modern Paradigm – Closures and Functional Programming

So far, we have been programming using the paradigm called **object-oriented programming**, where everything in a program is represented as an object that can be manipulated and passed around to other objects. This is the most popular way to create apps because it is a very intuitive way to think about software and it goes well with the way Apple has designed their frameworks. However, there are some drawbacks to this technique. The biggest one is that the state of data can be very hard to track and reason about. If we have a thousand different objects floating around in our app, all with different information, it can be hard to track down where the bugs occurred and it can be hard to understand how the whole system fits together. Another paradigm of programming that can help with this problem is called **functional programming**.

Some programming languages are designed to use only functional programming, but Swift is designed primarily as an object-oriented language with the ability to use functional programming concepts. In this chapter, we will explore how to implement these functional programming concepts in Swift and what they are used for. To do this, we will cover the following topics:

- Functional programming philosophy
- Closures
- Building blocks of functional programming in Swift
- Lazy evaluation
- Example

Functional programming philosophy

Before we jump into writing code, let's discuss the ideas and motivations behind functional programming.

State and side effects

Functional programming makes it significantly easier to think of each component in isolation. This includes things such as types, functions, and methods. If we can wrap our minds around everything that is input into these code components and everything that should be returned from them, we could analyze the code easily to ensure that there are no bugs and it performs well. Every type is created with a certain number of parameters and each method and function in a program has a certain number of parameters and return values. Normally, we think about these as the only inputs and outputs, but the reality is that often there are more. We refer to these extra inputs and outputs as **state**.

In a more general sense, state is any stored information, however temporary, that can be changed. Let's consider a simple `double` function:

```
func double(input: Int) -> Int {
    return input * 2
}
```

This is a great example of a **stateless** function. No matter what else is happening in the entire universe of the program, this method will always return the same value, if it is given the same input. An input of 2 will always return 4.

Now, let's look at a method with state:

```
struct Ball {
    var radius: Double

    mutating func growByAmount(amount: Double) -> Double {
        self.radius = self.radius + amount
        return self.radius
    }
}
```

If you call this method repeatedly, with the same input on the same `Ball` instance, you will get a different result every time. This is because there is an additional input in this method, which is the instance it is being called on. It is otherwise referred to as `self`. `self` is actually both an input and an output of this method, because the original value of radius affects the output and `radius` is changed by the end of the method. This is still not very difficult to reason about, as long as you keep in mind that `self` is always another input and output. However, you can imagine that with a more complex data structure, it can be hard to track every possible input and output from a piece of code. As soon as that starts to happen, it becomes easier for bugs to get created, because we will almost certainly have, unexpected inputs causing unexpected outputs.

Side effects are an even worse type of extra input or output. They are the unexpected changes to state, seemingly unrelated to the code being run. If we simply rename our preceding method to something a little less clear, its effect on the instance becomes unexpected:

```
mutating func currentRadiusPlusAmount(amount: Double) -> Double {
    self.radius = self.radius + amount
    return self.radius
}
```

Based on its name, you wouldn't expect this method to change the actual value of `radius`. This means that if you didn't see the actual implementation, you would expect this method to keep returning the same value if called with the same amount on the same instance. Unpredictability is a terrible thing to have as a programmer.

In its strictest form, functional programming eliminates all state and therefore side effects. We will never go that far in Swift, but we will often use functional programming techniques to reduce state and side effects to increase the predictability of our code, drastically.

Declarative versus imperative code

Besides predictability, the other effect that functional programming has on our code is that it becomes more **declarative**. This means that the code shows us how we expect information to flow through our application. This is in contrast to what we have been doing with object-oriented programming, which we call **imperative code**. This is the difference between writing a code that loops through an array to add only certain elements to a new array and running a filter on the array. The former would look similar to this:

```
var originalArray = [1,2,3,4,5]
var greaterThanThree = [Int]()
for num in originalArray {
```

```
        if num > 3 {
            greaterThanThree.append(num)
        }
    }
    print(greaterThanThree) // [4,5]
```

Running a filter on the array would look similar to this:

```
    var originalArray = [1,2,3,4,5]
    var greaterThanThree = originalArray.filter {$0 > 3}
    print(greaterThanThree) // [4,5]
```

Don't worry if you don't understand the second example yet. This is what we are going to cover in the rest of this chapter. The general idea is that with imperative codes, we are going to issue a series of commands with the intent of the code as a secondary, subtler idea. To understand that we are creating a copy of originalArray with only elements greater than 3, we have to read the code and mentally step through what is happening. In the second example, we are stating in the code itself that we are filtering the original array. Ultimately, these ideas exist on a spectrum and it is hard to have something be 100% declarative or imperative, but the principles of each are important.

So far, with our imperative code, most of it just defines what our data should look like and how it can be manipulated. Even with high quality abstractions, understanding a section of code can often involve jumping between lots of methods, tracing the execution. In declarative code, logic can be more centralized and often more easily read, based on well-named methods.

You can also think of imperative codes as if it were as a factory where each person makes a car in its entirety while thinking of declarative code as if it were a factory with an assembly line. In order to understand what the person is doing in a non-assembly line factory, you have to watch the whole process unfold one step at a time. They will probably be pulling in all kinds of tools at different times and it will be hard to follow. In a factory with an assembly line, you can determine what is happening by looking at each step in the assembly line one at a time.

Now that we understand some of the motivations of functional programming, let's look at the Swift features that make it possible.

Closures

In Swift, functions are considered first-class citizens, which means that they can be treated the same as any other type. They can be assigned to variables and be passed in and out of other functions. When treated this way, we call them **closures**. This is an extremely critical piece to write more declarative code because it allows us to treat functionalities like objects. Instead of thinking of functions as a collection of code to be executed, we can start to think about them more like a recipe to get something done. Just like you can give just about any recipe to a chef to cook, you can create types and methods that take a closure to perform some customizable behavior.

Closures as variables

Let's take a look at how closures work in Swift. The simplest way to capture a closure in a variable is to define the function and then use its name to assign it to a variable:

```
func double(input: Int) -> Int {
        return input * 2
}

var doubleClosure = double
print(doubleClosure(2)) // 4
```

As you can see, `doubleClosure` can be used just like the normal function name after being assigned. There is actually no difference between using `double` and `doubleClosure`. Note that we can now think of this closure as an object that will double anything passed to it.

If you look at the type of `doubleClosure` by holding the option key and click on the name, you will see that the type is defined as `(Int) -> Int`. The basic type of any closure is `(ParamterType1, ParameterType2, ...) -> ReturnType`.

Using this syntax, we can also define our closure inline, such as:

```
var doubleClosure2 = { (input: Double) -> Double in
    return input * 2
}
```

We begin and end any closure with curly brackets (`{ }`). Then, we follow the opening curly bracket with the type for the closure, which will include input parameters and a return value. Finally, we separate the type definition from the actual implementation with the `in` keyword.

An absence of a return type is defined as Void or (). Even though you may see that some programmers use parentheses, Void is preferred for return declarations:

```
var printDouble = { (input: Double) -> Void in
    print(input * 2)
}
```

Essentially, () is an empty tuple meaning it holds no value and it is more commonly used for the input parameters, in case the closure doesn't take any parameters at all:

```
var makeHelloWorld = { () -> String in
    return "Hello World!"
}
```

So far, even though we can change our thinking about the block of code by making it into a closure, it is not terribly useful. To really make closures useful, we need to start passing them into other functions.

Closures as parameters

We can define a function to take a closure as a parameter, using the same type syntax we saw previously:

```
func firstInNumbers(
    numbers: [Int],
    passingTest: (number: Int) -> Bool
    ) -> Int?
{
    for number in numbers {
        if passingTest(number: number) {
            return number
        }
    }
    return nil
}
```

Here, we have a function that can find the first number in an array that passes some arbitrary test. The syntax at the end of the function declaration may be confusing but it should be clear if you work from the inside out. The type for passingTest is (number: Int) -> Bool. That is then the second parameter of the whole firstInNumbers function, which returns an Int?. If we want to use this function to find the first number greater than three, we can create a custom test and pass that into the function:

```
let numbers = [1,2,3,4,5]
func greaterThanThree(number: Int) -> Bool {
```

```
        return number > 3
    }
    var firstNumber = firstInNumbers(numbers, greaterThanThree)
    print(firstNumber) // "Optional(4)"
```

Here, we are essentially passing a little bundle of functionality to the
firstInNumbers: function that lets us drastically enhance what a single function
can normally do. This is an incredibly useful technique. Looping through an array
to find an element can be very verbose. Instead, we can use this function to find an
element showing only the important part of the code: the test.

We can even define our test right in a call to the function:

```
    firstNumber = firstInNumbers(numbers, passingTest: { (number: Int) ->
    Bool in
        return number > 3
    })
```

Even though this is more concise, it's pretty complex; hence, Swift allows us to cut
out some of the unnecessary syntax.

Syntactic sugar

First, we can make use of type inference for the type of number. The
compiler knows that number needs to be Int based on the definition of
firstInNumbers:passingTest:. It also knows that the closure has to return
Bool. Now, we can rewrite our call, as shown:

```
    firstNumber = firstInNumbers(numbers, passingTest: { (number) in
        return number > 3
    })
```

This looks cleaner, but the parentheses around number are not required; we could
leave those out. In addition, if we have closure as the last parameter of a function,
we can provide the closure outside the parentheses for the function call:

```
    firstNumber = firstInNumbers(numbers) { number in
        return number > 3
    }
```

Note that the closing parenthesis for the function parameters moved from being after the closure to before it. This is looking pretty great, but we can go even further. For a single line closure, we don't even have to write the `return` keyword because it is implied:

```
firstNumber = firstInNumbers(numbers) { number in
    number > 3
}
```

Lastly, we don't always need to give a name to the parameters of closures. If you leave out the names altogether, each parameter can be referenced using the syntax `$<ParemterIndex>`. Just like with arrays, the index starts at 0. This helps us write this call very concisely in a single line:

```
firstNumber = firstInNumbers(numbers) { $0 > 3 }
```

This is a long way from our original syntax. You can mix and match all of these different techniques to make sure that your code is as understandable as possible. As we have discussed before, understandability is a balance between being concise and clear. It is up to you in each circumstance to decide how much syntax you want to cut out. To me, it is not immediately clear what the closure is without it having a name. My preferred syntax for this is to use the parameter name in the call:

```
firstNumber = firstInNumbers(numbers, passingTest: {$0 > 3})
```

This makes it clear that the closure is a test to see which number we want to pull out of the list.

Now that we know what a closure is and how to use one, we can discuss some of the core features of Swift that allow us to write a functional style code.

Building blocks of functional programming in Swift

The first thing to realize is that Swift is not a functional programming language. At its core, it will always be an object-oriented programming language. However, since functions in Swift are first-class citizens, we can use some of the core techniques. Swift provides some built-in methods to get us started.

Filter

The first method we are going to discuss is called **filter**. As the name suggests, this method is used to filter elements in a list. For example, we can filter our `numbers` array to include only even numbers:

```
var evenNumbers = numbers.filter({ element in
    element % 2 == 0
}) // [2, 4]
```

The closure we provide to filter will be called once for each element in the array. It is tasked with returning `true` if the element needs to be included in the result and `false` otherwise. The preceding closure takes advantage of the implied return value and simply returns `true` if the number has a remainder of zero when being divided by two.

Note that the filter does not change the `numbers` variable; it simply returns a filtered copy. Changing the value will modify the state, which we want to avoid.

This method provides us with a concise way to filter a list in virtually any way we want. It is also the beginning of building up a vocabulary of transformations, which we can perform on data. One could argue that all applications just transform data from one form to another, so this vocabulary helps us achieve the maximum functionality we want in any app.

Reduce

Swift also provides a method called **reduce**. The purpose of reduce is to condense a list down to a single value. Reduce works by iterating over every value and combining it with a single value that represents all previous elements. This is just like mixing a bunch of ingredients in a bowl for a recipe. We will take one ingredient at a time and combine it in the bowl until we are left with just a single bowl of ingredients.

Let's take a look at what the reduce function looks like in our code. We can use it to sum up the values in our number array:

```
var sum = numbers.reduce(0, combine: { previousSum, element in
    previousSum + element
}) // 15
```

As you can see, reduce takes two parameters. The first parameter is a value with which to start combining each item in the list. The second is a closure that will do the combining. Similar to filter, this closure is called once for each element in the array. The first parameter of the closure is the value after combing each of the previous elements with the initial value. The second parameter is the next element.

So the first time the closure is called, it is called with 0 (the initial value) and 1 (the first element of the list); it then returns 1. This means that it is then called again with 1 (the value from the last call) and 2 (the next element in the list) returning 3. This will continue until it is combining the running sum of 10, with the last element 5, returning a final result of 15. It becomes very simple once we break it down.

Reduce is another great vocabulary item to add to our skill-set. It can reduce any list of information into a single value by analyzing data to generate a document from a list of images and much more.

Also, we can start to chain our functions together. If we want to find the sum of all the even numbers in our list, we can run the following code:

```
var evenSum = numbers.filter({$0 % 2 == 0}).reduce(0, combine: {$0 +
$1}) // 6
```

Now, we can actually do one more thing to shorten this. Every arithmetic operation, including addition (+) is really just another function or closure. Addition is a function that takes two values of the same type and returns their sum. This means that we can simply pass the addition function as our combine closure:

```
evenSum = numbers.filter({$0 % 2 == 0}).reduce(0, combine: +) // 6
```

Now we are getting fancy!

Also, keep in mind that the combined value does not need to be the same type that is in the original list. Instead of summing the values, we could combine them all into one string:

```
let string = numbers.reduce("", combine: {"\($0)\($1)"}) // "12345"
```

Here I am using string interpolation to create a string that starts with the running value and ends with the next element.

Map

Map is a method to transform every element in a list to another value. For example, we can add one to every number in the list:

```
let plusOne = numbers.map({ element -> Int in
    return element + 1
}) // [2, 3, 4, 5, 6]
```

As you can probably guess, the closure that map takes is called once for each element in the list. As a parameter, it takes the element and is expected to return the new value to be added to the resulting array.

Just like with reduce, the transformed type does not need to match. We can convert all of our numbers to strings:

```
let strings = numbers.map {String($0)}
```

Map is incredibly versatile. It can be used to convert a list of data into a list of views to display the data, convert a list of image paths to their loaded images, and so on.

The map method is a great choice to perform calculations on each element of a list, but it should be used only when it makes sense to put the result of the calculation back into a list. You could technically use it to iterate through a list and perform some other action, but in that case, a for-in loop is more appropriate.

Sort

The last built-in functional method we will discuss is called **sorted**. As the name suggests, sorted allows you to change the order of a list. For example, if we want to reorder our numbers list to go from largest to smallest:

```
numbers.sort({ element1, element2 in
    element1 > element2
}) // [5, 4, 3, 2, 1]
```

The closure that is passed into sorted is called `isOrderedBefore`. This means that it takes two elements in the list as input and it should return `true` if the first element is to be ordered before the second element. We cannot rely on the closure to be called a certain number of times, nor the elements it will be called with, but it will be called until the sorting algorithm has enough knowledge to come up with a new order.

In our case, we return `true` any time the first argument is greater than the second argument. This results in larger elements always coming before smaller elements.

This is a great method because sorting is a very common task and often data will need to be sorted in multiple ways, depending on the user's interaction. Using this method, you could design multiple sorting closures and change the one being used based on the user's interaction.

How these affect the state and nature of code

There are more built-in functional methods and we will learn to write our own in the next chapter on generics, but these are a core few to help you start thinking about certain problems in a functional way. So how do these methods help us avoid state?

These methods, along with others, can be combined in infinite ways to transform data and perform actions. No matter how complex the combination is, there is no way to interfere with each individual step. There are no side effects because the only inputs are the result of the preceding step and the only outputs are what will be passed on to the next step.

You can also see that complex transformations can all be declared in a concise and centralized place. A reader of the code doesn't need to trace the changing values of many variables; they can simply look at the code and see what processes it will go through.

Lazy evaluation

A powerful feature of Swift is the ability to make these operations lazily evaluated. This means that, just like a lazy person would do, a value is only calculated when it is absolutely necessary and at the latest point possible.

First, it is important to realize the order in which these methods are executed. For example, what if we only want the first element of our numbers to be mapped to strings:

```
var firstString = numbers.map({String($0)}).first
```

This works well, except that we actually converted every number to a string to get to just the first one. That is because each step of the chain is completed in its entirety before the next one can be executed. To prevent this, Swift has a built-in method called **lazy**.

Lazy creates a new version of a container that only pulls specific values from it when it is specifically requested. This means that lazy essentially allows each element to flow through a series of functions one at a time, as it is needed. You can think about it like a lazy version of a worker. If you ask someone lazy to look up the capital of Cameroon, they aren't going to compile a list of the capitals of all countries before they get the answer. They are only going to do the work necessary to get that specific answer. That work may involve multiple steps, but they would only have to do those steps for the specific countries you ask for.

Now, let's look at what lazy looks like in code. You use it to convert a normal list into a lazy list:

```
firstString = numbers.lazy.map({String($0)}).first
```

Now, instead of calling map directly on `numbers`, we called it on the lazy version of `numbers`. This makes it so that every time a value is requested from the result, it only processes a single element out of the input array. In our preceding example, the `map` method will only have been performed once.

This even applies to looping through a result:

```
let lazyStrings = numbers.lazy.map({String($0)})
for string in lazyStrings {
    print(string)
}
```

Each number is converted to a string only upon the next iteration of the for-in loop. If we were to break out of that loop early, the rest of the values would not be calculated. This is a great way to save processing time, especially on large lists.

Example

Let's take a look at what this looks like in practice. We can use some of the techniques we learned in this chapter to write a different and possibly better implementation of our party inviter.

We can start by defining the same input data:

```
//: List of people to invite
let invitees = [
    "Sarah",
    "Jamison",
    "Marcos",
    "Roana",
```

```
        "Neena",
    ]

    //: Dictionary of shows organized by genre
    var showsByGenre = [
        "Comedy": "Modern Family",
        "Drama": "Breaking Bad",
        "Variety": "The Colbert Report",
    ]
```

In this implementation, we are making the invitees list, which is just a constant list of names and the shows by genre dictionary variable. This is because we are going to be mapping our invitees list to a list of invitation text. As we do the mapping, we will have to pick a random genre to assign to the current invitee, and in order to avoid assigning the same genre more than once, we can remove the genre from the dictionary.

So let's write the random genre function:

```
    func pickAndRemoveRandomGenre() -> (genre: String, example: String)? {
        let genres = Array(showsByGenre.keys)
        guard genres.count > 0 else {
            return nil
        }

        let genre = genres[Int(rand()) % genres.count]
        let example = showsByGenre[genre]!
        showsByGenre[genre] = nil
        return (genre: genre, example: example)
    }
```

We start by creating an array of just the keys of the shows by genre dictionary. Then, if there are no genres left, we simply return nil. Otherwise, we pick out a random genre, remove it from the dictionary, and return it and the show example.

Now we can use that function to map the invitees to a list of invitations:

```
    let invitations: [String] = invitees
    .map({ name in
        guard let (genre, example) = pickAndRemoveRandomGenre() else {
            return "\(name), just bring yourself"
        }
        return "\(name), bring a \(genre) show"
            + "\n\(example) is a great \(genre)"
    })
```

Here we try to pick a random genre. If we can't, we return an invitation saying that the invitee should just bring themselves. If we can, we return an invitation saying what genre they should bring with the example show. The one new thing to note here is that we are using the sequence "\n" in our string. This is a newline character and it signals that a new line should be started in the text.

The last step is to print out the invitations. To do that, we can print out the invitations as a string joined by newline characters:

```
print(invitations.joinWithSeparator("\n"))
```

This works pretty well but there is one problem. The first invitees we listed will always be assigned a genre because the order they are processed in never changes. To fix this, we can write a function to shuffle the invitees before we begin to map the function:

```
func shuffle(array: [String]) -> [String] {
    return array
        .map({ ($0, Int(rand())) })
        .sort({ $0.1 < $1.1 })
        .map({$0.0})
}
```

In order to shuffle an array, we go through three steps: First, we map the array to a tuple with the original element and a random number. Second, we sort the tuples based on those random numbers. Finally, we map the tuples back to just their original elements.

Now, all we have to do is add a call to this function to our sequence:

```
let invitations: [String] = shuffle(invitees)
.map({ name in
    guard let (genre, example) = pickAndRemoveRandomGenre() else {
        return "\(name), just bring yourself"
    }
    return "\(name), bring a \(genre) show"
        + "\n\(example) is a great \(genre)"
})
```

This implementation is not necessarily better than our previous implementations, but it definitely has its advantages. We have taken steps towards reducing the state by implementing it as a series of data transformations. The big hiccup in that is that we are still maintaining state in the genre dictionary. We can certainly do more to eliminate that as well, but this gives you a good idea of how we can start to think about problems in a functional way. The more ways in which we can think about a problem, the higher our odds of coming up with the best solution.

Summary

In this chapter, we have had to shift the way we think about code. At the very least, this is a great exercise so we don't get set in our programming ways. We have covered the philosophy behind functional programming and how it differs from object-oriented programming. We have looked into the specifics of closures and how they enable functional programming techniques in Swift. Lastly, we explored some of the specific functional methods that Swift has built in.

The sign of a truly great programmer is not someone who knows a lot about one tool, but one who knows which tool to use when. We get there by learning and practicing using lots of different tools and techniques without ever becoming too attached to a specific one.

Once you are comfortable with the concepts of closures and functional programming, you are ready to move on to our next topic, generics. Generics is our first opportunity to make the strongly typed nature of Swift really work for us.

6
Make Swift Work For You – Protocols and Generics

As we learned in *Chapter 2, Building Blocks – Variables, Collections, and Flow Control*, Swift is a strongly typed language, which means that every piece of data must have a type. Not only can we take advantage of this to reduce the clutter in our code, we can also leverage it to let the compiler catch bugs for us. The earlier we catch a bug, the better. Besides not writing them in the first place, the earliest place where we can catch a bug is when the compiler reports an error.

Two big tools that Swift provides to achieve this are called **protocols** and **generics**. Both of them use the type system to make our intentions clear to the compiler so that it can catch more bugs for us.

In this chapter, we will cover the following topics:

- Protocols
- Generics
- Extending existing generics
- Extending protocols
- Putting protocols and generics to use

Protocols

The first tool we will look at is **protocols**. A protocol is essentially a contract that a type can sign, specifying that it will provide a certain interface to other components. This relationship is significantly looser than the relationship a subclass has with its superclass. A protocol does not provide any implementation to the types that implement them. Instead, a type can implement them in any way that they like.

Let's take a look at how we define a protocol, in order to understand them better.

Defining a protocol

Let's say we have some code that needs to interact with a collection of strings. We don't actually care what order they are stored in and we only need to be able to add and enumerate elements inside the container. One option would be to simply use an array, but an array does way more than we need it to. What if we decide later that we would rather write and read the elements from the file system? Furthermore, what if we want to write a container that would intelligently start using the file system as it got really large? We can make our code flexible enough to do this in the future by defining a string container protocol, which is a loose contract that defines what we need it to do. This protocol might look similar to the following code:

```
protocol StringContainer {
    var count: Int { get }
    mutating func addString(string: String)
    func enumerateStrings(handler: (string: String) -> Void)
}
```

Predictably, a protocol is defined using the `protocol` keyword, similar to a class or a structure. It also allows you to specify computed properties and methods. You cannot declare a stored property because it is not possible to create an instance of a protocol directly. You can only create instances of types that implement the protocol. Also, you may notice that none of the computed properties or methods provide implementations. In a protocol, you only provide the interface.

Since protocols cannot be initialized on their own, they are useless until we create a type that implements them. Let's take a look at how we can create a type that implements our `StringContainer` protocol.

Implementing a protocol

A type "signs the contract" of a protocol in the same way that a class inherits from another class except that structures and enumerations can also implement protocols:

```
struct StringBag: StringContainer {
    // Error: Type 'StringBag' does not conform to protocol
'StringContainer'
}
```

As you can see, once a type has claimed to implement a specific protocol, the compiler will give an error if it has not fulfilled the contract by implementing everything defined in the protocol. To satisfy the compiler, we must now implement the count computed property, mutating function addString:, and function enumerateStrings: as they are defined. We will do this by internally holding our values in an array:

```
struct StringBag: StringContainer {
    var strings = [String]()
    var count: Int {
        return self.strings.count
    }

    mutating func addString(string: String) {
        self.strings.append(string)
    }

    func enumerateStrings(handler: (string: String) -> Void) {
        for string in self.strings {
            handler(string: string)
        }
    }
}
```

The count property will always just return the number of elements in our strings array. The addString: method can simply add the string to our array. Finally, our enumerateString: method just needs to loop through our array and call the handler with each element.

At this point, the compiler is satisfied that StringBag is fulfilling its contract with the StringContainer protocol.

Now, we can similarly create a class that implements the StringContainer protocol. This time, we will implement it using an internal dictionary instead of an array:

```
class SomeSuperclass {}
class StringBag2: SomeSuperclass, StringContainer {
    var strings = [String:Void]()
    var count: Int {
        return self.strings.count
    }
```

```swift
        func addString(string: String) {
            self.strings[string] = ()
        }

        func enumerateStrings(handler: (string: String) -> Void) {
            for string in self.strings.keys {
                handler(string: string)
            }
        }
    }
```

Here we can see that a class can both inherit from a superclass and implement a protocol. The superclass always has to come first in the list, but you can implement as many protocols as you want, separating each one with a comma. In fact, a structure and enumeration can also implement multiple protocols.

With this implementation we are doing something slightly strange with the dictionary. We defined it to have no values; it is simply a collection of keys. This allows us to store our strings without any regard to the order they are in.

Now, when we create instances, we can actually assign any instance of any type that implements our protocol to a variable that is defined to be our protocol, just like we can with superclasses:

```swift
    var someStringBag: StringContainer = StringBag()
    someStringBag.addString("Sarah")
    someStringBag = StringBag2()
    someStringBag.addString("Sarah")
```

When a variable is defined with our protocol as its type, we can only interact with it using the interface that the protocol defines. This is a great way to abstract implementation details and create more flexible code. By being less restrictive on the type that we want to use, we can easily change our code without affecting how we use it. Protocols provide the same benefit that superclasses do, but in an even more flexible and comprehensive way, because they can be implemented by all types and a type can implement an unlimited number of protocols. The only benefit that superclasses provide over protocols is that superclasses share their implementations with their children.

Using type aliases

Protocols can be made more flexible using a feature called **type aliases**. They act as a placeholder for a type that will be defined later when the protocol is being implemented. For example, instead of creating an interface that specifically includes strings, we can create an interface for a container that can hold any type of value, as shown:

```
protocol Container {
    typealias Element

    mutating func addElement(element: Element)
    func enumerateElements(handler: (element: Element) -> Void)
}
```

As you can see, this protocol creates a type alias called `Element` using the keyword `typealias`. It does not actually specify a real type; it is just a placeholder for a type that will be defined later. Everywhere we have previously used a string, we simply refer to it as `Element`.

Now, we can create another string bag that uses the new `Container` protocol with a type alias instead of the `StringContainer` protocol. To do this, we not only need to implement each of the methods, we also need to give a definition for the type alias, as shown:

```
struct StringBag3: Container {
    typealias Element = String

    var elements = [Element:Void]()

    var count: Int {
        return elements.count
    }

    mutating func addElement(element: Element) {
        self.elements[element] = ()
    }

    func enumerateElements(handler: (element: Element) -> Void) {
        for element in self.elements.keys {
            handler(element: element)
        }
    }
}
```

With this code, we have specified that the `Element` type alias should be a string for this implementation using an equal sign (=). This code continues to use the type alias for all of the properties and methods, but you can also use string since they are in fact the same thing now.

Using the type alias actually makes it really easy for us to create another structure that can hold integers instead of strings:

```
struct IntBag: Container {
    typealias Element = Int

    var elements = [Element:Void]()

    var count: Int {
        return elements.count
    }

    mutating func addElement(element: Element) {
        self.elements[element] = ()
    }

    func enumerateElements(handler: (element: Element) -> Void) {
        for element in self.elements.keys {
            handler(element: element)
        }
    }
}
```

The only difference between these two pieces of code is that the type alias has been defined to be an integer in the second case instead of a string. We could use copy and paste to create a container of virtually any type, but as usual, doing a lot of copy and paste is a sign that there is a better solution. Also, you may notice that our new `Container` protocol isn't actually that useful on its own because with our existing techniques, we can't treat a variable as just a `Container`. If we are going to interact with an instance that implements this protocol, we need to know what type it has assigned the type alias to.

Swift provides a tool called **generics** to solve both of these problems.

Generics

A generic is very similar to a type alias. The difference is that the exact type of a generic is determined by the context in which it is being used, instead of being determined by the implementing types. This also means that a generic only has a single implementation that must support all possible types. Let's start by defining a generic function.

Generic function

In *Chapter 5, A Modern Paradigm – Closures and Functional Programming*, we created a function that helped us find the first number in an array of numbers that passes a test:

```
func firstInNumbers(
    numbers: [Int],
    passingTest: (number: Int) -> Bool
    ) -> Int?
{
    for number in numbers {
        if passingTest(number: number) {
            return number
        }
    }
    return nil
}
```

This would be great if we only ever dealt with arrays of `integers`, but clearly it would be helpful to be able to do this with other types. In fact, dare I say, all types? We achieve this very simply by making our function generic. A generic function is declared similar to a normal function, but you include a list of comma-separated placeholders inside angled brackets (`<>`) at the end of the function name, as shown:

```
func firstInArray<ValueType>(
    array: [ValueType],
    passingTest: (value: ValueType) -> Bool
    ) -> ValueType?
{
    for value in array {
        if passingTest(value: value) {
            return value
        }
    }
    return nil
}
```

In this function, we have declared a single placeholder called `ValueType`. Just like with type aliases, we can continue to use this type in our implementation. This will stand in for a single type that will be determined when we go to use the function. You can imagine inserting `String` or any other type into this code instead of `ValueType` and it would still work.

We use this function similarly to any other function, as shown:

```
var strings = ["This", "is", "a", "sentence"]
var numbers = [1, 1, 2, 3, 5, 8, 13]
firstInArray(strings, passingTest: {$0 == "a"}) // "a"
firstInArray(numbers, passingTest: {$0 > 10}) // 13
```

Here, we have used `firstInArray:passingTest:` with both an array of strings and an array of numbers. The compiler figures out what type to substitute in for the placeholder based on the variables we pass into the function. In the first case, `strings` is an array of `String`. It compares that to `[ValueType]` and assumes that we want to replace `ValueType` with `String`. The same thing happens with our `Int` array in the second case.

So what happens if the type we use in our closure doesn't match the type of array we pass in?

```
firstInArray(numbers, passingTest: {$0 == "a"}) // Cannot convert
// value of type '[Int]' to expected argument type'[_]'
```

As you can see, we get an error that the types don't match.

You may have noticed that we have actually used generic functions before. All of the built in functions we looked at in *Chapter 5, A Modern Paradigm – Closures and Functional Programming*, such as `map` and `filter` are generic; they can be used with any type.

We have even experienced generic types before. Arrays and dictionaries are also generic. The Swift team didn't have to write a new implementation of array and dictionary for every type that we might want to use inside the containers; they created them as generic types.

Generic type

Similar to a generic function, a generic type is defined just like a normal type but it has a list of placeholders at the end of its name. Earlier in this chapter, we created our own containers for strings and `integers`. Let's make a generic version of these containers, as shown:

```
struct Bag<ElementType> {
    var elements = [ElementType]()
```

```
    mutating func addElement(element: ElementType) {
        self.elements.append(element)
    }

    func enumerateElements(
        handler: (element: ElementType) -> ()
        )
    {
        for element in self.elements {
            handler(element: element)
        }
    }
}
```

This implementation looks similar to our type alias versions, but we are using the `ElementType` placeholder instead.

While a generic function's placeholders are determined when the function is called, a generic type's placeholders are determined when initializing new instances:

```
var stringBag = Bag(elements: ["This", "is", "a", "sentence"])
var numberBag = Bag(elements: [1, 1, 2, 3, 5, 8, 13])
```

All future interactions with a generic instance must use the same types for its placeholders. This is actually one of the beauties of generics where the compiler does work for us. If we create an instance of one type and accidently try to use it as a different type, the compiler won't let us. This protection does not exist in many other programming languages, including Apple's previous language: Objective-C.

One interesting case to consider is if we try to initialize a bag with an empty array:

```
var emptyBag = Bag(elements: []) // Cannot invoke initilaizer for
// type 'Bag<_>' with an argument list of type '(elements: [_])'
```

As you can see, we get an error that the compiler could not determine the type to assign to our generic placeholder. We can solve this by giving an explicit type to the generic we are assigning it to:

```
var emptyBag: Bag<String> = Bag(elements: [])
```

This is great because not only can the compiler determine the generic placeholder types based on the variables we pass to them, it can also determine the type based on how we are using the result.

We have already seen how to use generics in a powerful way. We solved the first problem we discussed in the type alias section about copying and pasting a bunch of implementations for different types. However, we have not yet figured out how to solve the second problem: how do we write a generic function to handle any type of our `Container` protocol? The answer is that we can use **type constraints**.

Type constraints

Before we jump right into solving the problem, let's take a look at a simpler form of type constraints.

Protocol constraints

Let's say that we want to write a function that can determine the index of an instance within an array using an equality check. Our first attempt will probably look similar to the following code:

```
func indexOfValue<T>(value: T, inArray array: [T]) -> Int? {
    var index = 0
    for testValue in array {
        if testValue == value { // Error: Cannot invoke '=='
            return index
        }
        index++
    }
    return nil
}
```

With this attempt, we get an error that we cannot invoke the equality operator (`==`). This is because our implementation must work for any possible type that might be assigned to our placeholder. Not every type in Swift can be tested for equality. To fix this problem, we can use a type constraint to tell the compiler that we only want to allow our function to be called with types that support the equality operation. We add type constraints by requiring the placeholder to implement a protocol. In this case, Swift provides a protocol called `Equatable`, which we can use:

```
func indexOfValue<T: Equatable>(
    value: T,
    inArray array: [T]
    ) -> Int?
{
    var index = 0
    for testValue in array {
        if testValue == value {
```

```
        return index
    }
    index++
}
return nil
}
```

A type constraint looks similar to a type implementing a protocol using a colon (:) after a placeholder name. Now, the compiler is satisfied that every possible type can be compared using the equality operator. If we were to try to call this function with a type that is not equatable, the compiler would produce an error:

```
class MyType {}
var typeList = [MyType]()
indexOfValue(MyType(), inArray: typeList)
// Cannot convert value of type '[MyType]' to expected
// argument type '[_]'
```

This is another case where the compiler can save us from ourselves.

We can also add type constraints to our generic types. For example, if we tried to create a bag with our dictionary implementation without a constraint, we would get an error:

```
struct Bag2<ElementType> {
    var elements: [ElementType:Void]
    // Type 'ElementType' does not conform to protocol 'Hashable'
}
```

This is because the key of dictionaries has a constraint that it must be `Hashable`. Dictionary is defined as `struct Dictionary<Key : Hashable, Value>`. `Hashable` basically means that the type can be represented using an integer. In fact, we can look at exactly what it means if we write `Hashable` in Xcode and then click on it while holding down the *Command* Key. This brings us to the definition of `Hashable`, which has comments that explain that the hash value of two objects that are equal must be the same. This is important to the way that `Dictionary` is implemented. So, if we want to be able to store our elements as keys in a dictionary, we must also add the `Hashable` constraint:

```
struct Bag2<ElementType: Hashable> {
    var elements: [ElementType:Void]

    mutating func addElement(element: ElementType) {
        self.elements[element] = ()
    }
}
```

```
func enumerateElements(
    handler: (element: ElementType) -> ()
    )
{
    for element in self.elements.keys {
        handler(element: element)
    }
}
}
```

Now the compiler is happy and we can start to use our `Bag2` struct with any type that is `Hashable`. We are close to solving our `Container` problem, but we need a constraint on the type alias of `Container`, not `Container` itself. To do that, we can use a `where` clause.

Where clauses for protocols

You can specify any number of `where` clauses you want after you have defined each placeholder type. They allow you to represent more complicated relationships. If we want to write a function that can check if our container contains a particular value, we can require that the element type is equatable:

```
func container<C: Container where C.Element: Equatable>(
    container: C,
    hasElement element: C.Element
    ) -> Bool
{
    var hasElement = false
    container.enumerateElements { testElement in
        if element == testElement {
            hasElement = true
        }
    }
    return hasElement
}
```

Here, we have specified a placeholder `C` that must implement the `Container` protocol; it must also have an `Element` type that is `Equatable`.

Sometimes we may also want to enforce a relationship between multiple placeholders. To do that, we can use an equality test inside the `where` clauses.

Where clauses for equality

If we want to write a function that can merge one container into another while still allowing the exact types to vary, we could write a function that would require that the containers hold the same value:

```
func merged<C1: Container, C2: Container where C1.Element ==
C2.Element>(
    lhs: C1,
    rhs: C2
    ) -> C1
{
    var merged = lhs
    rhs.enumerateElements { element in
        merged.addElement(element)
    }
    return merged
}
```

Here, we have specified two different placeholders: C1 and C2. Both of them must implement the `Container` protocol and they must also contain the same `Element` type. This allows us to add elements from the second container into a copy of the first container that we return at the end.

Now that we know how to create our own generic functions and types, let's take a look at how we can extend existing generics.

Extending generics

The two main generics that we will probably want to extend are arrays and dictionaries. These are the two most prominent containers provided by Swift and are used in virtually every app. Extending a generic type is simple once you understand that an extension itself does not need to be generic.

Adding methods to all forms of a generic

Knowing that an array is declared as `struct Array<Element>`, your first instinct to extend an array might look something similar to this:

```
extension Array<Element> { // Use of undeclared type 'Element'
    // ...
}
```

However, as you can see, you would get an error. Instead, you can simply leave out the placeholder specification and still use the `Element` placeholder inside your implementations. Your other instinct might be to declare `Element` as a placeholder for your individual methods:

```
extension Array {
    func someMethod<Element>(element: Element) {
        // ...
    }
}
```

This is more dangerous because the compiler doesn't detect an error. This is wrong because you are actually declaring a new placeholder `Element` to be used within the method. This new `Element` has nothing to do with the `Element` defined in `Array` itself. For example, you might get a confusing error if you tried to compare a parameter to the method to an element of the Array:

```
extension Array {
    mutating func addElement<Element>(element: Element) {
        self.append(element)
        // Cannot invoke 'append' with argument list
        // of type '(Element)'
    }
}
```

This is because the `Element` defined in `Array` cannot be guaranteed to be the exact same type as the new `Element` defined in `addElement:`. You are free to declare additional placeholders in methods on generic types, but it is best to give them unique names so that they don't hide the type's version of the placeholder.

Now that we understand this, let's add an extension to the array that allows us to test if it contains an element passing a test:

```
extension Array {
    func hasElementThatPasses(
        test: (element: Element) -> Bool
    ) -> Bool
    {
        for element in self {
            if test(element: element) {
                return true
            }
        }
        return false
    }
}
```

As you can see, we continue to use the placeholder `Element` within our extension. This allows us to call the passed in test closure for each element in the array. Now, what if we want to be able to add a method that will check if an element exists using the equality operator? The problem that we will run into is that array does not place a type constraint on `Element` requiring it to be `Equatable`. To do this, we can add an extra constraint to our extension.

Adding methods to only certain instances of a generic

A constraint on an extension is written as a `where` clause, as shown:

```
extension Array where Element: Equatable {
    func containsElement(element: Element) -> Bool {
        for testElement in self {
            if testElement == element {
                return true
            }
        }
        return false
    }
}
```

Here we add a constraint that guarantees that our element is equatable. This means that we will only be able to call this method on arrays that have equatable elements:

```
[1,2,3,4,5].containsElement(4) // true
class MyType {}
var typeList = [MyType]()
typeList.containsElement(MyType()) // Type 'MyType' does not
// conform to protocol 'Equtable'
```

Again, Swift is protecting us from accidently trying to call this method on an array that it wouldn't work for.

These are the building blocks that we have to play with generics. However, we actually have one more feature of protocols that we have not discussed, which works really well in combination with generics.

Extending protocols

We first discussed how we can extend existing types in *Chapter 3, One Piece at a Time – Types, Scopes, and Projects*. In Swift 2, Apple added the ability to extend protocols. This has some fascinating implications, but before we dive into those, let's take a look at an example of adding a method to the `Comparable` protocol:

```
extension Comparable {
    func isBetween(a: Self, b: Self) -> Bool {
        return a < self && self < b
    }
}
```

This adds a method to all types that implement the Comparable. This means that it will now be available on any of the built-in types that are comparable and any of our own types that are comparable:

```
6.isBetween(4, b: 7) // true
"A".isBetween("B", b: "Z") // false
```

This is a really powerful tool. In fact, this is how the Swift team implemented many of the functional methods we saw in *Chapter 5, A Modern Paradigm – Closures and Functional Programming*. They did not have to implement the map method on arrays, dictionaries, or on any other sequence that should be mappable; instead, they implemented it directly on `SequenceType`.

This shows that similarly, protocol extensions can be used for inheritance, and it can also be applied to both classes and structures and types can also inherit this functionality from multiple different protocols because there is no limit to the number of protocols a type can implement. However, there are two major differences between the two.

First, types cannot inherit stored properties from protocols, because extensions cannot define them. Protocols can define read only properties but every instance will have to redeclare them as properties:

```
protocol Building {
    var squareFootage: Int {get}
}

struct House: Building {
    let squareFootage: Int
}

struct Factory: Building {
    let squareFootage: Int
}
```

Second, method overriding does not work in the same way with protocol extensions. With protocols, Swift does not intelligently figure out which version of a method to call based on the actual type of an instance. With class inheritance, Swift will call the version of a method that is most directly associated with the instance. Remember, when we called clean on an instance of our House subclass in *Chapter 3, One Piece at a Time – Types, Scopes, and Projects*, it calls the overriding version of clean, as shown:

```
class Building {
    // ...

    func clean() {
        print(
            "Scrub \(self.squareFootage) square feet of floors"
        )
    }
}

class House: Building {
    // ...

    override func clean() {
        print("Make \(self.numberOfBedrooms) beds")
        print("Clean \(self.numberOfBathrooms) bathrooms")
    }
}

let building: Building = House(
    squareFootage: 800,
    numberOfBedrooms: 2,
    numberOfBathrooms: 1
)
building.clean()
// Make 2 beds
// Clean 1 bathroom
```

Here, even though the building variable is defined as a Building, it is in fact a house; so Swift will call the house's version of clean. The contrast with protocol extensions is that it will call the version of the method that is defined by the exact type the variable is declared as:

```
protocol Building {
    var squareFootage: Int {get}
}
```

```swift
extension Building {
    func clean() {
        print(
            "Scrub \(self.squareFootage) square feet of floors"
        )
    }
}

struct House: Building {
    let squareFootage: Int
    let numberOfBedrooms: Int
    let numberOfBathrooms: Double

    func clean() {
        print("Make \(self.numberOfBedrooms) beds")
        print("Clean \(self.numberOfBathrooms) bathrooms")
    }
}

let house = House(
    squareFootage: 1000,
    numberOfBedrooms: 2,
    numberOfBathrooms: 1.5
)
house.clean()
// Make 2 beds
// Clean 1.5 bathrooms

(house as Building).clean()
// Scrub 1000 square feet of floors
```

When we call clean on the house variable which is of type `House`, it calls the house version; however, when we cast the variable to a `Building` and then call it, it calls the building version.

All of this shows that it can be hard to choose between using structures and protocols or class inheritance. We will look at the last piece of that consideration in the next chapter on memory management, so we will be able to make a fully informed decision when moving forward.

Now that we have looked at the features available to us with generics and protocols, let's take this opportunity to explore some more advanced ways protocols and generics are used in Swift.

Putting protocols and generics to use

One cool part of Swift is generators and sequences. They provide an easy way to iterate over a list of values. Ultimately, they boil down to two different protocols: GeneratorType and SequenceType. If you implement the SequenceType protocol in your custom types, it allows you to use the for-in loop over an instance of your type. In this section, we will look at how we can do that.

Generators

The most critical part of this is the GeneratorType protocol. Essentially, a generator is an object that you can repeatedly ask for the next object in a series until there are no objects left. Most of the time you can simply use an array for this, but it is not always the best solution. For example, you can even make a generator that is infinite.

There is a famous infinite series of numbers called the Fibonacci sequence, where every number in the series is the sum of the two previous numbers. This is especially famous because it is found all over nature from the number of bees in a nest to the most pleasing aspect ratio of a rectangle to look at. Let's create an infinite generator that will produce this series.

We start by creating a structure that implements the GeneratorType protocol. The protocol is made up of two pieces. First, it has a type alias for the type of elements in the sequence and second, it has a mutating method called next that returns the next object in the sequence.

The implementation looks similar to this:

```
struct FibonacciGenerator: GeneratorType {
    typealias Element = Int

    var values = (0, 1)

    mutating func next() -> Element? {
        self.values = (
            self.values.1,
            self.values.0 + self.values.1
        )
        return self.values.0
    }
}
```

We defined a property called `values` that is a tuple representing the previous two values in the sequence. We update `values` and return the first element of the tuple each time `next` is called. This means that there will be no end to the sequence.

We can use this generator on its own by instantiating it and then repeatedly calling next inside a while loop:

```
var generator = FibonacciGenerator()
while let next = generator.next() {
    if next > 10 {
        break
    }
    print(next)
}
// 1, 1, 2, 3, 5, 8
```

We need to set up some sort of a condition so that the loop doesn't go on forever. In this case, we break out of the loop once the numbers get above 10. However, this code is pretty ugly, so Swift also defines the protocol called `SequenceType` to clean it up.

Sequences

`SequenceType` is another protocol that is defined as having a type alias for a `GeneratorType` and a method called `generate` that returns a new generator of that type. We could declare a simple sequence for our `FibonacciGenerator`, as follows:

```
struct FibonacciSequence: SequenceType {
    typealias Generator = FibonacciGenerator

    func generate() -> Generator {
        return FibonacciGenerator()
    }
}
```

Every for-in loop operates on the `SequenceType` protocol, so now we can use a for-in loop on our `FibonacciSequence`:

```
for next in FibonacciSequence() {
    if next > 10 {
        break
    }
    print(next)
}
```

This is pretty cool; we can easily iterate over the Fibonacci sequence in a very readable way. It is much easier to understand the preceding code than it would be to understand a complicated while loop that has to calculate the next value of the sequence each time. Imagine all of the other type of sequences we can design such as prime numbers, random name generators, and so on.

However, it is not always ideal to have to define two different types to create a single sequence. To fix this, we can use generics. Swift provides a generic type called `AnyGenerator` with a companion function called `anyGenerator:`. This function takes a closure and returns a generator that uses the closure as its next method. This means that we don't have to explicitly create a generator ourselves; instead we can use `anyGenerator:` directly in a sequence:

```
struct FibonacciSequence2: SequenceType {
    typealias Generator = AnyGenerator<Int>

    func generate() -> Generator {
        var values = (0, 1)
        return anyGenerator({
            values = (values.1, values.0 + values.1)
            return values.0
        })
    }
}
```

In this version of `FibonacciSequence`, we create a new generator every time generate is called that takes a closure that does the same thing that our original `FibonacciGenerator` was doing. We declare the `values` variable outside of the closure so that we can use it to store the state between calls to the closure. If your generator is simple and doesn't require a complicated state, using the `AnyGenerator` generic is a great way to go.

Now let's use this `FibonacciSequence` to solve the kind of math problem that computers are great at.

Product of Fibonacci numbers under 50

What if we want to know what is the result of multiplying every number in the Fibonacci sequence under 50? We can try to use a calculator and painstakingly enter in all of the numbers, but it is much more efficient to do it in Swift.

Let's start by creating a generic `SequenceType` that will take another sequence type and limit it to stop the sequence once it has reached a maximum number. We need to make sure that the type of the maximum value matches the type in the sequence and also that the element type is comparable. For that, we can use a where clause on the element type:

```
struct SequenceLimiter<
    S: SequenceType where S.Generator.Element: Comparable
    >: SequenceType
{
    typealias Generator = AnyGenerator<S.Generator.Element>
    let sequence: S
    let max: S.Generator.Element

    init(_ sequence: S, max: S.Generator.Element) {
        self.sequence = sequence
        self.max = max
    }

    func generate() -> Generator {
        var g = self.sequence.generate()
        return anyGenerator({
            if let next = g.next() {
                if next <= self.max {
                    return next
                }
            }
            return nil
        })
    }
}
```

Notice that when we refer to the element type, we must go through the generator type.

When our `SequenceLimiter` structure is created, it stores the original sequence. This is so that it can use the result of its `generate` method each time `generate` is called on this parent sequence. Each call to `generate` needs to start the sequence over again. It then creates an `AnyGenerator` with a closure that calls `next` on the locally initialized generator of the original sequence. If the value returned by the original generator is greater than or equal to the maximum value, we return `nil`, indicating that the sequence is over.

We can even add an extension to `SequenceType` with a method that will create a limiter for us:

```
extension SequenceType where Generator.Element: Comparable {
    func limit(max: Generator.Element) -> SequenceLimiter<Self> {
        return SequenceLimiter(self, max: max)
    }
}
```

We use `Self` as a placeholder representing the specific type of the instance the method is being called on.

Now, we can easily limit our Fibonacci sequence to only values under 50:

```
FibonacciSequence().limit(50)
```

The last part we need to solve our problem is the ability to find the product of a sequence. We can do this with another extension. In this case, we are only going to support sequences that contain `Int`s so that we can ensure that the elements can be multiplied:

```
extension SequenceType where Generator.Element == Int {
    var product: Generator.Element {
        return self.reduce(1, combine: *)
    }
}
```

This method takes advantage of the reduce function to start with the value one and multiply it by every value in the sequence. Now we can do our final calculation easily:

```
FibonacciSequence().limit(50).product // 2,227,680
```

Almost instantaneously, our program will return the result 2,227,680. Now we can really understand why we call these devices computers.

Summary

Protocols and generics are definitely complex, but we have seen that they can be used to effectively let the compiler protect us from ourselves. In this chapter, we have covered how protocols are like contracts for types to sign. We have also seen that protocols can be made more flexible using type aliases. Generics allow us to take full advantage of protocols with type aliases and also allow us to create powerful and flexible types that adapt to the contexts in which they are used. Finally, we looked at how we can use protocols and generics in the form of sequences and generators to solve a complex math problem in a very clean and understandable way, as an inspiration to solve other types of problems just as cleanly.

At this point we have covered all of the core features of the Swift language. We are now ready to look a little bit deeper at how data is actually stored while a program is run and how we can best manage the resources used by our programs.

7
Everything Is Connected – Memory Management

When using an app, there is nothing worse than it being slow and unresponsive. Computer users have come to expect every piece of software to respond immediately to every interaction. Even the most feature-rich app will be ruined if it is unpleasant to use because it doesn't manage the device resources effectively. Also, with the growing popularity of mobile computers and devices, it is more important than ever to write software that uses battery power efficiently. One of the aspects of writing software that has the largest impact on both responsiveness and battery power is memory management.

In this chapter, we will discuss techniques specific to Swift that allow us to manage memory in order to ensure that our code remains responsive and minimizes its effect on battery life and other apps. We will do so by covering the following topics:

- Computer data storage
- Value types versus reference types
- Automatic reference counting
- Strong reference cycles
- Lost objects
- Structures versus classes

Computer data storage

Before we start looking at the code, we need to understand in some detail how data is represented in a computer. The common cliché is that all data in a computer is in 1s and 0s. This is true, but not so important when talking about memory management. Instead, we are concerned about *where* the data is stored. All computers, whether a desktop, laptop, tablet, or phone, store data in two places.

The first place we normally think of is the file system. It is stored on a dedicated piece of hardware; this is called a hard disk drive in many computers, but more recently, some computers have started to use solid-state drives. The other thing we hear about when buying computers is the amount of "memory" it has. Computer memory comes in "sticks" which hold less information than normal drives. All data, even if primarily stored on the Internet somewhere, must be loaded into the computer's memory so that we can interact with it.

Let's take a look at what that means for us as programmers.

File system

The file system is designed for long-term storage of data. It is far slower to access than memory, but it is much more cost effective for storing a lot of data. As the name implies, the file system is simply a hierarchical tree of files, which we as users can interact with directly using the *Finder* on a Mac. This file system still exists on iPhones and iPads but it is hidden from us. However, software can still read and write the file system, thus allowing us to store data permanently, even after turning the device off.

Memory

Memory is a little more complex than the file system. It is designed to store the necessary data, temporarily for the software running currently. Unlike with a file system, all memory is lost as soon as you turn off your device. The analogy is similar to how we humans have short-term and long-term memory. While we are having a conversation or thinking about something, we have a certain subset of the information we are actively thinking about and the rest is in our long-term memory. In order to actively think about something, we have to recall it from our long-term memory into our short-term memory.

Memory is quick to access, but it is much more expensive. When computers start to act abnormally slow, it is commonly because it is very close to using up all of its memory. This is because the operating system will automatically start using the file system as a backup when memory is low. Information that is meant for short-term storage is automatically written to the file system instead, making it much slower to access again.

This is similar to how we humans have a problem processing too much information at once. If we try to add two 20-digit numbers in our head, it is going to take us a long time or simply be impossible. Instead, we often write out the partial solution on paper, as we go along. In this case, the paper is acting as our file system. It would be faster if we could just remember everything instead of taking the time to write it down and read it back, but we simply can't process that much information at one time.

This is important to consider when programming because we want to reduce the amount of memory that we use at any given time. Using a lot of memory doesn't only negatively affect our own software; it can negatively affect the entire computer's performance. Also, when the operating system has to resort to using the file system, the extra processing and extra access to a second piece of hardware causes more power usage.

Now that we understand our goal, we can start discussing how we manage memory better in Swift.

Value types versus reference types

All variables and constants in Swift are stored in memory. In fact, unless you explicitly write data to the file system, everything you create is going to be in memory. In Swift, there are two different categories of types. These two categories are **value types** and **reference types**. The only way in which they differ is in the way they behave when they get assigned to new variables, passed into methods, or captured in closures. Essentially, they only differ when you try to assign a new variable or constant to the value of an existing variable or constant.

A value type is always copied when being assigned somewhere new while a reference type is not. Before we look at exactly what that means in more detail, let's go over how we determine if a type is a value type or a reference type.

Determining value type or reference type

A value type is any type that is defined as either a structure or an enumeration, while all classes are reference types. This is easy to determine for your own custom types based on how you declared them. Beyond that, all of the built-in types for Swift, such as strings, arrays, and dictionaries are value types. If you are ever uncertain, you can test any of the two types you want in a playground, to see if its behavior is consistent with a value type or a reference type. The simplest behavior to check is what happens on assignment.

Behavior on assignment

When a value type is reassigned, it is copied so that afterwards each variable or constant holds a distinct value that can be changed independently. Let's take a look at a simple example using a string:

```
var value1 = "Hello"
var value2 = value1
value1 += " World!"
print(value1) // "Hello World!"
print(value2) // "Hello"
```

As you can see, when `value2` is set to `value1` a copy gets created. This is so that when we append `" World!"` to `value1`, `value2` remains unchanged, as `"Hello"`. We can visualize them as two completely separate entities:

On the other hand, let's take a look at what happens with a reference type:

```
class Person {
    var name: String

    init(name: String) {
        self.name = name
    }
}
var reference1 = Person(name: "Kai")
var reference2 = reference1
reference1.name = "Naya"
print(reference1.name) // "Naya"
print(reference2.name) // "Naya"
```

As you can see, when we changed the name of `reference1`, `reference2` was also changed. So why is this? As the name implies, reference types are simply references to an instance. When you assign a reference to another variable or constant, both are actually referring to the exact same instance. We can visualize it as two separate objects referencing the same instance:

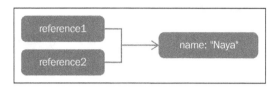

In the real world, this would be like two kids sharing a toy. Both can play with the toy but if one breaks the toy, it is broken for both kids.

However, it is important to realize that if you assign a reference type to a new value, it does not change the value it was originally referencing:

```
reference2 = Person(name: "Kai")
print(reference1.name) // "Naya"
print(reference2.name) // "Kai"
```

As you can see, we assigned `reference2` to an entirely different `Person` instance, so they can now be manipulated independently. We can then visualize this as two separate references on two separate instances, as shown in the following image:

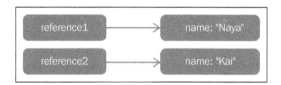

This will be like buying a new toy for one of the kids.

This shows you that a reference type is actually a special version of a value type. The difference is that a reference type is not itself an instance of any type. It is simply a way to refer to another instance, sort of like a placeholder. You can copy the reference so that you have two variables referencing the same instance, or you can give a variable a completely new reference to a new instance. With reference types, there is an extra layer of indirection based on sharing instances between multiple variables.

Now that we know this, the simplest way to verify if a type is a value type or a reference type is to check its behavior when being assigned. If the second value is changed when you modify the first value, it means that the type you are testing is a reference type.

Behavior on input

Another place where the behavior of a value type differs from a reference type is when passing them into functions and methods. However, the behavior is very simple to remember if you look at passing a variable or constant into a function as just another assignment. This means that when you pass a value type into a function, it is copied while a reference type still shares the same instance:

```
func setNameOfPerson(person: Person, var to name: String) {
    person.name = name
    name = "Other Name"
}
```

Here we have defined a function that takes both a reference type: `Person` and a value type: `String`. When we update the `Person` type within the function, the person we passed in is also changed:

```
var person = Person(name: "Sarah")
var newName = "Jamison"
setNameOfPerson(person, to: newName)

print(person.name) // "Jamison"
print(newName) // "Jamison"
```

However, when we change the string within the function, the `String` passed into it remains unchanged.

The place where things get a little more complicated is with `inout` parameters. An `inout` parameter is actually a reference to the passed-in instance. This means that, it will treat a value type as if it were a reference type:

```
func updateString(inout string: String) {
    string = "Other String"
}

var someString = "Some String"
updateString(&someString)
print(someString) // "Other String"
```

As you can see, when we changed the `inout` version of `string` within the function, it also changed the `someString` variable outside of the function just as if it were a reference type.

If we remember that a reference type is just a special version of a value type where the value is a reference, we can infer what will be possible with an `inout` version of a reference type. When we define an `inout` reference type, we actually have a reference *to a reference*; this reference is then the one that is pointing to a reference. We can visualize the difference between an `inout` value type and an `inout` reference type as shown:

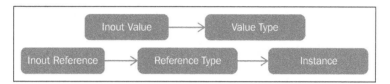

If we simply change the value of this variable, we will get the same behavior as if it were not an `inout` parameter. However, we can also change where the inner reference is referring to by declaring it as an `inout` parameter:

```
func updatePerson(inout insidePerson: Person) {
    insidePerson.name = "New Name"
    insidePerson = Person(name: "New Person")
}

var person2 = person
updatePerson(&person)
print(person.name) // "New Person"
print(person2.name) // "New Name"
```

We start by creating a second reference: `person2` to the same instance as the `person` variable that currently has the name `"Jamison"` from before. After this, we pass the original `person` variable into our `updatePerson:` method and have this:

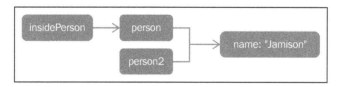

In this method, we first change the name of the existing person to a new name. We can see in the output that the name of person2 has also changed, because both insidePerson inside the function and person2 are still referencing the same instance:

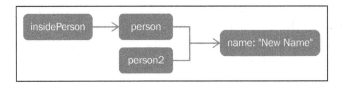

However, we then also assign insidePerson to a completely new instance of the Person reference type. This results in person and person2 outside of the function pointing at two completely different instances of Person leaving the name of person2 to be "New Name" and updating the name of person to "New Person":

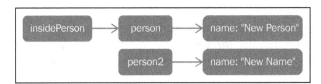

Here, by defining insidePerson as an inout parameter, we were able to change where the passed-in variable was referencing. It can help us to visualize all the different types as one type pointing to another.

At any point, any of these arrows can be pointed at something new using an assignment and the instance can always be accessed through the references.

Closure capture behavior

The last behavior we have to worry about is when variables are captured within closures. This is what we did not cover about closures in *Chapter 5, A Modern Paradigm – Closures and Functional Programming*. Closures can actually use the variables that were defined in the same scope as the closure itself:

```
var nameToPrint = "Kai"
var printName = {
    print(nameToPrint)
}
printName() // "Kai"
```

This is very different from normal parameters that we have seen before. We actually do not specify `nameToPrint` as a parameter, nor do we pass it in when calling the method. Instead, the closure captures the `nameToPrint` variable that is defined before it. These types of captures act similarly to `inout` parameters in functions.

When a value type is captured, it can be changed and it will change the original value as well:

```
var outsideName = "Kai"
var setName = {
    outsideName = "New Name"
}
print(outsideName) // "Kai"
setName()
print(outsideName) // "New Name"
```

As you can see, `outsideName` was changed after the closure was called. This is exactly like an `inout` parameter.

When a reference type is captured, any changes will also be applied to the outside version of the variable:

```
var outsidePerson = Person(name: "Kai")
var setPersonName = {
    outsidePerson.name = "New Name"
}
print(outsidePerson.name) // "Kai"
setPersonName()
print(outsidePerson.name) // "New Name"
```

This is also exactly like an `inout` parameter.

The other part of closure capture that we need to keep in mind is that changing the captured value after the closure is defined will still affect the value within the closure. We can take advantage of this to use the `printName` closure we defined in the preceding section to print any name:

```
nameToPrint = "Kai"
printName() // Kai
nameToPrint = "New Name"
printName() // "New Name"
```

As you can see, we can change what `printName` prints out by changing the value of `nameToPrint`. This behavior is actually very hard to track down when it happens accidently, so it is usually a good idea to avoid capturing variables in closures whenever possible. In this case, we are taking advantage of the behavior, but more often than not, it will cause bugs. Here, it would be better to pass what we want to print as an argument.

Another way to avoid this behavior is to use a feature called **capture lists**. With this, you can specify the variables that you want to capture by copying them:

```
nameToPrint = "Original Name"
var printNameWithCapture = { [nameToPrint] in
    print(nameToPrint)
}
printNameWithCapture() // "Original Name"
nameToPrint = "New Name"
printNameWithCapture() // "Original Name"
```

A capture list is defined at the beginning of a closure before any parameter. It is a comma-separated list of all the variables being captured, which we want to copy within square brackets. In this case, we requested `nameToPrint` to be copied, so when we change it later, it does not affect the value that is printed out. We will see more advanced uses of capture lists later in this chapter.

Automatic reference counting

Now that we understand the different ways in which data is represented in Swift, we can look into how we can manage the memory better. Every instance that we create takes up memory. Naturally, it wouldn't make sense to keep all data around forever. Swift needs to be able to free up memory so that it can be used for other purposes, once our program doesn't need it anymore. This is the key to managing memory in our apps. We need to make sure that Swift can free up all the memory that we no longer need, as soon as possible.

The way that Swift knows it can free up memory is when the code can no longer access an instance. If there is no longer any variable or constant referencing an instance, it can be repurposed for another instance. This is called "freeing the memory" or "deleting the object".

In *Chapter 3, One Piece at a Time – Types, Scopes, and Projects* we already discussed when a variable is accessible or not in the section about scopes. This makes memory management very simple for value types. Since value types are always copied when they are reassigned or passed into functions, they can be immediately deleted once they go out of scope. We can look at a simple example to get the full picture:

```
func printSomething() {
    let something = "Hello World!"
    print(something)
}
```

Here we have a very simple function that prints out "Hello World!". When `printSomething` is called, `something` is assigned to a new instance of `String` with the value `"Hello World!"`. After `print` is called, the function exits and therefore `something` is no longer in scope. At that point, the memory being taken up by `something` can be freed.

While this is very simple, reference types are much more complex. At a high level, an instance of a reference type is deleted at the point that there is no longer any reference to the instance in scope anymore. This is relatively straightforward to understand but it gets more complex in the details. The Swift feature that manages this is called **Automatic Reference Counting** or **ARC** for short.

Object relationships

The key to ARC is that every object has relationships with one or more variables. This can be extended to include the idea that all objects have a relationship with other objects. For example, a car object would contain objects for its four tires, engine, and so on. It will also have a relationship with its manufacturer, dealership, and owner. ARC uses these relationships to determine when an object can be deleted. In Swift, there are three different types of relationships: **strong**, **weak**, and **unowned**.

Strong

The first, and default type of relationship is a strong relationship. It says that a variable requires the instance it is referring to always exist, as long as the variable is still in scope. This is the only behavior available for value types. When an instance no longer has any strong relationships to it, it will be deleted.

A great example of this type of relationship is with a car that must have a
steering wheel:

```
class SteeringWheel {}

class Car {
    var steeringWheel: SteeringWheel

    init(steeringWheel: SteeringWheel) {
        self.steeringWheel = steeringWheel
    }
}
```

By default, the `steeringWheel` property has a strong relationship to the
`SteeringWheel` instance it is initialized with. Conceptually, this means that
the car itself has a strong relationship to the steering wheel. As long as a car exists,
it must have a relationship to a steering wheel that exists. Since `steeringWheel` is
declared as a variable, we could change the steering wheel of the car, which would
remove the old strong relationship and add a new one, but a strong relationship will
always exist.

If we were to create a new instance of `Car` and store it in a variable, that variable
would have a strong relationship to the car:

```
let wheel = SteeringWheel()
let car = Car(steeringWheel: wheel)
```

Lets break down all the relationships in this code. First we create the `wheel` constant
and assign it to a new instance of `SteeringWheel`. This sets up a strong relationship
from `wheel` to the new instance. We do the same thing with the `car` constant, but
this time we also pass in the `wheel` constant to the initializer. Now, not only does `car`
have a strong relationship to the new `Car` instance, but the `Car` initializer also creates
a strong relationship from the `steeringWheel` property to the same instance as the
`wheel` constant:

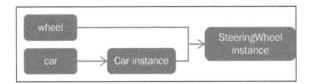

So what does this relationship graph mean for memory management? At this time, the Car instance has one strong relationship: the car constant, and the SteeringWheel instance has two strong relationships: the wheel constant and the steeringWheel property of the Car instance.

This means that the Car instance will be deleted as soon as the car constant goes out of scope. On the other hand, the SteeringWheel instance will only be deleted after both the wheel constant goes out of scope and the Car instance is deleted.

You can envision a strong reference counter on every instance in your program. Every time a strong relationship is setup to an instance the counter goes up. Every time an object strongly referencing it gets deleted, the counter goes down. If that counter ever goes back to zero, the instance is deleted.

The other important thing to realize is that all relationships are only in one direction. Just because the Car instance has a strong relationship to the SteeringWheel instance does not mean that the SteeringWheel instance has any relationship back. You could add your own relationship back by adding a car property to the SteeringWheel class, but you have to be careful when doing this, as we will see in the strong reference cycle section coming up.

Weak

The next type of relationship in Swift is a weak relationship. It allows one object to reference another without enforcing that it always exists. A weak relationship does not contribute to the reference counter of an instance, which means that the addition of a weak relationship does not increase the counter nor does it decrease the counter when removed.

Since a weak relationship cannot guarantee that it will always exist, it must always be defined as an optional. A weak relationship is defined using the weak keyword before the variable declaration:

```
class SteeringWheel {
    weak var car: Car?
}
```

This allows a SteeringWheel to have a car assigned to it, without enforcing that the car never be deleted. The car initializer can then assign this backwards reference to itself:

```
class Car {
    var steeringWheel: SteeringWheel
```

```
        init(steeringWheel: SteeringWheel) {
            self.steeringWheel = steeringWheel
            self.steeringWheel.car = self
        }
    }
```

If the car is ever deleted, the car property of `SteeringWheel` will automatically be set to nil. This allows us to gracefully handle the scenario that a weak relationship refers to an instance that has been deleted.

Unowned

The final type of relationship is an unowned relationship. This relationship is almost identical to a weak relationship. It also allows one object to reference another without contributing to the strong reference count. The only difference is that an unowned relationship does not need to be declared as optional and it uses the `unowned` keyword instead of `weak`. It acts similar to an implicitly unwrapped optional. You can interact with an unowned relationship as if it were a strong relationship, but if the unowned instance has been deleted and you try to access it, your entire program will crash. This means that you should only use unowned relationships in scenarios where the unowned object will never actually be deleted while the primary object still exists.

You may ask then, "Why would we not always use a strong relationship instead?" The answer is that sometimes unowned or weak references are needed to break something called a **strong reference cycle**.

Strong reference cycles

A strong reference cycle is when two instances directly or indirectly hold strong references to each other. This means that neither object can ever be deleted, because both are ensuring that the other will always exist.

This scenario is our first really bad memory management scenario. It is one thing to keep memory around longer than it is needed; it is a whole different level to create memory that can never be freed up to be reused again. This type of memory problem is called a memory leak, because the computer will slowly leak memory until there is no longer any new memory available. This is why you will sometimes see a speed improvement after restarting your device. Upon restart, all of the memory is freed up again. Modern operating systems will sometimes find ways to forcefully free up memory, especially when completely quitting an app, but we cannot rely on this as programmers.

So how can we prevent these strong reference cycles? First, let's take a look at what they look like. There are two main scenarios where these cycles can exist: between objects and with closures.

Between objects

A strong reference cycle between objects is when two types directly or indirectly contain strong references to each other.

Spotting

A great example of a strong reference cycle between objects is if we rewrite our preceding car example without using a weak reference from SteeringWheel to Car:

```
class SteeringWheel {
    var car: Car?
}

class Car {
    var steeringWheel: SteeringWheel

    init(steeringWheel: SteeringWheel) {
        self.steeringWheel = steeringWheel
        self.steeringWheel.car = self
    }
}
```

The only difference between this code and the preceding code is that the car property on SteeringWheel is no longer declared as weak. This means that when a car is created, it will set up a strong relationship to the SteeringWheel instance and then create a strong reference from the SteeringWheel instance back to the car:

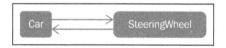

This scenario means that the reference count of both instances can never go down to zero and therefore they will never be deleted and the memory will be leaked.

Two objects can also indirectly hold strong references to each other through one or more third parties:

```
class Manufacturer {
    var cars: [Car] = []
}

class SteeringWheel {
    var manufacturer: Manufacturer?
}

class Car {
    var steeringWheel: SteeringWheel?
}
```

Here, we have the scenario where a `Car` can have a strong reference to a `SteeringWheel` that can have a strong reference to a `Manufacturer` that in turn has a strong reference to the original `Car`:

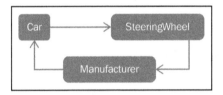

This is another strong reference cycle and it illustrates two more important points. First, optionals, by default, still create strong relationships when not nil. Also, the built in container types, such as arrays and dictionaries, also create strong relationships.

Clearly strong reference cycles can be difficult to spot, especially because they are hard to detect in the first place. An individual memory leak is rarely going to be noticeable to a user of your program, but if you continuously leak memory over and over again, it can cause their device to feel sluggish or even crash.

The best way as a developer to detect them is to use a tool built into Xcode called **Instruments**. Instruments can do many things, but one of those things is called **Leaks**. To run this tool you must have an Xcode Project; you cannot run it on a Playground. It is run by selecting **Product | Profile** from the menu bar.

This will build your project and display a series of profiling tools:

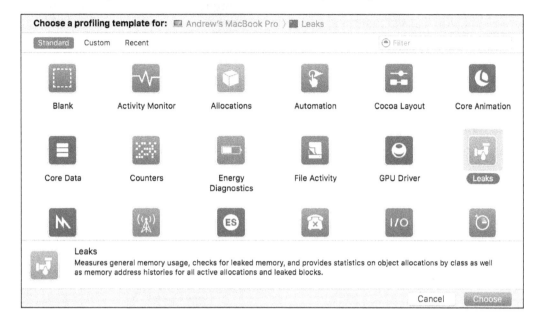

If you select the **Leaks** tool and press the record button in the upper-left corner, it will run your program and warn you of memory leaks which it can detect. A memory leak will look like a red X icon and will be listed as a leaked object:

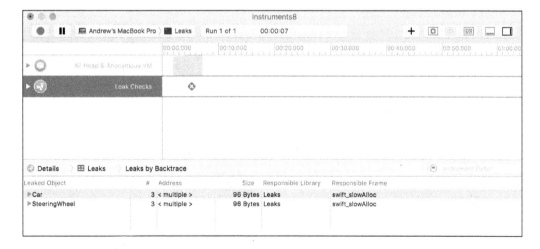

You can even select the **Cycles & Roots** view for the leaked objects and Instruments will show you a visual representation of your strong reference cycle. In the following screenshot, you can see that there is a cycle between `SteeringWheel` and `Car`:

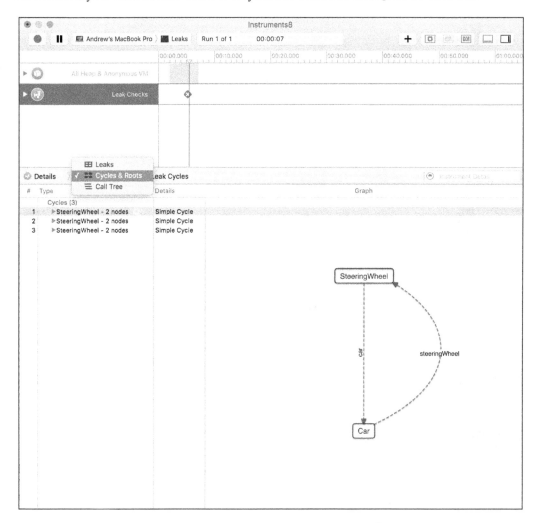

Clearly, Leaks is a powerful tool and you should run it periodically on your code, but it will not catch all strong reference cycles. The last line of defense is going to be you staying vigilant with your code, always thinking about the ownership graph.

Of course, spotting cycles is only part of the battle. The other part of the battle is fixing them.

Fixing

The easiest way to break a strong reference cycle is to simply remove one of the relationships completely. However, this is very often not going to be an option. A lot of the time, it is important to have a two-way relationship.

The way we fix cycles without completely removing a relationship is to make one or more of the relationships weak or unowned. In fact, this is the main reason that these other two types of relationships exist.

We fix the strong reference cycle in our original example by changing the car relationship back to weak:

```
class SteeringWheel {
    weak var car: Car?
}

class Car {
    var steeringWheel: SteeringWheel

    init(steeringWheel: SteeringWheel) {
        self.steeringWheel = steeringWheel
        self.steeringWheel.car = self
    }
}
```

Now `Car` has a strong reference to `SteeringWheel` but there is only a weak reference back:

How you break any given cycle is going to depend on your implementation. The only important part is that somewhere in the cycle of references there is a weak or unowned relationship.

Unowned relationships are good for scenarios where the connection will never be missing. In our example, there are times that a `SteeringWheel` exists without a car reference. If we change it so that the `SteeringWheel` is created in the `Car` initializer, we could make the reference unowned:

```
class SteeringWheel2 {
    unowned var car: Car
```

```
        init(car: Car) {
            self.car = car
        }
    }

    class Car {
        var steeringWheel: SteeringWheel2!

        init() {
            self.steeringWheel = SteeringWheel2(car: self)
        }
    }
```

Also, note that we had to define the `steeringWheel` property as an implicitly unwrapped optional. This is because we had to use `self` when initializing it but at the same time we cannot use `self` until all the properties have a value. Making it optional allows it to be nil while we are using `self` to create the steering wheel. This is safe as long as the `SteeringWheel2` initializer doesn't try to access the `steeringWheel` property of the passed in car.

With closures

As we found out in *Chapter 5, A Modern Paradigm – Closures and Functional Programming*, closures are just another type of object, so they follow the same ARC rules. However, they are subtler than classes because of their ability to capture variables from their surrounding scope. These captures create strong references from the closures to the captured variable that are often overlooked because capturing variables looks so natural compared to conditionals, for loops and other similar syntax.

Just as classes can create circular references, so can closures. Something can have a strong reference to a closure that directly or indirectly has a strong reference back to the original object. Let's take a look at how we can spot that.

Spotting

It is very common to provide closure properties that will be called whenever something occurs. These are generally called callbacks. Let's look at a ball class that has a callback for when the ball bounces:

```
    class Ball {
        var location: (x: Double, y: Double) = (0,0)

        var onBounce: (() -> ())?
    }
```

This type of setup makes it easy to inadvertently create a strong reference cycle:

```
let ball = Ball()
ball.onBounce = {
    print("\(ball.location.x), \(ball.location.y)")
}
```

Here, we are printing out the location of the ball every time it bounces. However, if you consider this carefully, you will see that there is a strong reference cycle between the closure and the ball instance. This is because we are capturing the ball within the closure. As we have learned already, this creates a strong reference from the closure to the ball. The ball also has a strong reference to the closure through the onBounce property. That is our circle.

You should always be conscious of what variables are being captured in your closures and if that variable directly or indirectly has a strong reference to the closure itself.

Fixing

To fix these types of strong reference cycles with closures we will again need to make one part of the circle weak or unowned.

Swift does not allow us to make closure references weak, so we have to find a way to capture the ball variable weakly instead of strongly.

To capture a variable weakly, we must use a capture list. Using a capture list, we can capture a weak or unowned copy of the original variable. We do so by specifying the weak or unowned variables before the capture list variable name:

```
ball.onBounce = { [weak ball] in
    print("\(ball?.location.x), \(ball?.location.y)")
}
```

By declaring the ball copy as weak, it automatically makes it optional. This means that we had to use optional chaining to print out its location. Just like with other weak variables, ball will be set to nil if the ball is deleted. However, based on the nature of the code, we know that this closure will never be called if ball is deleted, since the closure is stored right on the ball instance. In that case, it is probably better to use the unowned keyword:

```
ball.onBounce = { [unowned ball] in
    print("\(ball.location.x), \(ball.location.y)")
}
```

It is always nice to clean up your code by removing unnecessary optionals.

Lost objects

It is a great idea to always keep strong reference cycles in mind, but if we are too aggressive with the use of weak and unowned references, we can run into the opposite problem, where an object is deleted before we intended it to be.

Between objects

With an object this will happen if all of the references to the object are weak or unowned. This won't be a fatal mistake if we use weak references, but if this happens with an unowned reference it will crash your program.

For example, let's look at the preceding example with an extra weak reference:

```
class SteeringWheel {
    weak var car: Car?
}
class Car {
    weak var steeringWheel: SteeringWheel!

    init(steeringWheel: SteeringWheel) {
        self.steeringWheel = steeringWheel
        steeringWheel.car = self
    }
}

let wheel = SteeringWheel()
let car = Car(steeringWheel: wheel)
```

This code is the same as the preceding one except that both the `car` property of `SteeringWheel` and the `steeringWheel` property of `Car` are weak. This means that as soon as `wheel` goes out of scope, it will be deleted, resetting the `steeringWheel` property of the car to nil. There may be scenarios where you want this behavior, but often this will be unintentional and create confusing bugs.

The important thing is that you keep in mind all of the relationships an object has. There should always be at least one strong reference as long as you still want the object around and of course, there should never be a strong reference cycle.

With closures

This actually can't happen with closures because, as we discussed before, you cannot refer to a closure weakly. If you try, the compiler will give you an error:

```
class Ball2 {
    weak var onBounce: (() -> ())? // Error: 'weak' cannot be
    // applied to non-class type '() -> ()'
}
```

Swift saves us from yet another type of bug.

Structures versus classes

Now that we have a good understanding of memory management, we are ready to discuss the full trade-offs we make when we choose to design a type as a structure or a class. With our ability to extend protocols like we saw in the previous chapter, we can achieve very similar functionality to the inheritance we saw with classes in *Chapter 3, One Piece at a Time – Types, Scopes, and Projects*. This means that we are often choosing between using a structure or a class based on the memory implications, or in other words, whether we want our type to be a value type or a reference type.

Value types have an advantage because they are very simple to reason about. You don't have to worry about multiple variables referencing the same instance. Even better, you don't have to worry about all of the potential problems we have discussed with strong reference cycles. However, there is still an advantage to reference types.

Reference types are advantageous when it really makes sense to share an instance between multiple variables. This is especially true when you are representing some sort of physical resource that makes no sense to copy like a port on the computer or the main window of an application. Also, some will argue that reference types use memory more efficiently, because it doesn't take up more memory with lots of copies floating around. However, the Swift compiler will actually do a lot of optimizing of our code and reduce or eliminate most of the copying that actually occurs when possible. For example, if we pass a value type into a function that never modifies the value, there is no reason to actually create that copy. Ultimately, I don't recommend optimizing for something like that before it becomes necessary. Sometimes you will run into memory problems with your application and then it can be appropriate to convert large types to classes if they are being copied a lot.

Ultimately, I recommend using structures and protocols as a default, because they greatly reduce complexity and fall back to classes only when it is required. I even recommend using protocols instead of super classes when possible, because they are easier to shift around and make it an easier transition between value types and reference types.

Summary

Memory management is often considered difficult to understand, but when you break it down, you can see that it is relatively straightforward. In this chapter, we have seen that all data in a computer is either stored in the file system that is a slow permanent storage, or in memory, which is a fast but temporary location. The file system is used as a backup to memory, slowing down the computer greatly, so we as programmers want to minimize the amount of memory we are ever using at one time.

We saw that in Swift there are value types and reference types. These concepts are critical to understanding how you can reduce memory usage and eliminate memory leaks. Memory leaks are created when an object has a strong reference to itself, maybe through a third party, which is called a strong reference cycle. We must also be careful that we keep at least one strong reference to every object we want to stay around or we may lose it prematurely.

With practice programming, you will get better with both preventing and fixing memory problems. You will write streamlined apps that keep your users' computers running smoothly.

We are now ready to move on to the last feature of Swift that we will discuss before we get into the more artful side of computer programming called error handling.

Paths Less Traveled – Error Handling

8

One of the biggest changes in Swift 2 is that Apple added a feature called **error handling**. Handling error situations is often the least fun part of programming. It is usually much more exciting to handle a successful case, often referred to as the *happy path* because that is where the exciting functionality is. However, to make a truly great user experience and therefore a truly great piece of software, we must pay careful attention to what our software does when errors occur. The error-handling features of Swift help us in handling these situations succinctly and discourage us from ignoring errors in the first place.

In this chapter, we will discuss exactly what error-handling features Swift has and how they help us to write better software. We will do so by covering the following topics:

- Throwing errors
- Handling errors
- Cleaning up in error situations

Throwing errors

Before we talk about handling an error, we need to discuss how we can signal that an error has occurred in the first place. The term for this is *throwing an error*.

Defining an error type

The first part of throwing an error is defining an error that we can throw. Any type can be thrown as an error as long as it implements the `ErrorType` protocol, as shown:

```
struct SimpleError: ErrorType {}
```

This protocol doesn't have any requirements, so the type just needs to list it as a protocol it implements. It is now ready to be thrown from a function or method.

Defining a function that throws an error

Let's define a function that will take a string and repeat it until it is at least a certain length. This will be very simple to implement but there will be a problem scenario. If the passed in string is empty, it will never become longer, no matter how many times we repeat it. In this scenario, we should throw an error.

Any function or method can throw an error as long as it is marked with the `throws` keyword, as shown in the following code:

```
func repeatString(
    string: String,
    untilLongerThan: Int
    ) throws -> String
{
    // TODO: Implement
}
```

The `throws` keyword always comes after the parameters and before a return type.

Implementing a function that throws an error

Now, we can test if the passed in string is empty and throw an error if it is. To do this, we use the `throw` keyword with an instance of our error:

```
func repeatString(
    string: String,
    untilLongerThan: Int
    ) throws -> String
{
    if string.isEmpty {
```

```
            throw SimpleError()
    }

    var output = string
    while output.characters.count <= untilLongerThan {
        output += string
    }
    return output
}
```

An important thing to note here is that when we throw an error, it immediately exits the function. In the preceding case, if the string is empty, it goes to the throw line and then it does not execute the rest of the function. In this case, it is often more appropriate to use a `guard` statement instead of a simple `if` statement, as shown in the following code:

```
func repeatString(
    string: String,
    untilLongerThan: Int
) throws -> String
{
    guard !string.isEmpty else {
        throw SimpleError()
    }

    var output = string
    while output.characters.count < untilLongerThan {
        output += string
    }
    return output
}
```

Ultimately this doesn't act any differently from the previous implementation, but it reiterates that the rest of the function will not be executed if it fails the condition. We are now ready to try to use the function.

Handling errors

If we try to call a function, such as normal, Swift is going to give us an error, as shown in the following example:

```
let repeated1 = repeatString("Hello", untilLongerThan: 20)
// Error: Call can throw but is not market with 'try'
```

To eliminate this error, we must add the `try` keyword before the call. However, before we move forward, I would recommend that you wrap all of your code inside a function, if you are following along in a playground. This is because throwing errors at the root level of a playground will not be handled properly and may even cause the playground to stop working. To wrap your code in a function, you can simply add the following code:

```
func main() {
// The rest of your playground code
}
main()
```

This defines a function called `main` that contains all the normal playground code that is called once, at the end of the playground.

Now, let's get back to using the `try` keyword. There are actually three forms of it: `try`, `try?`, and `try!`. Let's start by discussing the exclamation point form, as it is the simplest form.

Forceful try

The `try!` keyword is called the **forceful try**. The error will completely go away if you use it, by using the following code:

```
let repeated2 = try! repeatString("Hello", untilLongerThan: 20)
print(repeated2) // "HelloHelloHelloHello"
```

The drawback of this approach might be intuitive, based on the exclamation point and what it has meant in the past. Just like with forced unwrapping and forced casting, an exclamation point is a sign that there will be a scenario which will crash the entire program. In this case, the crash will be caused if an error is thrown from the function. There may be times when you can really assert that an error will never be thrown from a call to a throwing function or method, but in general this isn't an advisable solution, considering the fact that we are trying to gracefully handle our error situations.

Optional try

We can also use the `try?` keyword, which is referred to as an **optional try**. Instead of allowing for the possibility of a crash, this will turn the result of the function into an optional:

```
let repeated3 = try? repeatString("Hello", untilLongerThan: 20)
print(repeated3) // Optional("HelloHelloHelloHello")
```

The advantage here is that if the function throws an error, `repeated3` will simply be set to `nil`. However, there are a couple strange scenarios with this. First, if the function already returns an optional, the result will be converted to an optional of an optional:

```
func aFailableOptional() throws -> String? {
    return "Hello"
}
print(try? aFailableOptional()) // Optional(Optional("Hello"))
```

This means that you will have to unwrap the optional twice in order to get to the real value. The outer optional will be nil if an error is thrown and the inner optional will be nil if the method returned nil.

The other strange scenario is if the function doesn't return anything at all. In this case, using an optional try will create an optional void, as shown:

```
func aFailableVoid() throws {
    print("Hello")
}
print(try? aFailableVoid()) // Optional(())
```

You can check the result for nil to determine if an error was thrown.

The biggest drawback to this technique is that there is no way to determine the reason an error was thrown. This isn't a problem for our `repeatString:untilLongerThan:` function because there is only one error scenario, but we will often have functions or methods that can fail in multiple ways. Especially, if these are called based on user input, we will want to be able to report to the user exactly why an error occurred.

To allow us to get more precise information on the reason for an error, we can use the final keyword, which is simply `try`.

Catching an error

To get an idea of the usefulness of catching an error, let's look at writing a new function that will create a list of random numbers. Our function will allow the user to configure how long the list should be and also what the range of possible random numbers should be.

The idea behind catching an error is that you get a chance to look at the error that was thrown. With our current error type, this wouldn't be terribly useful because there is no way to create different types of errors. A great option to fix this is to use an enumeration that implements the `ErrorType` protocol:

```
enum RandomListError: ErrorType {
    case NegativeListLength
    case FirstNumberMustBeLower
}
```

This enumeration has a case for both the errors which we will want to throw, so now we are ready to implement our function:

```
func createRandomListContaininingXNumbers(
    xNumbers: Int,
    between low: Int,
    and high: Int
) throws -> [Int]
{
    guard xNumbers >= 0 else {
        throw RandomListError.NegativeListLength
    }
    guard low < high else {
        throw RandomListError.FirstNumberMustBeLower
    }

    var output = [Int]()
    for _ in 0 ..< xNumbers {
        let rangeSize = high - low + 1
        let betweenZero = Int(rand()) % rangeSize
        let number = betweenZero + low
        output.append(number)
    }
    return output
}
```

This function begins by checking the error scenarios. It first checks to make sure that we are not trying to create a list of negative length. It then checks to make sure that the high value of the range is in fact greater than the low one. After that, we repeatedly add a random number to the output array for the requested number of times.

Note that this implementation uses the `rand` function, which we used in *Chapter 2, Building Blocks – Variables, Collections, and Flow Control*. To use it, you will need to `import Foundation` and also seed the random number with `srand` again.

Also, this use of random is a bit more complicated. Previously, we only needed to make sure that the random number was between zero and the length of our array; now, we need it to be between two arbitrary numbers. First, we determine the amount of different numbers we can generate, which is the difference between the high and low number plus one, because we want to include the high number. Then, we generate the random number within that range and finally, shift it to the actual range we want by adding the low number to the result. To make sure this works, let's think through a simple scenario. Lets say we want to generate a number between 4 and 10. The range size here will be `10 - 4 + 1 = 7`, so we will be generating random numbers between 0 and 6. Then, when we add 4 to it, it will move that range to be between 4 and 10.

So, we now have a function that throws a couple of types of errors. If we want to catch the errors, we have to embed the call inside a `do` block and also add the `try` keyword:

```
do {
    try createRandomListContaininingXNumbers(
        5,
        between: 5,
        and: 10
    )
}
```

However, if we put this into a playground, within the `main` function, we will still get an error that the errors thrown from here are not handled. This will not produce an error if you put it at the root level of the playground because the playground will handle any error thrown by default. To handle them within a function, we need to add catch blocks. A `catch` block works the same as a `switch` case, just as if the `switch` were being performed on the error:

```
do {
    try createRandomListContaininingXNumbers(
        5,
        between: 5,
        and: 10
    )
}
catch RandomListError.NegativeListLength {
    print("Cannot create with a negative number of elements")
}
catch RandomListError.FirstNumberMustBeLower {
    print("First number must be lower than second number")
}
```

A `catch` block is defined with the keyword `catch` followed by the case description and then curly brackets that contain the code to be run for that case. Each `catch` block acts as a separate switch case. In our preceding example, we have defined two different `catch` blocks: one for each of the errors where we print out a user-understandable message.

However, if we add this to our playground, we still get an error that all errors are not handled because the enclosing catch is not exhaustive. That is because `catch` blocks are just like switches in that they have to cover every possible case. There is no way to say if our function can only throw random list errors, so we need to add a final `catch` block that handles any other errors:

```
do {
    try createRandomListContaininingXNumbers(
        5,
        between: 5,
        and: 10
    )
}
catch RandomListError.NegativeListLength {
    print("Cannot create with a negative number of elements")
}
catch RandomListError.FirstNumberMustBeLower {
    print("First number must be lower than second number")
}
catch let error {
    print("Unknown error: \(error)")
}
```

The last `catch` block stores the error into a variable that is just of type `ErrorType`. All we can really do with that type is print it out. With our current implementation this will never be called, but it is possible that it will be called if we add a different error to our function later and forget to add a new `catch` block.

Note that currently there is no way to specify what type of error can be thrown from a specific function; so with this implementation there is no way for the compiler to ensure that we are covering every case of our error enumeration. We could instead perform a `switch` within a `catch` block, so that the compiler will at least force us to handle every case:

```
do {
    try createRandomListContaininingXNumbers(
        5,
        between: 5,
```

```
            and: 10
        )
    }
catch let error as RandomListError {
    switch error {
    case .NegativeListLength:
        print("Cannot create with a negative number of elements")
    case .FirstNumberMustBeLower:
        print("First number must be lower than second number")
    }
}
catch let error {
    print("Unknown error: \(error)")
}
```

This technique will not cause the compiler to give us an error if we throw a completely different type of error from our function, but it will at least give us an error if we add a new case to our enumeration.

Another technique that we can use would be to define an error type that includes a description that should be displayed to a user:

```
struct UserError: ErrorType {
    let userReadableDescription: String
    init(_ description: String) {
        self.userReadableDescription = description
    }
}

func createRandomListContaininingXNumbers2(
    xNumbers: Int,
    between low: Int,
    and high: Int
    ) throws -> [Int]
{
    guard xNumbers >= 0 else {
        throw UserError(
            "Cannot create with a negative number of elements"
        )
    }

    guard low < high else {
        throw UserError(
```

```
                "First number must be lower than second number"
            )
        }

        // ...
    }
```

Instead of throwing enumeration cases, we are creating instances of the `UserError` type with a text description of the problem. Now, when we call the function, we can just catch the error as a `UserError` type and print out the value of its `userReadableDescription` property:

```
do {
    try createRandomListContaininingXNumbers2(
        5,
        between: 5,
        and: 10
    )
}
catch let error as UserError {
    print(error.userReadableDescription)
}
catch let error {
    print("Unknown error: \(error)")
}
```

This is a pretty attractive technique but it has its own drawback. This doesn't allow us to easily run certain code if a certain error occurs. This isn't important in a scenario where we are just reporting the error to the user, but it is very important for scenarios where we might more intelligently handle errors. For example, if we have an app that uploads information to the Internet, we will often run into Internet connection problems. Instead of just telling the user to try again later, we can save the information locally and automatically try to upload it again later without having to bother the user. However, Internet connectivity won't be the only reason an upload might fail. In other error circumstances, we will probably want to do something else.

A more robust solution might be to create a combination of both of these techniques. We can start by defining a protocol for errors that can be reported directly to the user:

```
protocol UserErrorType: ErrorType {
    var userReadableDescription: String {get}
}
```

Now we can create an enumeration for our specific errors that implements that protocol:

```
enum RandomListError: String, UserErrorType {
    case NegativeListLength =
        "Cannot create with a negative number of elements"
    case FirstNumberMustBeLower =
        "First number must be lower than second number"

    var userReadableDescription: String {
        return self.rawValue
    }
}
```

This enumeration is set up to have a raw type that is a string. This allows us to write a simpler implementation of the userReadableDescription property that just returns the raw value.

With this, our implementation of the function looks the same as earlier:

```
func createRandomListContaininingXNumbers3(
    xNumbers: Int,
    between low: Int,
    and high: Int
    ) throws -> [Int]
{
    guard xNumbers >= 0 else {
        throw RandomListError.NegativeListLength
    }
    guard low < high else {
        throw RandomListError.FirstNumberMustBeLower
    }

    // ...
}
```

However, our error handling can now be more advanced. We can always just catch any UserErrorType and display it to the user, but we can also catch a specific enumeration case if we want to do something special in this scenario:

```
do {
    try createRandomListContaininingXNumbers3(
        5,
        between: 5,
```

```
            and: 10
        )
    }
    catch RandomListError.NegativeListLength {
        // Do something else
    }
    catch let error as UserErrorType {
        print(error.userReadableDescription)
    }
    catch let error {
        print("Unknown error: \(error)")
    }
```

Keep in mind that the order of our catch blocks is very important, just like the order of switch cases is important. If we put our `UserErrorType` block before the `NegativeListLength` block, we would always just report it to the user, because once a catch block is satisfied, the program will skip every remaining block.

This is a pretty heavy handed solution; so, you may want to use a simpler solution at times. You may even come up with your own solutions in the future, but this gives you some options to play around with.

Propagating errors

The last option for handling an error is to allow it to propagate. This is only possible when the containing function or method is also marked as throwing errors, but it is simple to implement if that is true:

```
func parentFunction() throws {
    try createRandomListContaininingXNumbers3(
        5,
        between: 5,
        and: 10
    )
}
```

In this case, the `try` call does not have to be wrapped in a do-catch, because all errors thrown by `createRandomListContainingXNumbers:between:and:` will be rethrown by `parentFunction`. In fact, you can still use a do-catch block, but the catch cases no longer need to be exhaustive, because any errors not caught will simply be rethrown. This allows you to only catch the errors relevant to you.

However, while this can be a useful technique, I would be careful not to do it too much. The earlier you handle the error situations, the simpler your code can be. Every possible error thrown is like adding a new road to a highway system; it becomes harder to determine where someone took a wrong turn if they are going the wrong way. The earlier we handle errors, the fewer chances we have to create additional code paths in the parent functions.

Cleaning up in error situations

So far, we have not had to be too concerned about what happens in a function after we throw an error. There are times when we will need to perform a certain action before exiting a function, regardless of if we threw an error or not.

Order of execution when errors occur

An important part to remember about throwing errors is that the execution of the current scope exits. This is easy to think about for functions if you think of it as just a call to return. Any code after the throw will not be executed. It is a little less intuitive within do-catch blocks. A do-catch can have multiple calls to functions that may throw errors, but as soon as a function throws an error, the execution will jump to the first catch block that matches the error:

```
do {
    try function1()
    try function2()
    try function3()
}
catch {
    print("Error")
}
```

Here, if `function1` throws an error, `function2` and `function3` will not be called. If `function1` does not throw but `function2` does, then only `function3` will not be called. Also note that we can prevent that skipping behavior using either of the two other `try` keywords:

```
do {
    try! function1()
    try? function2()
    try function3()
}
catch {
    print("Error")
}
```

Now if `function1` throws an error, the whole program will crash and if `function2` throws an error, it will just continue right on with executing `function3`.

Deferring execution

Now, as I hinted before, there will be circumstances where we need to perform some action before exiting a function or method regardless of if we throw an error or not. You could potentially put that functionality into a function which is called before throwing each error, but Swift provides a better way called a **defer block**. A defer block simply allows you to give some code to be run right before exiting the function or method. Let's take a look at an example of a personal chef type that must always clean up after attempting to cook some food:

```
struct PersonalChef {
    func clean() {
        print("Wash dishes")
        print("Clean counters")
    }

    func addIngredients() throws {}
    func bringToBoil() throws {}
    func removeFromHeat() throws {}
    func allowItToSit() throws {}

    func makeCrèmeBrûlée(URL: NSURL) throws {
        defer {
            self.clean()
        }

        try self.addIngredients()
        try self.bringToBoil()
        try self.removeFromHeat()
        try self.allowItToSit()
    }
}
```

In the make crème brûlée method, we start out with a defer block that calls the clean method. This is not executed right away; it's executed immediately after an error is thrown or immediately before the method exits. This ensures that no matter how the making of the crème brûlée goes, the personal chef will still clean up after itself.

In fact, defer even works when returning from a function or method at any point:

```
struct Ingredient {
    let name: String
}

struct Pantry {
    private let ingredients: [Ingredient]

    func openDoor() {}
    func closeDoor() {}

    func getIngredientNamed(name: String) -> Ingredient? {
        self.openDoor()

        defer {
            self.closeDoor()
        }

        for ingredient in self.ingredients {
            if ingredient.name == name {
                return ingredient
            }
        }
        return nil
    }
}
```

Here, we have defined a small ingredient type and a pantry type. The pantry has a list of ingredients and a method to help us get an ingredient out of it. When we go to get an ingredient, we first have to open the door, so we need to make sure that we close the door at the end, whether or not we find an ingredient. This is another perfect scenario for a defer block.

One last thing to be aware of with defer blocks is that you can define as many defer blocks as you like. Each defer block will be called in the reverse order to which they are defined. So, the most recent deferred block will be called first and the oldest deferred block will be called last. We can take a look at a simple example:

```
func multipleDefers() {
    defer {
        print("C")
    }
```

```
    defer {
        print("B")
    }
    defer {
        print("A")
    }
}
multipleDefers()
```

In this example, "A" will be printed first because it was the last block to be deferred and "C" will be printed last.

Ultimately, it is a great idea to use defer any time you perform some action that will require clean-up. You may not have any extra returns or throws when first implementing it, but it will make it much safer to make updates to your code later.

Summary

Error handling isn't usually the most fun part of programming, but as you can see, there can absolutely be some interesting design strategies around it. It is also absolutely critical in developing quality software. We like to think that our users will never run into any problems or unforeseen scenarios, but you might be amazed at how often that happens. We want to do the very best we can to make those scenarios work well, because users will form lasting negative impressions of your product if they get bogged down in unavoidable error situations.

We saw that Swift provides us with a paradigm to help with this called error handling. Functions and methods can be marked as possibly throwing errors and then we can throw any type that implements the ErrorType protocol. We can handle those thrown errors in different ways. We can assert that an error will never be thrown using the try! keyword, we can convert a throwing function or method into an optional with the try? keyword, or we can catch and inspect errors with do-catch blocks. Lastly, we went over defer blocks, that help us ensure certain actions happen no matter if we throw an error or return early.

Now that we've got error handling out of the way, we can jump into the more artful side of computer programming called design patterns.

9
Writing Code the Swift Way – Design Patterns and Techniques

Unless you are on the cutting edge of computer science, most of the software you write will be more focused on user experience and maintainability than on any particular advanced programming language. As you write more and more of this type of software, you will see a lot of patterns emerge, especially if you focus on readability and maintainability, as most of us should. However, we don't have to come up with all of these patterns on our own; people have been programming and coming up with patterns for years that transfer really well from language to language.

We call these patterns, **design patterns**. Design patterns is a massive topic with countless books, tutorials, and other resources. We spend our entire careers practicing, shaping, and perfecting the use of these patterns in practical ways. We give each pattern a name so that we can have smoother conversations with fellow programmers and also organize them better in our own minds.

In this chapter, we will take a look at some of the most common design patterns, especially the ones important to understand Apple's frameworks. You will have a much easier time understanding and making use of that code when you begin to recognize patterns while using other people's code. It will also help you write better code yourself. We will focus on the high level ideas behind each pattern and then how to implement them in Swift. We will then go past the classic design patterns and look at some advanced features of Swift that allow us to write particularly clean code.

To do all that, we will cover the following topics in this chapter:

- What is a design pattern?
- The behavioral patterns
- The structural patterns
- The creational patterns
- Using associated values effectively
- Extending system types to reduce code
- The lazy properties

What is a design pattern?

Let's delve a little deeper into what a design pattern is before we dive into the specific patterns. As you may have begun to understand, there are unlimited ways to write a program that does even a simple thing. A design pattern is a solution to solve a recurrent and common problem. These problems are often so ubiquitous, that even if you don't use a pattern deliberately, you will almost certainly be using one or more patterns inadvertently; especially, if you are using third-party code.

To better evaluate the use of design patterns, we will look at three high-level measurements: **coupling**, **cohesion**, and **complexity**.

Coupling is the degree to which individual code components depend on other components. We want to reduce the coupling in our code so that all our code components operate as independently as possible. We want to be able to look at them and understand each component on its own without needing a full understanding of the entire system. Low coupling also allows us to make changes to one component without drastically affecting the rest of the code.

Cohesion is a reference to how well different code components fit together. We want code components that can operate independently, but they should still fit together with other components in a cohesive and understandable way. This means that to have low coupling and high cohesion, we want code components that are designed to have a single purpose and a small interface to the rest of our code. This applies to every level of our code, from how the different sections of our app fit together, down to how functions interact with each other.

Both of these measurements have a high impact on our final measurement: complexity. Complexity is basically just how difficult it is to understand the code, especially when it comes to practical things like adding new features or fixing bugs. By having low coupling and high cohesion, we will generally be writing much less complex code. However, taken to their extremes, these principles can sometimes actually cause greater complexity. Sometimes the simplest solution is the quickest and most effective one because we don't want to get bogged down into architecting the perfect solution when we can implement a near perfect solution ten times faster. Most of us cannot afford to code on an unlimited budget.

Instead of having a single giant list, design patterns are usually organized according to how they are used into three main categories: **behavioral**, **structural**, and **creational**.

Behavioral patterns

Behavioral patterns are patterns that describe how objects will communicate with each other. In other words, it is how one object will send information to another object, even if that information is just that some event has occurred. They help to lower the code's coupling by providing a more detached communication mechanism that allows one object to send information to another, while having as little knowledge about the other object as possible. The less any type knows about the rest of the types in the code base, the less it will depend on those types. These behavior patterns also help to increase cohesion by providing straightforward and understandable ways to send the information.

This can often be the difference between doing something, such as calling your sister to ask your mom to ask your grandpa what he wants for his birthday and being able to ask your grandpa directly because you have a good communication channel open with him. In general, we will want to have the direct channel of communication open but sometimes it is actually better design to interact with fewer people, as long as we don't put too much burden on the other components. Behavioral patterns can help us with this.

Iterator

The first behavioral pattern we will discuss is called the **iterator pattern**. We are starting with this one because we have actually already made use of this pattern in *Chapter 6, Make Swift Work For You – Protocols and Generics*. The idea of the iterator pattern is to provide a way to step through the contents of a container independent of the way the elements are represented inside the container.

As we saw, Swift provides us with the basics of this pattern with the `GeneratorType` and `SequenceType` protocols. It even implements those protocols for its array and dictionary containers. Even though we don't know how the elements are stored within an array or dictionary, we are still able to step through each value contained within them. Apple can easily change the way the elements are stored within them and it would not affect how we loop through the containers at all. This shows a great decoupling between our code and the container implementations.

If you remember, we were even able to create a generator for the infinite Fibonacci sequence:

```swift
struct FibonacciGenerator: GeneratorType {
    typealias Element = Int

    var values = (0, 1)

    mutating func next() -> Element? {
        self.values = (
            self.values.1,
            self.values.0 + self.values.1
        )
        return self.values.0
    }
}
```

The "container" doesn't even store any elements but we can still iterate through them as if it did.

The iterator pattern is a great introduction to how we make real world use of design patterns. Stepping through a list is such a common problem that Apple built the pattern directly into Swift.

Observer

The other behavioral pattern that we will discuss is called the **observer pattern**. The basic idea of this pattern is that you have one object that is designed to allow other objects to be notified when something occurs.

Callback

In Swift, the easiest way to achieve this is to provide a closure property on the object that you want to be observable and have that object call the closure whenever it wants to notify its observer. The property will be optional, so that any other object can set their closure on this property:

```swift
class ATM {
    var onCashWithdrawn: ((amount: Double) -> ())?

    func withdrawCash(amount: Double) {
        // other work

        // Notify observer if any
        if let callback = self.onCashWithdrawn {
            callback(amount: amount)
        }
    }
}
```

Here we have a class that represents an ATM that allows for withdrawing cash. It provides a closure property called `onCashWithdrawn` that is called every time cash is withdrawn. This type of closure property is usually called a **callback**. It is a good idea to make its purpose clear by its name. I personally choose to name all event-based callbacks by starting them with the word "on."

Now, any object can define its own closure on the callback and be notified whenever cash is withdrawn:

```swift
class RecordKeeper {
    var transactions = [Double]()

    func watchATM(atm: ATM) {
        atm.onCashWithdrawn = { [weak self] amount in
            self?.transactions.append(amount)
        }
    }
}
```

In this case, `ATM` is considered the observable object and the `RecordKeeper` is the observer. The `ATM` type is completely disconnected from whatever process might be keeping a record of its transactions. The record keeping mechanism can be changed without making any changes to the `ATM` and the `ATM` can be changed without any change to the `RecordKeeper` as long as the new `ATM` implementation still calls `onCashWithDrawn` whenever cash is withdrawn.

However, the `RecordKeeper` needs to be passed an ATM instance for this connection to be made. There can also only ever be one observer at a time. If we need to allow multiple observers, we can potentially provide an array of callbacks, but that can make removing observers more difficult. A solution that solves both of those problems is to implement the observer pattern using a notification center instead.

Notification center

A notification center is a central object that manages events for other types. We can implement a notification center for ATM withdrawals:

```
class ATMWithdrawalNotificationCenter {
    typealias Callback = (amount: Double) -> ()
    private var observers: [String:Callback] = [:]

    func trigger(amount: Double) {
        for (_, callback) in self.observers {
            callback(amount: amount)
        }
    }

    func addObserverForKey(key: String, callback: Callback) {
        self.observers[key] = callback
    }

    func removeObserverForKey(key: String) {
        self.observers[key] = nil
    }
}
```

With this implementation, any object can start observing by passing a unique key and callback to the `addObserverForKey:callback:` method. It doesn't have to have any reference to an instance of an ATM. An observer can also be removed by passing the same unique key to `removeObserverForKey:`. At any point, any object can trigger the notification by calling the `trigger:` method and all the registered observers will be notified.

If you really want to challenge yourself with advanced protocols and generics, you can try to implement a completely generic notification center that can store and trigger multiple events at once. The ideal notification center in Swift would allow any object to trigger an arbitrary event and any object to observe that arbitrary event, as long as it knows about it. The notification center should not have to know anything about any specific events. It should also allow an event to contain any type of data.

Structural patterns

Structural patterns are patterns that describe how objects should relate to each other so that they can work together to achieve a common goal. They help us lower our coupling by suggesting an easy and clear way to break down a problem into related parts and they help raise our cohesion by giving us a predefined way that those components will fit together.

This is like a sports team defining specific roles for each person on the field so that they can play together better as a whole.

Composite

The first structural pattern we are going to look at is called the **composite pattern**. The concept of this pattern is that you have a single object that can be broken down into a collection of objects just like itself. This is like the organization of many large companies. They will have teams that are made up of smaller teams, which are then made up of even smaller teams. Each sub-team is responsible for a small part and they come together to be responsible for a larger part of the company.

Hierarchies

A computer ultimately represents what is on the screen with a grid of pixel data. However, it does not make sense for every program to be concerned with each individual pixel. Instead, most programmers use frameworks, often provided by the operating system, to manipulate what is on the screen at a much higher level. A graphical program is usually given one or more windows to draw within and instead of drawing pixels within a window; a program will usually set up a series of "views". A view will have lots of different properties but they will most importantly have a position, size, and background color.

We can potentially build up an entire window with just a big list of views but programmers have devised a way of using the composite pattern to make the whole process much more intuitive. A view can actually contain other views, which are generally referred to as subviews. In this sense, you can look at any view like a tree of subviews. If you look at the very root of the tree, you will see a complete image of what will be displayed on the window. However, you can look at any of the tree branches or leaves and see a smaller part of that view. This is the same as looking at a large team as a whole versus looking at a small team within that larger team. In all of this, there is no difference between a view at the root of the tree and a view at the leaf of the tree, except the root has more sub-views.

Let's look at our own implementation of a `View` class:

```swift
class View {
    var color: (red: Float, green: Float, blue: Float)
        = (1, 1, 1) // white
    var position: (x: Float, y: Float) = (0, 0)
    var size: (width: Float, height: Float)
    var subviews = [View]()

    init(size: (width: Float, height: Float)) {
        self.size = size
    }
}
```

This is a pretty simple class, but by adding the `subviews` property, which is an array of additional views, we are using the composite pattern to make this a very powerful class. You can imagine a virtually infinite hierarchy of views that are all contained within a single parent view. That single view could be passed to some other class that could draw the entire hierarchy of views.

As an example, let's set up a view that has red in the left-half, green in the upper-right half, and blue in the lower-right half:

To produce this with our class, we could write a code similar to:

```swift
let rootView = View(size: (width: 100, height: 100))

let leftView = View(size: (width: rootView.size.width / 2, height:
rootView.size.height))
leftView.color = (red: 1, green: 0, blue: 0)
rootView.subviews.append(leftView)

let rightView = View(size: (width: rootView.size.width / 2, height:
rootView.size.height))
rightView.color = (red: 0, green: 0, blue: 1)
rightView.position = (x: rootView.size.width / 2, y: 0)
```

```
rootView.subviews.append(rightView)

let upperRightView = View(size: (width: rightView.size.width, height:
rootView.size.height / 2))
upperRightView.color = (red: 0, green: 1, blue: 0)
rightView.subviews.append(upperRightView)
```

In this implementation, we actually have a red left half as defined by `leftView` and a blue right half as defined by `rightView`. The reason the upper-right half is green instead of blue is that we added `upperRightView` as a subview to `rightView` and only made it half the height. This means that our view hierarchy looks similar to the following image:

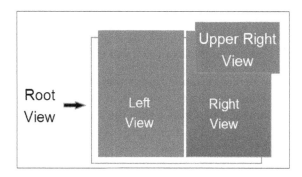

It is important to note that the position of `upperRightView` is left at *0, 0*. That is because the positioning of all sub-views will always be relative to their immediate parent view. This allows us to pull any view out of the hierarchy without affecting any of its sub-views; drawing `rightView` within `rootView` will look exactly the same as if it were drawn on its own.

You could also set up separate objects to manage the contents of different subsections of the main view. For example, to create a program like Xcode, we might have one object that manages the contents of the file list on the left and a different object that manages the display of the selected file. Clearly, Xcode is much more complex than that, but it gives us an idea of how we can build incredibly powerful and complex software with relatively simple concepts.

You may, however, have noticed a potential problem with our view class. What would happen if we added a view to its own subview hierarchy somewhere. That is most likely going to cause an infinite loop when another part of our code goes to draw the view. As another challenge to you, try to update our `View` class to prevent this from happening. I suggest you start by making `subviews` private and providing methods for adding and removing subviews. You will probably also want to add an optional `superview` property that will reference the parent view.

Alternative to subclassing

As you can see, the composite pattern is ideal for any situation where an object can be broken down into pieces that are just like it. This is great for something seemingly infinite like a hierarchy of views, but it is also a great alternative to subclassing. Subclassing is actually the tightest form of coupling. A subclass is extremely dependent on its superclass. Any change to a superclass is almost certainly going to affect all of its subclasses. We can often use the composite pattern as a less coupled alternative to subclassing.

As an example, let's explore the concept of representing a sentence. One way to look at the problem is to consider the sentence a special kind of string. Any kind of specialization like this will usually lead us to create a subclass; after all, a subclass is a specialization of its superclass. So we could create a `Sentence` subclass of `String`. This will be great because we can build strings using our sentence class and then pass them to methods that are expecting a normal string.

However, there is an important obstacle to this method: we don't have control of the `String` code and even worse we can't even look at the code so we don't even know how the characters are stored. This means that the code can be changed underneath us with an update from Apple without our knowledge. Even with our knowledge, this could cause a maintenance headache.

A better solution would be to use the composite pattern and implement a `Sentence` type that contains strings:

```
struct Sentence {
    var words: [String]

    enum Type: String {
        case Statement = "."
        case Question = "?"
        case Exclamation = "!"
    }

    var type: Type
}
```

Here, we were able to give more meaningful names to the parts of the sentence with various words and we set up a `Type` enumeration that allows us to use different end punctuations. As a convenience, we can even add a `string` calculated property so that we can use the sentence as a normal string:

```
struct Sentence {
    // ..

    var string: String {
        return self.words.joinWithSeparator(" ")
            + self.type.rawValue
    }
}

let sentence = Sentence(words: [
    "This", "is",
    "a", "sentence"
], type: .Statement)
print(sentence.string) // "This is a sentence."
```

This is a much better alternative to subclassing in this scenario.

Delegate

One of the most commonly used design patterns in Apple's frameworks is called the **delegate pattern**. The idea behind it is that you set up an object to let another object handle some of its responsibilities. In other words, one object will delegate some of its responsibilities to another object. This is like a manager hiring employees to do a job that the manager cannot or does not want to do themselves.

As a more technical example, on iOS, Apple provides a user interface class called `UITableView`. As the name suggest, this class provides us with an easy way to draw a list of elements. On its own, a `UITableView` isn't enough to make an interface. It needs data to display and it needs to be able to handle all kinds of user interactions, such as tapping, reordering, deleting, and so on.

One instinct is to create your own subclass of `UITableView`, maybe something like `PeopleTableView`. This is an OK option until you remember how we discussed that subclassing is actually the strongest type of coupling between two objects. In order to properly subclass a `UITableView`, you would have to be pretty intimately aware of how the superclass works. This is especially difficult when you are not even allowed to see the code of the superclass.

Another option is to set data on the table view and use the observer pattern to handle user interactions. This is better than the subclassing option, but most data you will want to display is not static and therefore it would be cumbersome to make updates to the table view. It will also still be hard to implement an object that can be reused easily for other ways of displaying a list of information.

So instead, what Apple did is, they created two different properties on `UITableView`: `delegate` and `dataSource`. These properties are there so that we can assign our own objects to handle various responsibilities for the table. The data source is primarily responsible for providing the information to be shown in the table and the delegate's responsibility is to handle user interaction. Of course, if these objects could be of any type, the table view would not really be able to interact with them. Also, if these objects were of a specific type, we would still run into the same subclassing problem. Instead, they are defined to implement the `UITableViewDelegate` and `UITableViewDataSource` protocols respectively.

These protocols define only the methods necessary to allow the table view to properly function. This means that the `delegate` and `dataSource` properties can be any type as long as they implement the necessary methods. For example, one of the critical methods the data source must implement is `tableView:numberOfRowsInSection:`. This method provides the table view and an integer referring to the section that it wants to know about. It requires that an integer be returned for the number of rows in the referenced section. This is only one of multiple methods that data source must implement, but it gives you an idea of how the table view no longer has to figure out what data it contains. It simply asks the data source to figure it out.

This provides a very loosely coupled way to implement a specific table view and this same pattern is reused all over the programming world. You would be amazed at what Apple has been able to do with its table view, with very little to no pain inflicted on third party developers. The table view is incredibly optimized to handle thousands upon thousands of rows if you really wanted it to. The table has also changed a lot since the first developer kit for iOS, but these protocols have very rarely been changed except to add additional features.

Model view controller

Model view controller is one of the highest levels and most abstract design patterns. Variations of it are pervasive across a huge percentage of software, especially Apple's frameworks. It really can be considered the foundational pattern for how all of Apple's code is designed and therefore how most third party developers design their own code. The core concept of model view controller is that you split all of your types into three categories, often referred to as layers: **model**, **view**, and **controller**.

The model layer is for all of the types that represent and manipulate data. This layer is the real foundation of what your software can do for its user, so it is also often referred to as the business logic. For example, the model layer from an address book app would have types representing contacts, groups, and so on. It would also contain logic to create, delete, modify, and store those types.

The view layer is for all types involved in the display and interaction of your software. It consists of types like tables, text view, and buttons. Essentially, this layer is responsible for displaying information to the user and providing the affordances for how a user can interact with your application. The view in an address book app would consist of the displayed list of contacts, groups, and contact information.

The final layer, controller, is mostly just the glue code between the model and view layers. It will instruct the view of what to display based on the data in the model layer and it will trigger the right business logic depending on the interactions coming from the view layer. In our address book example, the controller layer would connect something such as a contact add button in the view, to the logic defined in the model for creating a new contact. It will also connect things like the on screen table view to the list of contacts in the model.

In the ideal implementation of model view controller, no model type should ever have any knowledge of the existence of a view type and no view type should know about a model type. Often, a model view controller is visualized sort of like a cake:

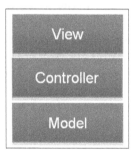

The user sees and interacts with the top of the cake and each layer only communicates with its adjacent layers. This means that all communication between the view and the model layers should go through the controller layer. At the same time, the controller layer should be pretty lightweight, because the model layer is doing the heavy lifting on the logic side of the application and the view layer is doing the heavy lifting on drawing to the screen and accepting user input.

One of the main benefits of this design pattern is that it provides a logical and consistent way to break down many pieces of software. This greatly increases your ability to share your code with other developers and understand their code. It gives everyone a frame of reference for when they try to understand another large code base that they haven't seen before. The naming of classes also gives strong clues to developers about what role a type will play in the overall system. Virtually every view class in iOS has the word "view" in it: `UITableView`, `UIView`, `UICollectionViewCell`, etc. Also, most of the controller layer classes that Apple provides have the word controller in them: `UIViewController`, `UITableViewController`, `MFMailComposeViewController`, etc. The model layer is mostly left to third party developers, other than the basic data types, since Apple isn't going to be able to help much with the business logic of your software. However, even among third party developers, these classes are often nouns named after the data they are representing or manipulating: Person, AddressBook, Publisher, and so on.

Another huge benefit of model view controller is that most components will be very reusable. You should be able to easily reuse views with different types of data like you can use a table view to display virtually any kind of data without changing the table view type and you should be able to display something like an address book in lots of different ways without changing the address book type.

As useful as this pattern is, it is also extremely hard to stick to. You will probably spend your entire development career evolving your sense for how to effectively breakdown your problems into these layers. It is often helpful to create explicit folders for each layer, forcing yourself to put every type into only one of the categories. You will also probably find yourself creating a bloated controller layer, especially in iOS, because it is often convenient to stick business logic there. More than any other design pattern, model view controller is probably the one that can be most described as something you strive for but rarely ever perfectly achieve.

Creational patterns

The final type of design patterns we will discuss is called **creational patterns**. These patterns relate to the initialization of new objects. At first, the initialization of an object probably seems simple and not a very important place to have design patterns. After all, we already have initializers. However, in certain circumstances, creational patterns can be extremely helpful.

Singleton/shared instance

The first patterns we will discuss are the **singleton** and **shared instance** patterns. We are discussing them together because they are extremely similar. First we will discuss shared instance, because it is the less strict form of the singleton pattern.

The idea of the shared instance pattern is that you provide an instance of your class to be used by other parts of your code. Let's look at a quick example of this in Swift:

```
class AddressBook {
    static let sharedInstance = AddressBook()

    func logContacts() {
        // ...
    }
}
```

Here, we have a simple address book class but we are providing a static constant called `sharedInstance` that any other code can use without having to create its own instance. This is a very convenient way to allow otherwise separate code to collaborate. Instead of having to pass around a reference to the same instance all over your code, any code can refer the shared instance right through the class itself:

```
AddressBook.sharedInstance.logContacts()
```

Now, the different thing about the singleton pattern is that you would write your code in such a way that it is not even possible to create a second instance of your class. Even though our preceding address book class provides a shared instance, there is nothing to stop someone from creating their own instance using the normal initializers. We could pretty easily change our address book class to a singleton instead of a shared instance, as shown:

```
class AddressBook {
    static let singleton = AddressBook()

    private init() {}

    func logContacts() {
        // ...
    }
}

AddressBook.singelton.logContacts()
```

Besides changing the name of the static constant, the only difference with this code is that we declared the initializers as private. This makes it so that no code outside of this file can use the initializer and therefore, no code outside of this file can create a new instance.

The singleton pattern is great for when multiple instances of the same class are going to cause a problem. This is especially important for classes that represent a finite physical resource but it can also be a way to simplify a class that would be more difficult and unnecessary to implement in a way that would allow multiple instances. For example, there isn't actually much of a reason to ensure there is only ever one address book in an application. Perhaps the user will want to have two address books: one for business and one for personal. They should be able to operate independently as long as they are working from a different file, but maybe in your application you know that there will only ever be a single address book and it always has to be driven by a single file. Instead of requiring your code to create an address book with a specific file path, and instead of dealing with the danger of having multiple instances reading and writing to the same file, you can use the singleton version above and have the file path be fixed.

In fact, the singleton and shared instance patterns are so convenient that many developers over use them. So let's discuss some of the drawbacks of these patterns. It is nice to be able to access an instance from anywhere, but when it is easy to do so, it is also easy to create a very complex web of dependencies on that object. That goes against the principle of low coupling that we are trying to achieve. Imagine trying to change a singleton class when you have 20 different pieces of code all using it directly.

Using these patterns can also create hidden dependencies. Usually, it is pretty clear what dependencies an instance has based on what it must be initialized with, but a singleton or shared instance does not get passed into the initializer, so it can often go unnoticed as a dependency. Even though there is some initial extra overhead to passing an object into an initializer, it will often reduce the coupling and maintain a clearer picture of how your types interact. The bottom line is, like with any other pattern, think carefully about each use of the singleton and shared instance patterns and be sure it is the best tool for the job.

Abstract factory

The final pattern we will discuss here is called **abstract factory**. It is based on a simpler pattern called **factory**. The idea of a factory pattern is that you implement an object for creating other objects, much like you would create a factory for assembling cars. The factory pattern is great when the initializing of a type is very complex or you want to create a bunch of similar objects. Let's take a look at the second scenario. What if we were creating a two-player ping-pong game and we had some scenario in the game where we would add additional balls that a specific player needed to keep in play? The ball class might look something like this:

```
struct Ball {
    let color: String
    let owningPlayer: Int
}
```

Every time we needed a new ball we could assign a new color and owning player to it. Or, we could create a separate ball factory for each player:

```
struct BallFactory {
    let color: String
    let owningPlayer: Int

    func createNewBall() -> Ball {
        return Ball(
            color: self.color,
            owningPlayer: self.owningPlayer
        )
    }
}

let player1Factory = BallFactory(
    color: "Red", owningPlayer: 1
)
let player2Factory = BallFactory(
    color: "Green", owningPlayer: 1
)

let ball1 = player1Factory.createNewBall()
```

Now, we could pass this factory into whatever object is responsible for handling the ball creation event and that object is no longer responsible for determining the color of the ball or any other properties we might want. This is great for reducing the number of responsibilities that object has and also keeps the code very flexible to add additional ball properties in the future without having to change the ball creation event object.

An abstract factory is a special form of factory where the instances the factory creates may be one of many subclasses of a single other class. A great example of this would be an image creation factory. As we discussed in *Chapter 3*, *One Piece at a Time – Types, Scopes, and Projects*, computers have an enormous number of ways to represent images. In that chapter we hypothesized having a superclass called just "Image" that would have a subclass for each type of image. This would help us write classes to handle any type of image very easily by always having them work with the image superclass. Similarly, we could create an image factory that would virtually eliminate any need for an external type to know anything about the different types of images. We could design an abstract factory that takes the path to any image, loads the image into the appropriate subclass, and returns it simply as the image superclass. Now, neither the code that loads an image, nor the code that uses the image, needs to know what type of image they are dealing with. All of the complexity of different image representations is abstracted away inside the factory and the image class hierarchy. This is a huge win for making our code easier to understand and more maintainable.

Using associated values effectively

Good programming is about more than just grand, universal concepts of how to write effective code. The best programmers know how to play to the strengths of the tools at hand. We are now going to move from looking at the core tenants of programming design to some of the gritty details of enhancing your code with the power of Swift.

The first thing we will look at is making effective use of the associated value of an enumeration. Associated values are a pretty unique feature of Swift, so they open up some pretty interesting possibilities.

Replacing class hierarchies

We have already seen in *Chapter 3, One Piece at a Time – Types, Scopes, and Projects* that we can use an enumeration with associated values to represent a measurement like distance in multiple measurement systems:

```
enum Height {
    case Imperial(feet: Int, Inches: Double)
    case Metric(meters: Double)
    case Other(String)
}
```

We can generalize this use case as using an enumeration to flatten out a simple class hierarchy. Instead of the enumeration, we could have created a height superclass or protocol with subclasses for each measurement system. However, this would be a more complex solution and we would lose the benefits of using a value type instead of a reference type. The enumeration solution is also very compact, making it very easy to understand at a glance instead of having to analyze how multiple different classes fit together.

Let's look at an even more complex example. Let's say we want to create a fitness app and we want to be able to track multiple types of workouts. Sometimes people workout to do a certain number of repetitions of various movements; other times they are just going for a certain amount of time. We could create a class hierarchy for this, but an enumeration with associated values works great:

```
enum Workout {
    case ForTime(seconds: Int)
    case ForReps(movements: [(name: String, reps: Int)])
}
```

Now, when we want to create a workout, we only need to define values relevant to the type of workout we are interested in without having to use any classes at all.

Concisely representing state

Another great use of enumerations with associated values is to represent the state of something. The simplest example of this would be a result enumeration that can either contain a value or an error description if an error occurs:

```
enum NumberResult {
    case Success(value: Int)
    case Failure(reason: String)
}
```

This allows us to write a function that can fail and give a reason that it failed:

```
func divide(first: Int, by second: Int) -> NumberResult {
    guard second != 0 else {
        return .Failure(reason: "Cannot divide by zero")
    }
    return .Success(value: first / second)
}
```

This is an alternative to normal error handling and can make sense for functions where the failure case is treated similarly to a success case instead of as a rare exception.

A slightly more complex idea is to use an enumeration to represent a process that will go through various stages over time, often called a state machine. We could write an enumeration for the process of a download:

```
enum DownloadState {
    case Pending
    case InProgress(percentComplete: Float)
    case Complete(data: String)
}
```

While the download is in progress we can access how complete it is and once it is complete we can access the data that it downloaded. This information is only accessible when it is applicable. This enumeration will also make it easier to make sure our download is always in a reasonable and clearly defined state. There is no possibility for a middle ground where, for example, the download might be complete but the data hasn't been processed yet. If we wanted to represent an additional processing step, we could easily add another case and it would be clear from then on out that a download will go through that additional state.

Extending system types to reduce code

Another powerful feature that we briefly covered in *Chapter 3, One Piece at a Time – Types, Scopes, and Projects* is the ability to extend existing types. We saw that we could add an extension to the string type that would allow us to repeat the string multiple times. Let's look at a more practical use case for this and discuss its benefits in terms of improving our code.

Perhaps we are creating a grade-tracking program where we are going to be printing out a lot of percentages. A great way to represent percentages is by using a float with a value between zero and one. Floats are great for percentages because we can use the built-in math functions and they can represent pretty granular numbers. The hurdle to cross when using a float to represent a percentage is printing it out. If we simply print out the value, it will most likely not be formatted the way we would want. People prefer percentages to be out of 100 and have a percent symbol after it.

Worst case scenario, we are going to write something, such as `print("\(myPercent * 100)%")`, every time we need to print out a percentage. This is not very flexible; what if we wanted to tweak all percentage outputs to have leading spaces, so it prints out right aligned? We would have to go through and change every print statement. Instead, we could write our own function like `printPercentage`. This will allow us to share the same code in lots of places.

This is a good step, but we can do one better using Swift's ability to extend system types. If we have an arbitrary function called `printPercentage`, we are going to have a hard time remembering it is there and other developers will have a hard time discovering it in the first place. It would be much nicer if we could easily get a printable version of a float directly from the float itself. We can make this possible by adding an extension to `Float`:

```swift
extension Float {
    var percentString: String {
        return "\(self * 100)%"
    }
}
let myPercent: Float = 0.32
print(myPercent.percentString) // 32.0%
```

Now we can use auto-complete to help us remember what formats we have defined for a float. Over time, you will probably develop a collection of useful and generic extensions like this that are extremely reusable because they are independent of any of your other program specific code. Writing these in such a reusable way makes it very easy to bring them into a new program, greatly accelerating each new project you start.

However, you do want to be careful that you don't end up creating too many extensions. For more complex situations, it is often more appropriate to use the composite pattern instead. For example, we could have written this as a `Percent` type that can be constructed with a `Float`:

```
struct Percent: CustomStringConvertible {
    let value: Float

    var description: String {
        return "\(self.value * 100)%"
    }
}
print(Percent(value: 0.3))
```

In this case it may not warrant the complexity of its own class, but you should at least consider how you might want to extend the idea of a percentage in the future.

Lazy properties

One feature we have not yet discussed is the concept of lazy properties. Marking a property as lazy allows Swift to wait to initialize it until the first time it is accessed. This can be useful in at least a few important ways.

Avoiding unnecessary memory usage

The most obvious way to use lazy properties is to avoid unnecessary memory usage. Let's look at a very simple example first:

```
struct MyType {
    lazy var largeString = "Some String"
}
let instance = MyType()
```

Even though we created a new instance of `MyType` in the preceding code, `largeString` is not set until we try to access it. This is great if we have a large variable that may not be needed on every instance. Until it is accessed, it is not taking up any memory.

Avoiding unnecessary processing

We can also take this idea of a lazy property even further using a closure to calculate the value:

```
class Directory {
    lazy var subFolders: [Directory] = {
        var loaded = [Directory]()
        // Load subfolders into 'loaded'
        return loaded
    }()
}
```

Here we are actually making use of a self-evaluating closure. We did this by adding the open and close parentheses to the end of the closure. By doing this, we are assigning the subFolders property to the result of executing the closure; because it is a lazy property, the closure will not be executed until the subFolders property is accessed for the first time. Just like the plain lazy property that can help us avoid taking up unnecessary memory, this technique allows us to avoid running time-consuming operations when we don't have to.

Localizing logic to the concerned property

An alternative to using lazy properties to achieve our goals above would be to use optional properties instead and simply assign those values later as needed. This is an OK solution, especially if our only goal is to reduce unnecessary memory usage or processing. However, there is one other great benefit to the lazy property solution. It produces more legible code by connecting the logic to calculate a property's value right by its definition. If we simply had an optional property it would have to be initialized in either an initializer or by some other method. It would not be immediately clear when looking at the property what its value will be and when it will be set, if it will be set at all.

This is a critically important advantage as your code base grows in size and age. It is very easy to get lost in a code base, even if it is your own. The more straight lines you can draw from one piece of logic to another, the easier it will be able to find the logic you are looking for when you come back to your code base later.

Summary

We have covered a lot of very large design concepts in a short period of time. We have looked at a number of specific design patterns, that help reduce the complexity of our code by reducing inter-object dependencies, commonly referred to as low coupling, and increasing the simplicity in which those objects work together, otherwise referred to as high cohesion.

We learned that there are three types of design patterns that focus on fixing different types of problems. Behavioral patterns help objects communicate with each other better, structural patterns facilitate the breaking down of complex structures into smaller and simpler ones, and creational patterns help with the initialization of new objects.

We also looked at some very specific features of Swift and how they can help us achieve similar goals to the ones we achieve with design patterns. We saw how to use enumerations with associated values to reduce the complexity of our type system and represent state better; we used extensions to system types to reduce the amount of code we write, and we wrote more efficient and understandable code using lazy properties.

As I said in the beginning, design patterns is a huge topic and not something you will master quickly, if ever. Figuring out how to best use the feature of a specific language is also a huge topic. I strongly recommend you use this chapter as a reference when you start to develop larger software and want to find ways to make it less complex. I also strongly encourage you to research more patterns and try to implement them on your own. Each design pattern is another tool in your toolbox. The more tools you have and the more experienced you are with each of them, the better you will be able to choose the right tool for the right job. That is the art of programming.

Now we are ready for the next chapter, where we will take a step back into the past to look at Objective-C so that we can leverage the vast resources targeted at Objective-C that are still very relevant to us as Swift developers.

10
Harnessing the Past – Understanding and Translating Objective-C

While Apple's platforms have been around for many years, Swift is still a very new language. Even before the release of the first iPhone, Apple's primary language of choice was Objective-C. This means that there are a vast number of resources in the world for developing on Apple's platforms using Objective-C. There are many amazing tutorials, code libraries, articles, and more, that are written in Objective-C that are still incredibly valuable for a Swift developer.

To take advantage of these resources, you must have at least a basic understanding of Objective-C, so that you can translate the concepts learned in tutorials and articles into Swift, as well as make use of the time tested Objective-C libraries.

In this chapter, we will develop a basic understanding of Objective-C with a focus on how it compares to Swift with the following topics:

- Swift's relationship to Objective-C
- Background of Objective-C
- Constants and variables
- Containers
- Control flow
- Functions
- Types
- Projects
- Calling Objective-C code from Swift

Swift's relationship to Objective-C

As we discussed already, Objective-C was previously the primary language for developing on Apple's platforms. This means that Objective-C had a lot of influence on Swift; the largest of which is that Swift was designed to interoperate with Objective-C. Swift code can call Objective-C code and, likewise, Objective-C code can call Swift code.

Ultimately, Swift was designed, and is still is being designed, to be the next step in programming languages, without having to throw away all of our Objective-C code. Apple's stated goals for the language are for Swift to be more modern, interactive, safe, fast, and powerful. These words would be pretty much meaningless if we didn't already have a baseline to compare Swift against. Since Swift was designed primarily for Apple's platforms, that baseline is largely Objective-C.

Background of Objective-C

Before we can talk about the details of Objective-C, we need to acknowledge its history. Objective-C is based on a language called simply "C". The C programming language was one of the first highly portable languages. Portable means that the same C code could be compiled to run on any processor as long as someone writes a compiler for that platform. Before that, most of the code was written in Assembly; which always had to be written specifically for each processor it would run on.

C is what is commonly referred to as a procedural programming language. It is built on the concept of a series of functions that call each other. It has a very basic support to create your own types, but it has no built in concept of objects. Objective-C was developed as an object-oriented extension to C. Just as Swift is backwards compatible with Objective-C, Objective-C is backwards compatible with C. Really, it simply adds object-oriented features on top of C with some new syntax and built-in libraries.

The real important thing is that Apple developed their current APIs: Cocoa and Cocoa Touch, for Objective-C. This is one of the biggest reasons why Objective-C is still very relevant to us as Swift developers. Even though we are primarily writing Swift code, we are still going to be regularly interacting with the Cocoa and Cocoa Touch libraries written in Objective-C.

Constants and variables

Now, we are ready to dive into the basics of the Objective-C language. Objective-C has constants and variables very similar to Swift but they are declared and worked with slightly differently. Let's take a look at declaring a variable in both Swift and Objective-C:

```
var number: Int
int number;
```

The first line should look familiar, as it is Swift. The Objective-C version doesn't actually look all that different. The important difference is that the type of the variable is declared before the name instead of after. It is also important to note that Objective-C has no concept of type inference. Every time a variable is declared, it must be given a specific type. You will also see that there is a semicolon after the name. This is because every line of code in Objective-C must end with a semicolon. Lastly, you should notice that we have not explicitly declared `number` as a variable. This is because all information is assumed to be variable in Objective-C unless specified otherwise. To define `number` as a constant, we will add the `const` keyword before its type:

```
let number = 10
const int number = 10;
```

Objective-C has value and reference types just like Swift. However, in Objective-C, the difference between them is more conceptual.

Value types

The number we declared above is a value type in both languages. They are copied if they are passed to another function and there cannot be more than one variable referencing the exact same instance.

It is actually easier to determine if a variable is a value type or a reference type in Objective-C because, as we will see, virtually all reference types are declared with an asterisk (*). If there is an asterisk, you can be safe to assume that it is a reference type.

Reference types

Objective-C actually allows you to make any type a reference type by adding an asterisk:

```
int *number;
```

This declares a reference to a number variable, more commonly referred to as a **pointer**. In a pointer declaration, the asterisk should always come after the type and before the name.

In Objective-C, reference types are actually loosely mixed with the concept of optional in Swift. All reference types are optional because a pointer can always point to nil:

```
int *number = nil;
```

A pointer can also always be tested for nil:

```
number == nil;
```

To access the referenced value, you must dereference it:

```
int actualNumber = *number;
```

You can dereference a pointer by adding an asterisk before it.

This is how pointers are similar to optionals in Swift. The difference is that there is no way to declare a non-optional reference type in Objective-C. Every reference type could technically be nil, even if you design it to never actually be nil. This can often add a lot of unnecessary nil checking and means every function you write that accepts a reference type should probably deal with the nil case.

Finally, the other difference between reference types in the two languages is that Objective-C is not very strict when it comes to what type the pointer is referencing. For example, Objective-C won't complain if we create a new double reference that points at the same thing as the int pointer:

```
double *another = (double *)number;
```

Now, we have two variables: number and another; they are pointing at the same value but assuming that they both are of different types. One of them is clearly going to be wrong, but Objective-C will happily try to use the same value as both a double and an int if you try. This is just one bug that Swift makes impossible by design.

So far, all of the Objective-C code we have looked at is actually strict C. We have not used any of the features that Objective-C added onto C. The main thing that Objective-C adds to C is its class system.

Lets take a look at our first actual Objective-C type called NSString compared to the Swift String type:

```
var myString = "Hello World!"
NSString *myString = @"Hello World!";
```

Just like in Swift, you can create a string instance using double quotes; however, in Objective-C you must put an @ sign before it.

One big thing to remember with the Objective-C class system is that it is not possible to create an instance of a class that is a value type. All instances must be referenced by a reference type. We cannot create a plain NSString. It must always be an NSString* pointer.

Containers

Objective-C has the same exact core containers that Swift does, with the two exceptions being that they are named slightly differently, and all of the containers in Objective-C are reference types because of the basic requirement that all Objective-C types must be reference types.

Arrays

In Objective-C arrays are called NSArray. Let's take a look at the initialization of an array in both Swift and Objective-C side-by-side:

```
var array = [Int]()
NSArray *array = [NSArray alloc];
array = [array init];
```

We have defined a variable called array that is a reference to the type NSArray. We then assign it to a newly allocated instance of NSArray. The square bracket notation in Objective-C allows us to call methods on a type or on an instance. Each separate call is always contained within a single set of square brackets. In this case, we are first calling the alloc method on the NSArray class. This returns a newly allocated variable that is of the type NSArray.

In contrast to Swift, Objective-C requires a two-step process to initialize a new instance. First, the memory must be allocated and then it must be initialized. Allocating means that we are reserving the memory for that object and initializing it means that we are setting it to its default value. This is what we are doing in the second line. The second line asks the instance to initialize itself. We reassign the array to the result of the call to init, because it is possible for init to return nil. Note that we are not dereferencing the array variable in order to make a call on it. We actually call the methods directly on the pointer.

Now, it is kind of a waste to use two lines to initialize a new instance, so often the calls are chained together:

```
NSArray *array = [[NSArray alloc] init];
```

This calls `alloc` on `NSArray` and then immediately calls on `init` on the result of that. The `array` variable is then assigned to the result of the `init` call. Be aware that it is possible for `alloc` to return nil, in which case we would be calling `init` on nil. In Objective-C this is OK; if you call a method on nil, it will simply always return nil. This is similar to how optional chaining works in Swift.

There is also an alternative to calling `alloc` and `init`; it's called simply `new`:

```
NSArray *array = [NSArray new];
```

This class method allocates and initializes the instance at the same time. This is great when you are not passing any arguments into `init`, but you will still need to call `alloc` separately when you are passing arguments into it. We will see examples of this later on.

You may have noticed that we have not specified what type this array is supposed to hold. This is because it is actually not possible. All arrays in Objective-C can contain any mix of types as long as they are not C types. This means that an `NSArray` cannot contain an `int` (there is an `NSNumber` class instead), but it can contain any mix of `NSStrings`, `NSArrays`, or any other Objective-C type. The compiler will not do any form of type checking for you, which means that we can write code expecting the wrong type to be in the array. This is yet another classification of bug that Swift makes impossible.

So how do we add objects to our array? The reality is that the `NSArray` class does not allow us to add or remove objects from it. In other words, `NSArray` is immutable. Instead, there is a version of an array called `NSMutableArray` that allows us to add and remove objects. Then we can use the `addObject:` method:

```
NSMutableArray *array = [NSMutableArray new];
[array addObject:@"Hello World!"];
```

Methods in Objective-C and Swift are named in the same way with a colon indicating each argument. In Objective-C, the colon is also used when calling the method to indicate the following code is the value to pass into the method.

The existence of a plain `NSArray` is to serve the same basic purpose as a constant array in Swift. In fact, we will see that all Objective-C containers are split into mutable and non-mutable versions. A mutable container can be passed into a method and treated like the non-mutable version to add some safety by not allowing unwanted code to modify the array.

Now, to access a value in an NSArray we have two options. The full way is to use the objectAtIndex: method:

```
NSString *myString = [array objectAtIndex:0];
```

We can also use square brackets, similar to Swift:

```
NSString *myString = array[0];
```

Note that we are just assuming that the type returned from the array is an NSString. We can just as easily assume that it is another type, say NSArray:

```
NSArray *myString = array[0];
```

As we know, this will be wrong and will almost certainly cause bugs later in the code but the compiler will not complain.

Lastly, to remove an object from a mutable array, we can use the removeObjectAtIndex: method:

```
[array removeObjectAtIndex:0];
```

The other important feature that you will need to be aware of is that Objective-C also has array literals, so you don't have to build them up dynamically:

```
NSArray *array = @[@"one", @"two", @"three"];
```

Array literals start with an @ symbol just like a string, but then it is defined by a list of objects within square brackets just like Swift.

There is a lot more that arrays can do, but you should be able to understand what each method does when you see it because most are well named. The methods are also often named the same in each language or you can look them up online, where Apple has extensive documentation. The purpose of this chapter is just to get you comfortable enough to have a high-level understanding of Objective-C code.

Dictionaries

Following the same pattern as arrays, dictionaries in Objective-C are called NSDictionary and NSMutableDictionary. A dictionary is initialized in the exact same way as shown:

```
NSMutableDictionary *dict = [[NSMutableDictionary alloc] init];
NSDictionary *dict2 = [NSDictionary new];
```

To set a value, we use the setObject:forKey: method:

```
[dict setObject:@"World" forKey:@"Hello"];
```

Just like with arrays, we cannot set new objects on non-mutable dictionaries. Also, this is our first example of a method that takes more than one argument. As you can see, each argument is contained within the square brackets but separated by a space and the label for that argument. In this pattern, Objective-C methods can have a number of arguments.

Now to access a value we can use the `objectForKey:` method or square brackets again:

```
NSString *myString = [dict objectForKey:@"Hello"];
NSString *myString2 = dict[@"Hello"];
```

Again, we are assuming that the resulting object being returned is a string, because we know what we just put into the dictionary. This assumption isn't always safe and we also need to always be aware that this method will return nil if an object does not exist for that key.

Lastly, to remove an object, we can use the `removeObjectForKey:` method:

```
[dict removeObjectForKey:@"Hello"];
```

This is all relatively straightforward, especially when you are reading the code. This verbosity was always a great feature of Objective-C to write understandable code and this was definitely carried forward into Swift.

Dictionaries also have literals, but unlike `NSArrays` and Swift array literals, dictionary literals in Objective-C are declared using curly brackets. Otherwise, it looks very similar to Swift:

```
NSDictionary *dict3 = @{@1: @"one", @2: @"two", @3: @"three"};
```

Again, we have to start our literal with an @ symbol. We can also see that we can use numbers as objects in our containers as long as we put an @ symbol before each one. Instead of creating something such as an `int` type, this creates an `NSNumber` instance. You shouldn't need to know much about the `NSNumber` class except that it is a class to represent many different forms of numbers as objects.

Control flow

Objective-C has many of the same control flow paradigms as Swift. We will go through each of them quickly, but before we do, let's take a look at the Objective-C equivalent of `print`:

```
var name = "Sarah"
println("Hello \(name)")

NSString *name = @"Sarah";
NSLog(@"Hello %@", name);
```

Instead of `print`, we are using a function called `NSLog`. Objective-C does not have string interpolation, so `NSLog` is a somewhat more complex solution than `print`. The first argument to `NSLog` is a string that describes the format to be printed out. This includes a placeholder for each piece of information we want to log that indicates the type it should expect. Every placeholder starts with a percent symbol. In this case, we are using an at-symbol to indicate what we are going to be substituting in a string. Every argument after the initial format will be substituted for the placeholders in the same order they are passed in. Here, this means that it will end up logging **Hello Sarah** just like the Swift code.

Now, we are ready to look at the different methods of control flow in Objective-C.

Conditionals

A conditional looks exactly the same in both Swift and Objective-C except parentheses are required in Objective-C:

```
var invitees = ["Sarah", "Jamison", "Roana"]
if invitees.count > 20 {
    print("Too many people invited")
}
NSArray *invitees = @[@"Sarah", @"Jamison", @"Roana"];
if (invitees.count > 20) {
    NSLog(@"Too many people invited");
}
```

You can also include those parentheses in Swift, but they are optional. Here, you also see that Objective-C still has the idea of the dot syntax for calling some methods. In this case, we have used `invitees.count` instead of `[invitees count]`. This is only an option when we are accessing a property of the instance or we are calling a method that takes no arguments and returns something, as if it were a calculated property.

Switches

Switches in Objective-C are profoundly less powerful than switches in Swift. In fact, switches are a feature of strict C and are not enhanced at all by Objective-C. Switches cannot be used like a series of conditionals; they can only be used to do equality comparisons:

```
switch invitees.count {
    case 1:
        print("One person invited")
    case 2:
```

```
            print("Two people invited")
        default:
            print("More than two people invited")
    }
    switch (invitees.count) {
        case 1:
            NSLog(@"One person invited");
            break;

        case 2:
            NSLog(@"Two people invited");
            break;

        default:
            NSLog(@"More than two people invited");
            break;
    }
```

Again, parentheses are required in Objective-C, where they are optional in Swift. The most important difference with Objective-C switches is that by default, one case will flow into the next unless you specifically use the break keyword to get out of the switch. That is the opposite of Swift, where it will only flow into the next case if you use the fallthrough keyword. In practice, this means that the vast majority of Objective-C switch cases will need to end with break.

Objective-C switches are not powerful enough to allow us to create cases for ranges of values and certainly cannot test a list of arbitrary conditionals like we can in Swift.

Loops

Just like conditionals, loops in Objective-C are very similar to Swift. While-loops are identical except that the parentheses are required:

```
var index = 0
while index < invitees.count {
    print("\(invitees[index]) is invited");
    index++
}
int index = 0;
while (index < invitees.count) {
    NSLog(@"%@ is invited", invitees[index]);
    index++;
}
```

The for-in loops are slightly different, in this you must specify the type of the variable you are looping through with the following:

```
var showsByGenre = [
    "Comedy": "Modern Family",
    "Drama": "Breaking Bad"
]
for (genre, show) in showsByGenre {
    print("\(show) is a great \(genre)")
}

NSDictionary *showsByGenre=@{
    @"Comedy":@"Modern Family",
    @"Drama":@"Breaking Bad"
};
for (NSString *genre in showsByGenre) {
    NSLog(@"%@ is a great %@", showsByGenre[genre], genre);
}
```

You may have also noticed that when we are looping through an NSDictionary in Objective-C you only get the key. This is because tuples do not exist in Objective-C. Instead, you must access the value from the original dictionary, using the key as you loop through.

The other feature that is missing from Objective-C is ranges. To loop through a range of numbers, Objective-C programmers must use a different kind of loop called a for loop:

```
for number in 1 ... 10 {
    print(number)
}
for (int number = 1; number <= 10; number++) {
    NSLog(@"%i", number);
}
```

This loop is made up of three parts: an initial value, a condition to run until, and an operation to perform after each loop. This version loops through the numbers 1 to 10 just like the Swift version. Clearly, it is still possible to translate the Swift code into Objective-C; it just isn't as clean.

Even with that limitation, you can see that Objective-C and Swift loops are pretty much the same except for the parentheses requirement.

Functions

So far we have called some Objective-C functions but we have not defined any yet. Let's see what the Objective-C versions are of the functions we defined in *Chapter 2, Building Blocks – Variables, Collections, and Flow Control.*

Our most basic function definition didn't take any arguments and didn't return anything. The Objective-C version looks similar to the following code:

```
func sayHello() {
    print("Hello World!");
}
sayHello()
void sayHello() {
    NSLog(@"Hello World!");
}
sayHello();
```

Objective-C functions always starts with the type that the function returns instead of the keyword `func`. In this case, we aren't actually returning anything, so we use the keyword `void` to indicate that.

Functions that take arguments and return values have more of a disparity between the two languages:

```
func addInviteeToListIfSpotAvailable
    (
    invitees: [String],
    newInvitee: String
    )
    -> [String]
{
    if invitees.count >= 20 {
        return invitees
    }
    return invitees + [newInvitee]
}
addInviteeToListIfSpotAvailable(invitees, newInvitee: "Roana")

NSArray *addInviteeToListIfSpotAvailable
    (
    NSArray *invitees,
    NSString *newInvitee
    )
{
```

```
    if (invitees.count >= 20) {
        return invitees;
    }
    NSMutableArray *copy = [invitees mutableCopy];
    [copy addObject:newInvitee];
    return copy;
}
addInviteeToListIfSpotAvailable(invitees, @"Roana");
```

Again, the Objective-C version defines what it is returning at the beginning of the function. Also, just like variables, parameters to functions must have their type defined before their name instead of after. The rest however, is pretty similar: the arguments are contained within parentheses and separated by commas; the code of the function is contained within curly brackets and we use the `return` keyword to indicate what we want to return.

This specific implementation actually brings up an interesting requirement for dealing with arrays in Objective-C. Just like we want to avoid mutable arrays in Swift, we normally want to avoid them in Objective-C. In this case, we still don't want to modify the passed in array, we just want to add the new invitee to the end of a copied version. In Swift, because arrays are value types, the copy is made for us and we can use the addition operator to add on the new invitee. In Objective-C, we need to explicitly make a copy of the array. More than that, we need the copy to be mutable so that we can add the new invitee to it.

All in all, the biggest difference between Swift functions and Objective-C methods is the definition of the return value being at the beginning or the end of the parameters. The memory is handled in the same way in both languages. When passing in a pointer in Objective-C, the pointer itself is copied but both versions are going to reference the exact same instance. When a value type is passed into a function in Swift, the value is simply copied and the two versions have nothing to do with each other after that.

Types

The type system in Objective-C is a little bit more disparate than Swift. This is because the structures and enumerations in Objective-C come from C. Only classes and categories come from the Objective-C extension.

Structures

In Swift, structures are very similar to classes, but in Objective-C, they are much more different. Structures in Objective-C are essentially just a way of giving a name to a collection of individual types. They cannot contain methods. Even more restrictive than that, structures can't contain Objective-C types. This leaves us with only basic possibilities:

```
struct Cylinder {
    var radius: Int
    var height: Int
}
var c = Cylinder(radius: 10, height: 10)

typedef struct {
    int radius;
    int height;
} Cylinder;
Cylinder c;
c.radius = 10;
c.height = 5;
```

Structures in Objective-C start with the keyword `typedef`, which is short for type definition. This is then followed by the `struct` keyword and the different components of the structure contained within curly brackets. Finally, after the curly brackets is the name of the structure.

Advanced C programmers will do a lot more with structures. There are ways to simulate some features of inheritance with structures and to do other more advanced things, but that is beyond the scope of this book and not very relevant in most modern programming projects. There are some types in Apple's APIs that are structures like CGRect so you should know how to interact with them, but you most likely won't have to deal with custom structure definitions when looking at Objective-C resources.

Enumerations

Enumerations are also much more restrictive in Objective-C. They are really just a simple mechanism to represent a finite list of related possible values. This allows us to still represent possible primary colors:

```
enum PrimaryColor {
    case Red
    case Green
    case Blue
}
```

```
var color = PrimaryColor.Blue

typedef enum {
    PrimaryColorRed,
    PrimaryColorGreen,
    PrimaryColorBlue,
} PrimaryColor;
PrimaryColor color = PrimaryColorBlue;
```

Just like with structures, Objective-C enumerations start with the keyword `typedef` followed by `enum` with the name at the end of the definition. Each case is contained within the curly brackets and separated by a comma.

Notice that every case of the enumeration starts with the name of the enumeration. This is a very common convention, to make it easy for code completion and to show all possible values of an enumeration. This is because in Objective-C, you cannot specify a specific enumeration value through the name of the enumeration itself. Instead, every case is its own keyword. This is why when we are assigning our `color` variable to blue; we use the case name by itself.

Enumerations in Objective-C cannot have methods, associated values, or represent any other values except for integers. In fact, in Objective-C enumerations, every case has a numeric value. If you don't specify any, they start at 0 and go up by 1 for each case. If you want, you can manually specify a value for one or more of the cases:

```
typedef enum {
    PrimaryColorRed,
    PrimaryColorGreen = 10,
    PrimaryColorBlue,
} PrimaryColor;
```

Each case after a manually specified case will continue to increase by one. This means that in the preceding code `PrimaryColorRed` is still 0 but `PrimaryColorBlue` is 11.

Classes

Unlike Objective-C structures and enumerations, classes are very similar to their Swift counterparts. Objective-C classes can contain methods and properties, use inheritance, and get initialized. However, they look pretty different. Most notably, a class in Objective-C is split into two parts: its interface and its implementation. The interface is intended to be the public interface to the class, while the implementation includes the implementation of that interface in addition to any other private methods.

Basic class

Let's start by looking again at our contact class from *Chapter 3, One Piece at a Time – Types, Scopes, and Projects* and what it looks like in Objective-C:

```
class Contact {
    var firstName: String = "First"
    var lastName: String = "Last"
}

@interface Contact : NSObject {
    NSString *firstName;
    NSString *lastName;
}
@end

@implementation Contact
@end
```

Already Objective-C is taking a lot more lines of code. First, we have the interface declaration. This begins with the `@interface` keyword and ends with the `@end` keyword. Within the square brackets is a list of attributes. These are essentially the same as the attributes of a structure, except that you can include Objective-C objects in the attributes. These attributes are not commonly written like this because using the properties will create these automatically, as we will see later.

You will also notice that our class is inheriting from a class called `NSObject`, as indicated by `: NSObject`. This is because every class in Objective-C must inherit from `NSObject`, which makes `NSObject` the most basic form of class. However, don't let the term "basic" fool you; `NSObject` provides a lot of functionality. We won't really get into that here, but you should at least be aware of it.

The other part of the class is the implementation. It starts with the `@implementation` keyword followed by the name of the class we are implementing and then ends again with the `@end` keyword. Here, we have not actually added any extra functionality to our contact class. However, you may notice that our class is missing something that the Swift version has.

Initializers

Objective-C does not allow specifying default values for any attributes or properties. This means that we have to implement an initializer that sets the default values:

```
@implementation Contact
- (id)init {
    self = [super init];
    if (self) {
```

```
        firstName = @"First";
        lastName = @"Last";
    }
    return self;
}
@end
```

In Objective-C, initializers are the exact same as a method, except that by convention they start with the name `init`. This is actually just a convention but it is important, as it will cause problems down the line with memory management and interacting with the code from Swift.

The minus sign at the beginning indicates that this is a method. Next, the return type is specified within parentheses, which is then followed by the name of the method: in this case `init`. The body of the method is contained in curly brackets just like a function.

The return type for all initializers is going to be `id` by convention. This allows us to easily override initializers of subclasses.

Virtually all initializers will follow this same pattern. Just like in Swift, `self` references the instance that this method is being called on. The first line assigns the `self` reference to the result by calling the superclass's initializer with `[super init]`. We then allow for the possibility that the initializer fails and returns nil by testing it for nil in the `if (self)` statement. The `if` statement will fail if `self` is nil. If it is not nil, we assign the default values. Finally, we return self, so that calling code can maintain a reference to the newly initialized object. However, this is just a convention and Objective-C does not have any protection around properly initializing properties.

Properties

The Objective-C version of the contact class still isn't exactly like the Swift version because the `firstName` and `lastName` attributes are not accessible from outside the class. To make them accessible we need to define them as public properties and we can drop them from being explicit attributes:

```
@interface Contact : NSObject {
}
@property NSString *firstName;
@property NSString *lastName;
@end
```

Note that the properties are defined outside of the curly brackets but still within the `@interface`. In fact, you can leave off the curly brackets altogether if you have nothing to define in it. Properties automatically generate attributes by the same name except with an underscore at the beginning:

```
@implementation Contact
- (id)init {
    self = [super init];
    if (self) {
        _firstName = @"First";
        _lastName = @"Last";
    }
    return self;
}
@end
```

Alternatively, you can just set the values using `self`:

```
@implementation Contact
- (id)init {
    self = [super init];
    if (self) {
        self.firstName = @"First";
        self.lastName = @"Last";
    }
    return self;
}
@end
```

There are nuances to each approach but for just general reading purposes, it doesn't matter which one is used.

Also, just as you can define weak references in Swift, you can do so in Objective-C:

```
@interface SteeringWheel : NSObject
@property (weak) Car *car;
@end
```

If you want, you can replace weak with strong, but just like Swift, all properties are strong by default. Weak references in Objective-C will automatically be set to nil if the referenced object gets deallocated. You can also use the `unsafe_unretained` keyword, which is equivalent to unowned in Swift. However, this is rarely used as the only difference between the two in Objective-C is that `unsafe_unretained` does not reset the value to nil; instead, it will reference an invalid object if the object gets deallocated causing confusing crashes if used.

In addition to `weak` or `strong`, you can also specify that a property is `readonly` or `readwrite`:

```
@interface SteeringWheel : NSObject
@property (weak, readonly) Car *car;
@end
```

Each property attribute should be written inside the parentheses separated by a comma. As the `readonly` name implies, this makes it so that the property can be read but not written to. Every property is read-write by default, so normally it is not necessary to include it.

Note that you may also see the keyword `nonatomic` in the parentheses. This is a more advanced topic that is beyond the scope of this book.

Methods

We have already seen an example of a method in the form of an initializer, but let's take a look at some methods that take parameters:

```
@implementation Contact
- (NSArray *)addToInviteeList:(NSArray *)invitees
includeLastName:(BOOL)include {
    NSMutableArray *copy = [invitees mutableCopy];
    if (include) {
        NSString *newString = [self.firstName
            stringByAppendingFormat:@" %@", self.lastName
        ];
        [copy addObject:newString];
    }
    else {
        [copy addObject:self.firstName];
    }
    return copy;
}
@end
```

Each parameter is defined with a public label followed by a colon, its type in parentheses, and an internal name. Then, each parameter is separated by a space or new line.

You can also see an example way to format a long method call with the creation of the `newString` instance. Similar to Swift, any space can be converted to a new line instead. This allows us to convert a single long line into multiple lines, as long as we don't put semicolons after the partial lines.

Like Swift, Objective-C also has the idea of class methods. Class methods are indicated with a plus sign instead of a minus sign:

```
@implementation Contact
+ (void)printAvailablePhonePrefixes {
    NSLog(@"+1");
}
@end
```

So now you can call the method directly on the class:

```
[Contact printAvailablePhonePrefixes];
```

Inheritance

Just as all of our classes so far have inherited from NSObject, any class can inherit from any other class just like in Swift and all the same rules apply. Methods and properties are inherited from their superclass and you can choose to override methods in subclasses. However, the compiler enforces the rules much less. The compiler does not force you to specify that you intend your method to override another. The compiler does not enforce any rules around initializers and whom they call. However, all the conventions exist because those conventions were the inspiration for the Swift requirements.

Categories

Categories in Objective-C are just like Swift extensions. They allow you to add new methods to existing classes. They look very similar to plain classes:

```
extension Contact {
    func fullName() -> String {
        return "\(self.firstName) \(self.lastName)"
    }
}

@interface Contact (Helpers)
- (NSString *)fullName;
@end

@implementation Contact (Helpers)
- (NSString *)fullName {
    return [self.firstName stringByAppendingFormat:@" %@", self.
lastName];
}
@end
```

We know that this is a category instead of a normal class because we added a name within parentheses after the class name. Every category on a class must have a unique name. In this case, we are calling it `Helpers` and we are adding a method to return the contact's full name.

Here, for the first time, we are declaring a method inside the interface. This is also possible with classes. A method definition looks exactly like an implementation except that it ends in a semicolon instead of the code inside the curly brackets. This will allow us to call the method from outside the current file, as we will see in more detail in the upcoming projects section.

Categories can also add properties, but you will have to define your own getter and setter methods because just like Swift extensions can't add stored properties, Objective-C categories can't add attributes:

```
@interface Contact (Helpers)
@property NSString *fullName;
@end

@implementation Contact (Helpers)
- (NSString *)fullName {
    return [self.firstName stringByAppendingFormat: @" %@",
        self.lastName
    ];
}
- (void)setFullName:(NSString *)fullName {
    NSArray *components = [fullName
        componentsSeperatedByString:@" "];
    ];
    if (components.count > 0) {
        self.firstName = components[0];
    }
    if (components.count > 1) {
        self.lastName = components[1];
    }
}
@end
```

These types of properties are very similar to calculated properties. If you need to allow reading from a property, you must implement a method with the exact same name that takes no parameters and returns the same type. If you want to be able to write to the property you will have to implement a method that starts with `set`, followed by the same property name with a capital first letter, that takes the property type as a parameter and returns nothing. This allows outside classes to interact with the property as if it were an attribute, when in fact it is just another set of methods. Again, this is possible within a class or a category.

Protocols

Like Swift, Objective-C has the idea of protocols. Their definition looks similar to this:

```
protocol StringContainer {
    var count: Int {get}
    func addString(string: String)
    func enumerateStrings(handler: () -> ())
}

@protocol StringContainer
@property (readonly) NSInteger count;
- (void)addString:(NSString *)string;
- (void)enumerateStrings:(void(^)(NSString *))handler;
@end
```

Here, we are using the `@protocol` keyword instead of `@interface` and it still ends with the `@end` keyword. We can define any properties or methods that we want. We can then say that a class implements the protocol similar to this:

```
@interface StringList : NSObject <StringContainer>
@property NSMutableArray *contents;
@end
```

The list of protocols that a class implements should be listed within angled brackets after the class it inherits from separated by commas. In this case we are only implementing a single protocol so we don't need any commas. This code also declares a `contents` property, so that we can implement the protocol as shown:

```
@implementation StringList

- (NSInteger)count {
    return [self.contents count];
}

- (void)addString:(NSString *)string {
    if (self.contents == nil) {
        self.contents = [NSMutableArray new];
    }
    [self.contents addObject:string];
}

- (void)enumerateStrings:(void (^)(NSString *))handler {
    for (NSString *string in self.contents) {
        handler(string);
    }
}

@end
```

Note that we don't do anything special in the implementation to implement a protocol; we just need to make sure the proper methods and computed properties are implemented.

The other thing you should be aware of is that protocols in Objective-C are not used in the same way as classes. You can't just define a variable to be a protocol; instead, you must give it a type and require that it implement the protocol. Most commonly, this is done with the id type:

```
id<StringContainer> container = [StringList new];
```

Any variable declaration can require that it not only inherits from a specific type, but also implements certain protocols.

Blocks

Lastly, blocks are the Objective-C alternative to closures in Swift. They are actually a late addition to Objective-C so their syntax is somewhat complex:

```
int (^doubleClosure)(int) = ^(int input){
    return input * 2;
};
doubleClosure(2);
```

Let's break this down. We start like any other variable with the variable's name and type before the equals sign. The name starts with a carrot symbol (^) inside the first set of parentheses. In this case, we are calling it doubleClosure. The actual type of the closure surrounds that. The type it starts with is the type the closure returns, which in this case is an int. The second set of parentheses lists the types of the parameters the closure accepts. In total, this means that we are defining a closure called doubleClosure that accepts int and returns int.

Then, we move on to the business of implementing the closure. All closure implementations start with a carrot symbol followed by any arguments in parentheses and curly brackets with the actual implementation. Once a closure is defined, it can be called similar to any other function. However, you should always be aware that it is possible for a closure to be nil, in which calling it will cause the program to crash.

It is also possible to define a function or method that accepts a closure as a parameter. First, a function:

```
id firstInArrayPassingTest(NSArray *array, BOOL(^test)(id)) {
    for (id element in array) {
        if (test(element)) {
            return element;
```

```
            }
        }
        return nil;
    }
    firstInArrayPassingTest(array, ^BOOL(id test) {
        return false;
    });
```

Note that the type `id` signifies any Objective-C object and even though it doesn't have an asterisk, it is a reference type. The usage above looks exactly like a standalone block usage. However, the syntax looks somewhat different in a method:

```
    - (id)firstInArray:(NSArray *)array
        passingTest:(BOOL(^)(id test))test
    {
        for (id element in array) {
            if (test(element)) {
                return element;
            }
        }
        return nil;
    }
    [self firstInArray:array passingTest:^BOOL(id test) {
        return false;
    }];
```

This is because a method's parameter name is separated by parentheses. This causes the name of the parameter to be moved from being with the carrot to after the parentheses. In the end, we can say that the nuances of the syntax aren't too important when reading Objective-C code and translating to Swift, as long as you recognize that a carrot symbol indicates a block. Many Objective-C programmers look up the syntax of a block on a regular basis.

All of the same memory concerns exist in Objective-C with blocks. By default, all arguments are captured strongly and the syntax to capture them weakly is much more convoluted. Instead of including the weak captures in the block itself, you must create weak variables outside of the block and use them:

```
    @interface Ball : NSObject
    @property int xLocation;
    @property (strong) void (^onBounce)();
    @end
    @implementation Ball
    @end
```

```
Ball *ball = [Ball new];
__weak Ball *weakBall = ball;
ball.onBounce = ^{
    NSLog(@"%d", weakBall.xLocation);
};
```

Here we use the keyword __weak (that has two underscores) to indicate that the weakBall variable should only have a weak reference to ball. We can then safely reference the weakBall variable within the block and not create a circular reference.

Projects

Now that we have a pretty good understanding of Objective-C, let's discuss what Objective-C code looks like in a project. Unlike the Swift code, Objective-C is written in two different types of files. One of the types is called a header file and ends in the extension h. The other type is called an implementation file and ends in the extension m.

Before we can really discuss what the difference is between the two, we first have to discuss code exposure. In Swift, all the code you write is accessible to all other code in your project. This is not true with Objective-C. In Objective-C, you must explicitly indicate that you want to have access to the code in another file.

Header files

The header files are the types of files that can be included by other files. This means that header files should only contain the interfaces of types. In fact, this is why the separation exists between class interfaces and implementations. Any file can import a header file and that essentially inserts all the code of one file into the file that is importing it:

```
#import <Foundation/Foundation.h>
#import "Car.h"

@interface SteeringWheel : NSObject
@property (weak) Car *car;
@end
```

This allows us to separate each class into its own file just as we like to do in Swift. The danger is that we must only put code that can be safely imported into headers. If you try to put implementations in a header, you will end up with duplicate implementations for every time you import the header.

In the preceding example, we actually imported one header file into another. This means that if a different file now includes this header file, it will essentially be importing both header files.

You will also notice that there are two different ways to import a file. We import foundation with angled brackets and imported our car header with quotes. Angled brackets are used for importing header files from frameworks, while quotes are used for importing header files within the same framework or application.

A lot of the time it isn't actually necessary for one header file to include another because all it needs to know about is the existence of the class. If it doesn't need to know any actual details about the class, it can simply indicate that the class exists using the @class keyword:

```
@class Car;

@interface SteeringWheel : NSObject
@property (weak) Car *car;
@end
```

Now, the compiler will not complain that it doesn't know what Car is. However, you will most likely still need to import the car header in the implementation file because you will probably be interacting with some part of that class.

Implementation files

As you might have guessed, implementation files are generally for the implementation of your types. These files are not imported into others; they simply fulfill the promises of what the interface files have defined. This means that header and implementation files generally exist in pairs. If you are defining a steering wheel class, you will most likely create a SteeringWheel.h header and a SteeringWheel.m implementation file. Any other code that needs to interact with the details of the steering wheel class will import the header and at compile time, the compiler will make all of the implementations available to the running program.

Implementation files are also a great place to hide private code, because they cannot be imported by other code. Since the code is not visible anywhere else, it is unlikely to be interacted with. This means that people will sometimes add class interfaces to implementation files if their use is localized to just that file. It is also very common to add what is called an anonymous category to an implementation file:

```
@interface SteeringWheel ()
@property NSString *somePrivateProperty;
- (void)somePrivateMethod;
@end
```

This is considered anonymous because the category was not actually given a name. This means there is no way to pair an implementation directly with that category. Instead, the implementation should be defined within the normal implementation of the class. This provides a great way to define any private properties and methods at the top of an implementation file. You don't technically need to define any private methods because as long as they are implemented in the same file, they can be interacted with. However, it is often nice to have a concise list of the available properties and methods at the top of the file.

This brings up another point, that only methods that you intend to use from outside files should be declared in the header. You should always consider a header to be the public interface of your class and it should be as minimal as possible. It is always written from the perspective of outside files. This is the way that Objective-C implements access control. It isn't formally built into the language but the compiler will warn you if you try to interact with code that has not been imported. It is actually still possible to interact with these private interfaces, especially if you duplicate the interface declaration somewhere else, but it is considered best practice to not do that and Apple will actually reject your apps during review if you try to interact with private parts of their API.

Organization

Other than the obvious difference, the Objective-C projects will have two different types of files. They are organized in the exact same way as Swift files. It is still considered to be a good practice to create folders to group related files together. Most of the time you will want to keep header file and implementation file pairs together, as people will be switching between the two types of files a lot. However, people can also use the keyboard shortcuts *Control/Command* up arrow or *Control/Command* down arrow to quickly swap between a header file and its implementation file.

Calling Objective-C code from Swift

The last and possibly the most critical component of understanding Objective-C for our purpose is to be able to call Objective-C code from Swift. This is actually pretty straightforward in most circumstances. We will not take any time to discuss calling Swift code from Objective-C because this book assumes that you are only writing Swift code.

Bridging header

The most important part of being able to call Objective-C code from Swift is how to make the code visible to Swift. As we now know, Objective-C code needs to be imported to be visible to other code. This still holds true with Swift, but Swift has no mechanism to import individual files. Instead, when you add your first Objective-C code to a Swift project, Xcode is going to ask you if you want to add what is called a **bridging header**:

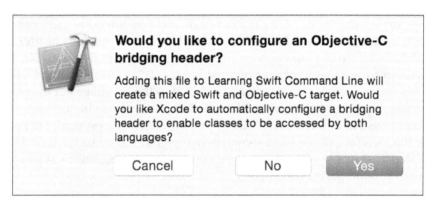

You should select **Yes** and then Xcode will automatically create a header file named after the project ending in `Bridging-Header.h`. This is the file where you need to import any Objective-C headers that you want to expose to Swift. It will just be a file with a list of imports. You still do not need to import any of the implementation files.

Using functions

After you have exposed the headers to Swift, it is very simple to call functions. You can simply call the functions directly as if they didn't have parameter names:

```
NSArray *addInviteeToListIfSpotAvailable
    (
    NSArray *invitees,
    NSString *newInvitee
    );

addInviteeToListIfSpotAvailable(inviteeList, "Sarah")
```

Xcode will even autocomplete the code for you. From your Swift files point of view, there is no way to know if that function is implemented in Objective-C or Swift.

Using types

You can use types the same way you use functions. Once the proper header files are imported in the bridging header, you can just use the type as if it were a Swift type:

```
@interface Contact : NSObject
@property NSString *firstName;
@property NSString *lastName;
- (NSArray *)addToInviteeList:(NSArray *)invitees
includeLastName:(BOOL)include;
@end

var contact = Contact()
contact.firstName = "First"
contact.lastName = "Last"
contact.addToInviteeList(inviteeList, includeLastName: false)
```

Again, from Swift's point of view, there is absolutely no difference between how we write the code that uses our Objective-C class and how we would write it if the class were implemented in Objective-C. We were even able to call the `addToInviteeLis t:includeLastName:` method with the same parameter names. This makes it even more clear that Swift was designed with backwards compatibility in mind.

The only real restrictions are that all classes defined in Objective-C are still going to inherit from `NSObject` and Objective-C enumerations aren't going to translate perfectly into Swift enumerations. Instead, they are still exposed as individual constants:

```
typedef enum {
    PrimaryColorRed,
    PrimaryColorGreen,
    PrimaryColorBlue,
} PrimaryColor;

var color: PrimaryColor = PrimaryColorRed
```

Containers

You may have also noticed that the `NSString` and `NSArray` types seem to translate transparently to `String` and `Array` classes in the preceding code. This is another wonderful feature of the bridge between Swift and Objective-C. These types, as well as dictionaries, translate almost perfectly. The only difference is that since Objective-C does require an element type when defining a container, they are translated into Swift as containing objects of type `AnyObject`. If you want to treat them as a more specific type, you will have to cast them:

```
inviteeList = contact.addToInviteeList(
    inviteeList,
    includeLastName: false
    ) as! [String]
```

The actual return value of this method when translated to Swift is [AnyObject]!. Therefore, if you are sure that the method never returns nil and always returns an array of Strings, it is safe to do the forced casting that we did above. Otherwise, you should still check for nil and do an optional casting (as?).

Annotations

You will note that this acts as a pattern when Objective-C types are translated to Swift. Any reference type is going to be translated, by default, to an implicitly unwrapped optional because of the nature of Objective-C reference types. The compiler can't automatically know if the value returned could be nil or not, so it doesn't know if it should be translated as a regular optional or a non-optional. However, Objective-C developers can add annotations to let the compiler know if a value can be nil or not.

Nullability

The first thing Objective-C developers can add annotations for is whether a specific variable can be null or not:

```
- (NSArray * __nonnull)addToInviteeList:
        (NSArray * __nullable)invitees;
```

The __nonnull keyword indicates that it cannot be nil, so it will be translated in Swift to a non-optional and the __nullable keyword indicates that it can be nil, so in Swift it will translated to a regular optional.

Container element types

Objective-C developer can also annotate their container types to say what type they contain. For this, use the angled brackets just like Swift:

```
- (NSArray<NSString *> * __nonnull)addStringToInviteeList:
        (NSArray<NSString *> * __nullable)invitees;
```

Now, this method will really work just like Swift methods in that it will take an optional array of strings and return a non-optional array of strings; there will be no casting necessary:

```
inviteeList = contact.addStringToInviteeList(inviteeList)
```

If you have control over the Objective-C code you are importing then you may want to add it. Otherwise, you might be able to ask the developer of the code to add the annotations to make your Swift coding much easier and more clean.

Summary

While Swift is the hot new language right now in the Apple development community, there is no immediate sign that Objective-C is getting replaced fully. All of Apple's APIs are still written in Objective-C and it would be a lot of work for Apple to rewrite them, if they even wanted to. Apple definitely designed Swift to be able to live alongside Objective-C, so for now we have to assume that Objective-C is here to stay. This makes understanding and being able to interact with Objective-C very valuable, even as a Swift developer.

In this chapter, we have gotten an overview of the most pertinent Objective-C features and syntax from the point of view of a primarily Swift developer. We have learned how Swift is basically a part of a long line of evolving languages. It was heavily influenced by Apple's desire to make it backwards compatible with Objective-C and Objective-C was actually an evolution of C which was an evolution of Assembly and so on. Objective-C is still a powerful language with the ability to express many of the same concepts as Swift. Objective-C has similar concepts of constants and variables with more of a stress on variables. It also has the same basic containers but control flow is slightly different in the two languages. Swift has more powerful switches and ranges, but the underlying concepts are still very much the same. Functions are almost identical between the two languages but the type system in Objective-C is somewhat more limited because it can only express classes unlike Swift which has a powerful concept of classes, structures, and enumerations. Structures and enumerations still exist in Objective-C, but they really come directly from C and can do a lot less. Finally, we saw that organizing Objective-C in a project is very much the same and calling Objective-C code from Swift is actually quite straightforward.

There is some debate in the Apple developer community about how relevant Objective-C will be moving forward. There are people that have jumped into Swift development full time and there are others that are waiting for Swift to mature even more before they commit energy to truly learning it. However, there is little debate over the fact that Objective-C knowledge is still going to be relevant for a while, most notably because of the vast resources that exist and the fact that all existing Apple APIs are written in Objective-C. We will put those APIs to use in our next chapter: *Chapter 11, A Whole New World – Developing an App,* when we will finally dive into some real app development.

11
A Whole New World – Developing an App

Until this point, we have been concentrating almost exclusively on learning Swift without learning much about the platforms that it was designed for. This is because learning a new platform is a completely different world from learning a language. Learning a programming language is like learning the basic grammar of a spoken language. The grammar between the spoken languages generally expresses similar concepts but the specific words of the languages are often more varied, even if they are sometimes recognizable. Learning a programming language is learning how to connect the specific vocabulary of your desired platform. This chapter will be about learning some of the vocabulary of the iOS framework.

We will do this by going through the process of starting to develop a simple camera app. Along the way, we will learn some of the most critical vocabularies to get started with any other kind of iOS app and many of the concepts will be transferable to OS X development. More specifically, we will cover:

- Conceptualizing the app
- Setting up the app project
- Configuring the user interface
- Running the app
- Temporarily saving a photo
- Populating our photo grid
- Refactoring to respect model-view-controller
- Permanently saving a photo

Conceptualizing the app

Before we even open up Xcode, we should have a good sense of what we plan to develop. We want to know the basics of what kind of data we are going to need to represent and what the user interface is going to be like. We don't yet need pixel perfect designs for every screen, but we should have a good idea of the flow of the app and what features we want to include in our first version.

Features

As we already discussed, we are going to develop a basic camera app. This leaves us with a very clear list of features, which we would want in a first version:

- Take a photo
- View gallery of previously taken photos
- Label photos
- Delete photos

These are the highly critical features of a camera app. Clearly, we don't have any differentiating features that will make this app valuable above other existing apps, but this will be enough to learn the most critical parts of making an iOS app.

Interface

Now that we have a list of features, we can come up with the basic flow of the app, otherwise referred to as a wireframe. The first screen of our app will be a gallery of any picture the user has already taken. There will be a button on the screen, which will allow them to take a new picture. It will also have the ability to activate the editing mode where they can delete photos or change their label:

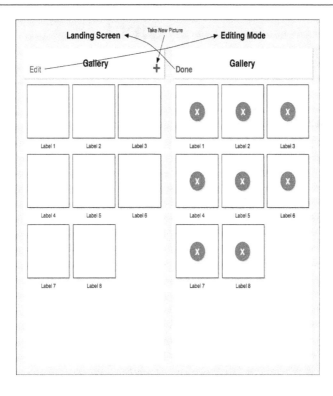

This interface will allow us to take advantage of the built-in picture-taking interface that we will look at in more detail later. This interface will also allow us to make it flexible to work on all the different phone and tablet screens. It may seem simple, but there are many components that have to fit together to make this application work. On the other hand, once you have a good understanding of the different components, it will start to seem simple again.

Data

Now that we know roughly how the app needs to work for the user, we can come up with at least a high-level concept of how the data should be stored. In this case, we simply have a flat list of images with different labels. The easiest way for us to store these files is in the local file system, with each image named after the user chosen label. The only thing to keep in mind with this system is that we will have to find a way to allow two different images with the same exact label. We will solve that problem in more detail when we get around to implementing it.

Setting up the app project

Now that we have finished conceptualizing our app, we are ready to start coding. In *Chapter 3, One Piece at a Time – Types, Scopes, and Projects*, we created a command-line project. This time, we are going to create an iOS Application. Once again, in Xcode, navigate to **File | New | Project...**. When a window appears, select the **Single View Application** from the **iOS | Application** menu:

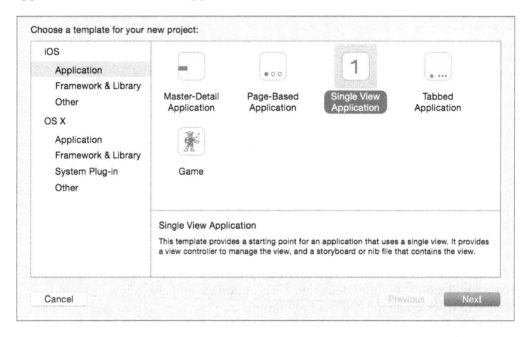

From there, click on **Next** and then give the project the name LearningCamera. Any **Organization Name** and **Identifier** are fine. Finally, make sure that **Swift** is selected from the Language drop down menu and **Universal** is selected from the **Devices** drop down. Now select **Next** again and create the project.

Xcode will then present you with a project development window that looks somewhat different from a command-line project:

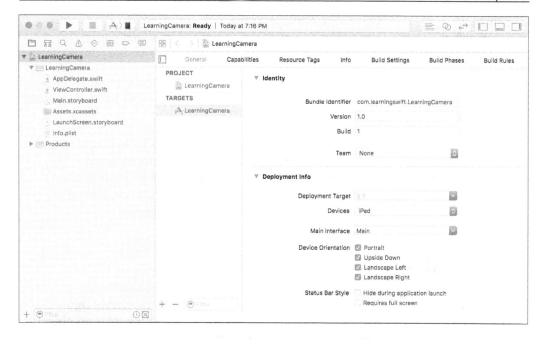

This default screen allows us to configure various attributes of the app including the version number, target devices, and much more. For our purposes, all of the defaults are fine. When you decide to submit an app to the app store, this screen will become much more important.

Xcode has also created a few different files and folders for us. We will be working exclusively in the LearningCamera folder. The LearningCameraTests folder is for automated tests; they are a fantastic idea but beyond the scope of this book. The final folder is the Products folder, which you won't have to change.

In the LearningCamera folder, we have several important files. The first file is AppDelegate.swift, which is the entry point of the application. It has a class that was created for you, called AppDelegate that has a number of methods that are called at different points during the application life cycle. We won't have to modify this file for our purposes but it is an important file in many applications.

The second file is ViewController.swift. This holds a UIViewController subclass that is used to manage the interaction between the app's default view and the business logic. We will be doing a lot of work in there.

The third file is `Main.storyboard`. This file contains the interface design for our views. Currently, it has only a single view that is managed by `ViewController`. We will be working with this file later to add and configure our visual components.

The fourth file is `Assets.xcassets`. This is a container for all of the images that we would want to display in our app. Almost every app you make will have at least one image so this is a very important file too.

Finally, the last file is `LaunchScreen.storyboard`. This file lets us manage the display while our app is launching. This is an extremely important part of a production application because this is the first thing a user sees every time they launch it; a well-designed launch process can make a huge difference. However, we do not have to do anything to this file for our learning purpose.

Configuring the user interface

Now that we have our bearings within the project, let's jump into configuring the user interface of our app. As we discussed earlier, this is done within the `Main.storyboard` file. When we select that file, we are presented with a graphical editing tool, generally referred to as **Interface Builder**:

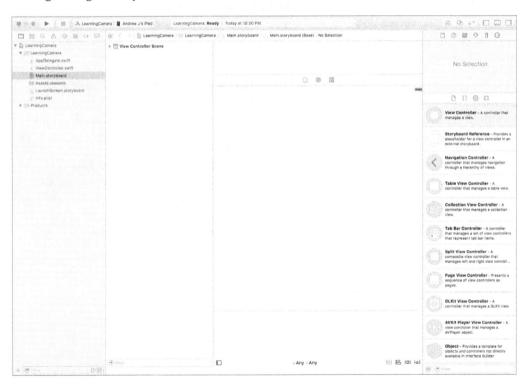

In the center, there is a main view that is controlled by a `ViewController` instance. This is a blank canvas where we can add all of the interface elements we want.

The first thing we want to do is add the bar along the top that is in our wireframes. This bar is called a **navigation bar** and we can add it directly, as it is one of the elements in our library. However, the frameworks will handle many complications for us if we use a **Navigation Controller** instead. A Navigation Controller is a view controller that contains other view controllers. Specifically, it adds a navigation bar to the top and allows us to push child view controllers onto it in the future. This controller creates the animation of a view being pushed on from the right in many applications. For example, when you select an e-mail in the Mail app, it animates in the contents of the e-mail; this uses a navigation controller. We will not have to push any view controllers on in this app, but it is good to be set up for the future and this is a superior way of getting a navigation bar at the top.

Along the right, we have a library of elements we can drag onto the canvas, let's start by finding the **Navigation Controller**. Drag it from the library to the pane on the left where the **View Controller Scene** is listed. This is going to add two new view controllers to the list:

We don't want the new **Root View Controller**, only the **View Controller Scene** so let's delete it. To do this, click on the **Root View Controller** with the yellow icon and press the *Delete* key. Next, we want to make the **View Controller Scene** the root view controller. The root view controller is the first controller to be shown within the **Navigation Controller**. To do this, right-click on the **Navigation Controller** with the yellow icon and drag it to the **View Controller** with the yellow icon below. The **View Controller** will be highlighted blue:

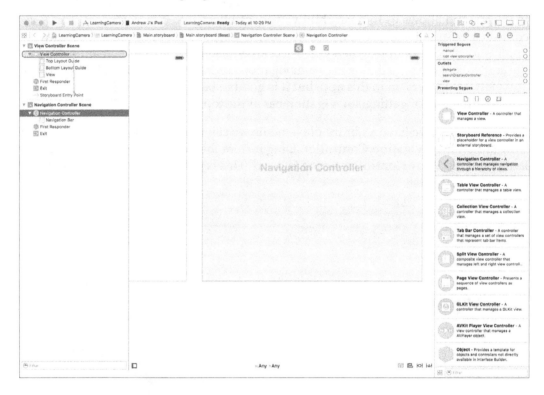

Once you let go of the right mouse button, a menu will come up and you should click on **Root View Controller**. Finally, we want to make the navigation controller the first view controller to appear in the app. Select the **Navigation Controller** with the yellow icon and navigate to **View | Utilities | Show Attributes Inspector** from the main menu, and then scroll-down and check the **Is Initial View Controller** checkbox. Note that you can drag around the view controllers on the screen however, you want to make the file easier to navigate.

Now we are ready to customize our main view. To focus the view, select **View Controller** from the pane on the left. Now double-click on the title and change it to Gallery:

Next, we want to add the "Take a Picture" button to our navigation bar. All buttons in toolbars are called **bar button items**. Find them in the library and then drag it to the right side of the toolbar (the place where you can drop it will turn blue when you get close to it). By default, the button will say **Item**, but we want it to be an add button instead. One option would be to change the text to an addition symbol, but there is a better option. After adding the button, you should be able to see it appear in the hierarchy that is to the left of the main view. In there, you will see the navigation bar with the new button item nested inside the **Gallery** title. If you select that item in the hierarchy, you will see some options we can configure about the item along the right-hand side of the screen. We want to change the System Item to **Add**:

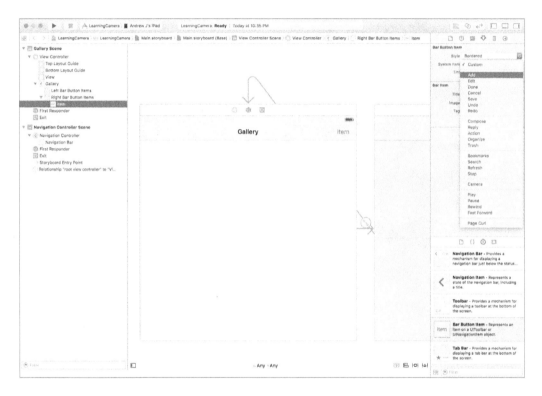

Now, you can do the same thing for the left-hand side of the navigation bar with the **Edit** identifier.

Finally, we need to add the gallery of photos. For this, we are going to use the **Collection View** from the library. Drag one onto the center of the view. A collection view is made of a variable amount of cells laid out in a grid. Each cell is a copy of a template cell and it can be configured in code to display specific data. When you dragged the collection view on, it also created a template cell for you. We will configure that soon.

First, we need to define the rules for the sizing of the collection view. This will allow the interface to adapt well to each different screen size. The tool we use to do this is called **Auto Layout**. Click on the collection view and then select the **Pin** icon in the lower right of the screen:

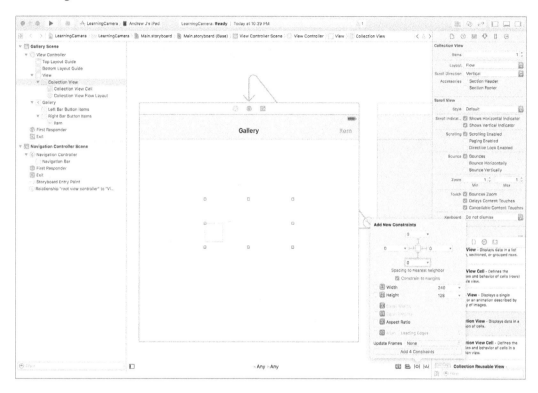

Configure this window to match the preceding screenshot. Click on each of the four struts so that they are highlighted red, uncheck **Constrain to margins**, and change each of the measurements to zero. After everything is configured, click on **Add 4 Constraints**. This will cause some yellow lines to appear that indicate that the view's placement is not consistent with the rules we just created. We can resize the views ourselves to make it match or we can let Xcode do it for us: there will be a yellow icon next to the **Gallery Scene** on the left-hand side of the screen. Click on that and you will get a list of misplaced views. In there, you can click on the yellow triangle and click on **Fix Misplacement**. We also want to make the background white instead of black. Select the collection view and then change its **Background** to white in the Attributes Inspector.

The last thing we need to configure on this screen is the **collection view cell**. This is the box in the upper-left corner of the collection view. We need to change the size and add both an image and a label; let's start by changing the size. Click on the **Collection View** if it isn't already selected and navigate to **View | Utilities | Show Size Inspector** from the main menu. Change the **Cell Size** to be 110 points wide and 150 points tall.

Now, we can drag in our image. In the library, this is called an **Image View**. Drag it into the cell and then change the height and width in the **Size Inspector** to 110 and **x** and **y** to 0. Next, we want to drag a **Label** below the image view. Once it is placed, we want to configure the placement rules within the cell.

First, select the **Image View**. We have to make it the full width and attach it to the top of the cell, so select the pin icon again and configure it as follows:

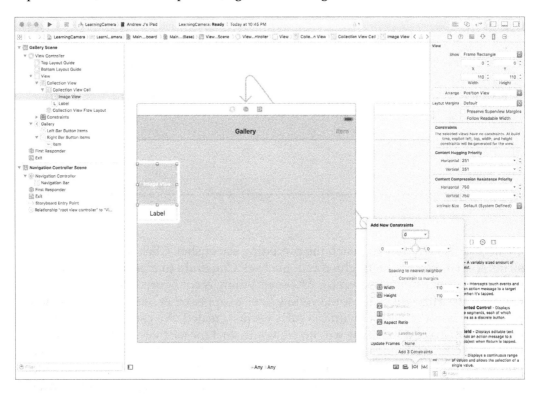

It is pinned to the left, top, and right without constraining to margins and values of zero for all three measurements. Click on **Add 3 Constraints** and we are ready to define the rules for the label. We want the label to be full width and vertically centered. A label is going to automatically center the text, so we want the label to be tall enough to have a reasonable margin above and below the text. Click on the label and configure it as follows:

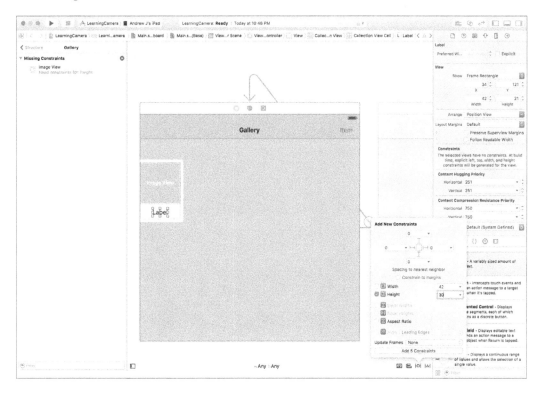

It is pinned in every direction without constraining to the margins and has zero for all measurements. It is also constrained to be 30 points tall by checking the **Height** checkbox. Click **Add 5 Constraints** and then have Xcode resize it for you again from the menu on the left. Also, make sure to select the center alignment in the Attributes Inspector and reduce the font size to 12.

Running the app

Now we have most of our interface configured without writing a single piece of code. We can run the app to see what it looks like. To do this, first select the simulator you want to run it on from the menu in the top bar. Then you can click on the run button, which is the one with the black triangle. This will open up a new simulator window running your app:

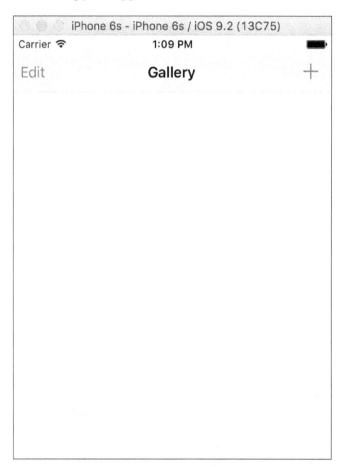

You can rotate the virtual device from the **Hardware** menu to see what happens when you rotate it and you can try running it on various different simulators. We have configured our view so far to adapt to any screen size.

Allowing picture taking

Now we are ready to move onto the programming. The first thing we need to allow the user to do is to take a new picture. In order to do that, we are going to need some code to run every time the user taps on the add button. We achieve this by connecting the trigger action of the add button to a method on our view controller. Normally we make a connection by right-click dragging from the button to the code; however, we can't do this if we can't see the interface and the code at the same time. The easiest way to do this is to show the **Assistant Editor**. You can do this by navigating to **View | Assistant Editor | Show Assistant Editor**. Also, make sure it is configured to be automatic by clicking on the bar at the top of the editor:

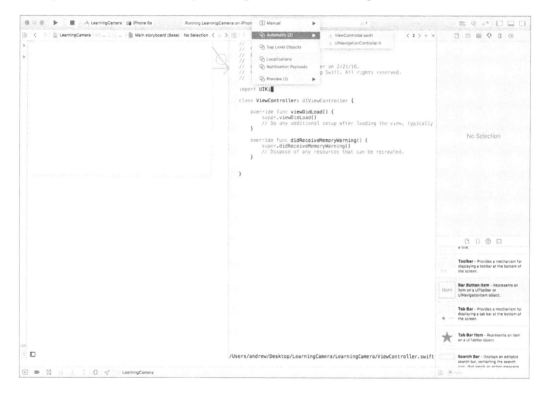

This mode causes the second view to automatically change to the most appropriate file according to what you have selected on the left. In this case, because we are working with the interface of our view controller, it shows the code for the view controller.

Our view controller code is generated with two methods to start. `viewDidLoad`
is called when the view for the view controller is loaded. Most of the time this
happens when the view controller is about to be displayed for the first time.
`didReceiveMemoryWarning` is called when the system starts to run low on memory.
This provides you an opportunity to help the system find more memory by deleting
anything that isn't necessary.

We want to start by creating a connection from the button to a new method.
You can do so by right clicking on the add button and dragging to below the
`didReceiveMemoryWarning` method:

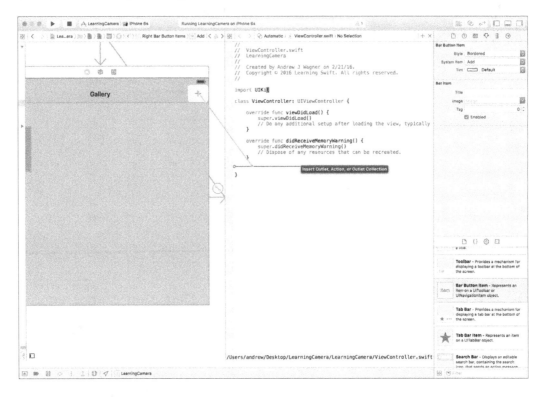

When you release the right mouse button, a little window will appear. There you
should select **Action** from the **Connection** menu and enter `didTapTakePhotoButton`.
When you click on **Connect**, Xcode will create a new method for you and connect it
to the button. You know it is connected because there is a filled in gray circle to the
left of the method. Now, every time the user taps the button, this method will be
executed. Note that this method has `@IBAction` at the beginning of it. This is needed
for any method that is connected to an interface element.

We want this method to present the user with an interface to take a picture. Apple provides a class for us called `UIImagePickerController` that makes this very easy for us. All we need to do is create an instance of `UIImagePickerController`, configure it to allow taking pictures, and present it to the screen. The code looks like this:

```
@IBAction func didTapTakePhotoButton(sender: AnyObject) {
    let imagePicker = UIImagePickerController()
    if UIImagePickerController.isSourceTypeAvailable(.Camera) {
        imagePicker.sourceType = .Camera
    }
    self.presentViewController(
        imagePicker,
        animated: true,
        completion: nil
    )
}
```

Lets break this code down. On the first line, we are creating our image picker. On the second line, we are checking if the current device has a camera by using the `isSourceTypeAvailable:` class method of `UIImagePickerController`. If the camera source is available, we set that as the source type for the image picker on line three. Otherwise, by default, an image picker lets the user pick an image from their photo library. Since the simulator doesn't support taking a picture, you are going to be presented with an image picker instead of a camera when simulating the app. Finally, the last line asks our view controller to present our image picker by animating it on the screen. `presentViewController:animated:completion:` is a method implemented within the `UIViewController` class, the superclass of our `ViewController`, to make it easy for us to present new view controllers. If you run the app and click on the add button, you will be asked for permission to access the photos and then it will display the photo picker. You can tap the **Cancel** button in the upper right and the image picker controller will be dismissed. However, if you select a photo, nothing will happen.

We need to write some code to handle the picking of a photo. To make this possible, image picker can have a delegate that receives a method call when an image is picked. We are going to make our view controller the delegate of the image picker and implement its protocol. First, we have to add a line to our action method above, that assigns our view controller as the delegate of the image picker. Add this line above the call to present the image picker:

```
imagePicker.delegate = self
```

When we do that, we will get a compiler error that says that we can't make this assignment because our view controller doesn't implement the necessary protocols. Lets change that. I like to implement each protocol as a separate extension in the same file to allow for better code separation. We need to implement both `UIImagePickerControllerDelegate` and `UINavigationControllerDelegate` according to the error. The only method that is important to us in either of these protocols is the one that is called when an image is picked. That leaves us with the following code:

```
extension ViewController: UINavigationControllerDelegate {}

extension ViewController: UIImagePickerControllerDelegate {
    func imagePickerController(
        picker: UIImagePickerController,
        didFinishPickingImage image: UIImage!,
        editingInfo: [NSObject : AnyObject]!
        )
    {
        self.dismissViewControllerAnimated(true, completion: nil)
    }
}
```

Our implementation for the `UINavigationControllerDelegate` delegate is empty but we have a simple implementation for the `imagePickerController:picker:di dFinishPickingImage:editingInfo:` method. This is where we are going to add our handling code, but for now, we are just dismissing the presented view controller to return the user to the previous screen. This method does not force us to specify the view controller we are dismissing because the view controller already knows which one it is presenting. Now, if you run the app and select a photo, you will return to the previous screen but nothing else will happen. In order to make something meaningful happen with the photo, we are going to have to put a lot of other code in place. We have to both save the picture and implement our view controller to display the picture inside our collection view.

Temporarily saving a photo

To start, we are only going to concern ourselves with temporarily storing our pictures in memory. To do this, we can add an image array as a property of our view controller:

```
class ViewController: UIViewController {

    var photos = [UIImage]()

    // ...
}
```

As we saw in the image picker delegate method, UIKit provides a class UIImage that can represent images. Our photos property can store an array of these instances. This means that the first step for us is to add new images to our property when the callback is called:

```
func imagePickerController(
    picker: UIImagePickerController,
    didFinishPickingImage image: UIImage!,
    editingInfo: [NSObject : AnyObject]!
    )
{
    self.photos.append(image)
    self.dismissViewControllerAnimated(true, completion: nil)
}
```

Now every time the user takes or picks a new photo, we add it to our list, which stores all of the images in memory. However, this isn't quite enough, we also want to require a label for each photo.

To support this feature, let's create a new structure called Photo that has an image and label property. At this point, I would create three groups in the LearningCamera folder: Model, View, and Controller by right-clicking on the LearningCamera folder and choosing **New Group**. I would move ViewController.swift into the **Controller** group and then create a new Photo.swift file by right-clicking on the **Model** group and selecting **New File...**. Just a plain **Swift File** is fine.

You should define your photo structure in that file:

```
import UIKit

struct Photo {
    let image: UIImage
    let label: String
}
```

We have to import UIKit because that is what defines UIImage. The rest of our structure is straightforward as it just defines our two desired properties. The default initializer will be fine for now.

Now, we can return to our ViewController.swift file and update our photos property to be of the type Photo instead of UIImage:

```
var images = [Photo]()
```

This now creates a new problem for us. How do we ask the user for the label for the image? Let's do that in a standard alert. To display an alert, UIKit has a class called `UIAlertController`. To use this, we will have to rework our function some. UIKit does not allow you to present more than one view controller from the same view controller at the same time. This means that we have to dismiss the photo picker and wait for that to complete before displaying our alert:

```
self.dismissViewControllerAnimated(true) {
    // Ask User for Label

    let alertController = UIAlertController(
        title: "Photo Label",
        message: "How would you like to label your photo?",
        preferredStyle: .Alert
    )

    alertController.addTextFieldWithConfigurationHandler()
    {
        textField in
        let saveAction = UIAlertAction(
            title: "Save",
            style: .Default
            ) { action in
            let label = textField.text ?? ""
            let photo = Photo(image: image, label: label)
            self.photos.append(photo)
        }
        alertController.addAction(saveAction)
    }

    self.presentViewController(
        alertController,
        animated: true,
        completion: nil
    )
}
```

Lets break down this code, as it is somewhat complex. To start, we are using the trailing closure syntax for the `dismissViewControllerAnimated:completion:` method. This closure is called once the view controller has finished animating off the screen.

Next, we are creating an alert controller with a title, message, and `Alert` as its style. Before we can display the alert controller, we have to configure it with a text field and a save action. We start by adding the text field and use the trailing closure again on `addTextFieldWithConfigurationHandler:`. This closure is called to give us an opportunity to configure the text field. We are OK with the defaults but we are going to want to know the text contained in the text field when saving so we can create our save action directly within this alert and save ourselves the hassle of getting a reference to it later.

Each action of an alert must be of the type `UIAlertAction`. In this case, we create one with the title `Save` with the default style. The last parameter of the `UIAlertAction` initializer is a closure that will be called when the user chooses that action. Again, we use the trailing closure syntax.

Inside that callback, we get the text from the text field and use that, along with our image, to create a new `Photo` instance and add it to our `photos` array.

Finally, we have to add our save action to the alert controller and then display the alert controller.

Now if you run the app, it will ask you for a label for each photo after it is chosen but it still won't appear to be showing it because we are not displaying the saved photos yet. That is our next task.

Populating our photo grid

Now that we are maintaining a list of photos, we need to display it in our collection view. A collection view is populated by providing it with a data source that implements its `UICollectionViewDataSource` protocol. Probably the most common thing to do is to have the view controller be the data source. We can do this by opening the `Main.storyboard` back up and *control* dragging from the collection view to the view controller:

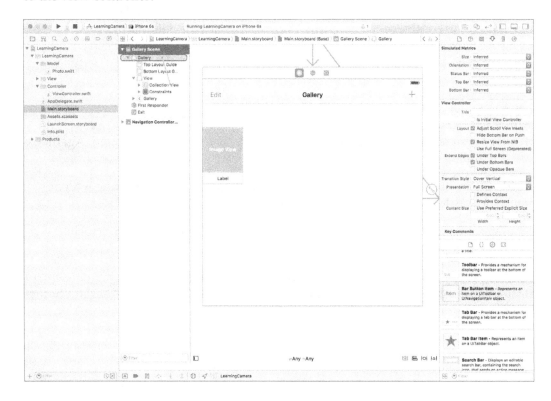

When you let go, select **dataSource** from the menu. After that, all we need to do is implement the data source protocol. The two methods we need to implement are `collectionView:numberOfItemsInSection:` and `collectionView:cellForItem AtIndexPath:`. The former allows us to specify how many cells should be displayed and the latter allows us to customize each cell for a specific index into our list. It is easy for us to return the number of cells that we want:

```
extension ViewController: UICollectionViewDataSource {
    func collectionView(
        collectionView: UICollectionView,
        numberOfItemsInSection section: Int
        ) -> Int
    {

        return self.photos.count

    }
}
```

All we have to do is return the number of elements in our `photos` property.

Configuring the cell is going to take a little bit more preparation. First, we need to create our own cell subclass that can reference the image and label we created in the storyboard. All collection view cells must subclass `UICollectionViewCell`. Let's call ours `PhotoCollectionViewCell` and create a new file for it in the **View** group. Like we needed a connection from the storyboard to our code for tapping the add button, we need a connection for both the image and the label. However, this is a different type of connection. Instead of an action, this type of connection is called an outlet, which adds the object as a property to the view controller. We could use the same click and drag technique we used for the action, but this time we will set up the code in advance ourselves:

```
import UIKit

class PhotoCollectionViewCell: UICollectionViewCell {
    @IBOutlet var imageView: UIImageView!
    @IBOutlet var label: UILabel!
}
```

Here we have specified two properties, each with a prefix of @IBOutlet. This prefix is what allows us to make the connection in Interface Builder just like we did with the data source. Both types are defined as implicitly unwrapped optionals because these connections cannot be set when the instance is initialized. Instead, they are connected when loading the view.

Now that we have that setup, we can go back to the storyboard and make the connections. Currently the cell is still just the type of a generic cell so first we need to change it to our class. Find the cell inside the view hierarchy on the left and click on it. Select **View | Utilities | Show Identify Inspector**. In this inspection, we can set the class of the cell to our class by entering PhotoCollectionViewCell in the class field. Now if you navigate to **View | Utilities | Show Connections Inspector** you will see our two outlets listed as possible connections. Click and drag from the hollow gray circle next to **imageView** to the image view in the cell:

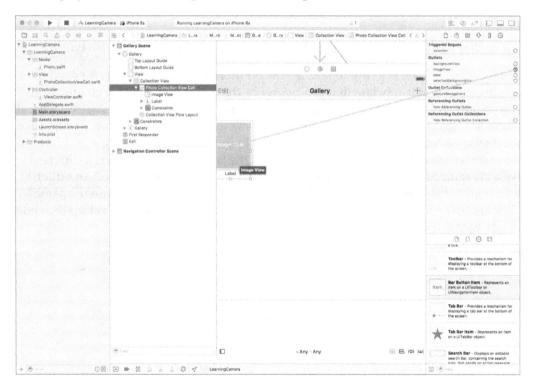

Once you let go, the connection will be made. Do the same thing with the **label** connection to the label we created before. We also need to set a reuse identifier for our cell so that we can reference this template in code. You can do this by returning to the Attributes Inspector and entering `DefaultCell` into the **Identifier** text field:

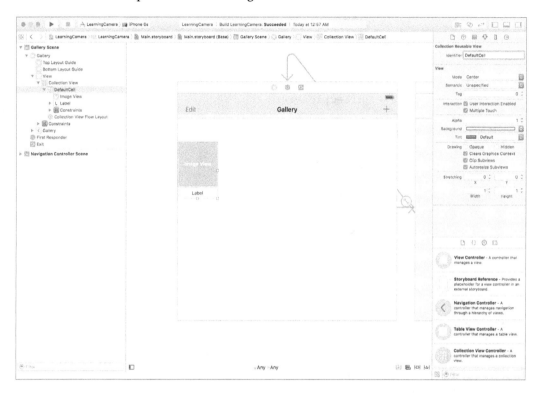

We are also going to need a reference to the collection view from within our view controller. This is because we will need to ask the collection view to add a cell each time a photo is saved. You can add this by writing the code first or by right clicking and dragging from the collection view to the code. Either way, you should end up with a property like this on the view controller:

```swift
class ViewController: UIViewController {
    @IBOutlet var collectionView: UICollectionView!

    // ...
}
```

Then we are ready to implement the remaining data source method:

```
extension ViewController: UICollectionViewDataSource {
    // ...

    func collectionView(
        collectionView: UICollectionView,
        cellForItemAtIndexPath indexPath: NSIndexPath
    ) -> UICollectionViewCell
    {
        let cell = collectionView
            .dequeueReusableCellWithReuseIdentifier(
            "DefaultCell",
            forIndexPath: indexPath
            ) as! PhotoCollectionViewCell

        let photo = self.photos[indexPath.item]
        cell.imageView.image = photo.image
        cell.label.text = photo.label

        return cell
    }
}
```

The first line of this implementation asks the collection view for a cell with our
DefaultCell identifier. To understand this fully, we have to understand a little
bit more about how a collection view works. A collection view is designed to
handle virtually any number of cells. We could want to display thousands of cells
at once but it would not be possible to have thousands of cells in memory at one
time. Instead, the collection view will automatically reuse cells that have been
scrolled off the screen to save on memory. We have no way of knowing whether
the cell we get back from this call is new or reused, so we must always assume it
is being reused. This means that anything we configure on a cell in this method,
must always be reset on each call, otherwise, some old configurations may still
exist from its previous configuration. We end that call by casting the result to our
PhotoCollectionViewCell class so that we can configure our subviews properly.

Our second line is getting the correct photo out of our list. The item property on
the indexPath variable is the index of the photo that we are using to configure the
cell. At any time, this method could be called with any index between zero and the
number returned in our previous data source method. This means that in our case, it
will always be a number within our photos array, making it safe to assume that the
index is properly within its bounds.

The next two lines set the image and label according to the photo and finally, the last line returns that cell so that the collection view can display it.

At this point, if you ran the app and added a photo you still wouldn't see anything because the collection view will not automatically reload its data when an element is added to the photos array. That is because the `collectionView:numberOfIte msInSection:` method is a callback. Callbacks are only called when other code initiates it. This method is called once when the collection view is first loaded but we must ask it to be called again manually from then on. The easiest way to do this is to call `reloadData` on the collection view when we add a photo to the list. This causes all of the data and cells to be loaded again. However, this does not look very good because the cell will just pop into existence. Instead, we want to use the `insertItemsAtIndexPaths` method. When used properly, this will cause a cell to be animated onto the screen. The important thing to remember with this method is that you must only call it after `collectionView:numberOfItemsInSection:` returns the updated amount after the insertion. This means we must call it after we have already added our photo to our property:

```
let saveAction = UIAlertAction(
    title: "Save",
    style: .Default
    ) { action in
    let label = textField.text ?? ""
    let photo = Photo(image: image, label: label)
    self.photos.append(photo)

    let indexPath = NSIndexPath(
        forItem: self.photos.count - 1,
        inSection: 0
    )
    self.collectionView.insertItemsAtIndexPaths([indexPath])
}
```

Only the last two lines of this are new. First, we create an index path for where we want to insert our new item. An index path consists of both an item and a section. All of our items exist in a single section, so we can always set that to zero. We want the item to be one less than the total count of photos because we just added it to the end of the list. The last line is simply making the call to the insert items method that takes an array of index paths.

Now you can run your app and all saved photos will be displayed in the collection view.

Refactoring to respect model-view-controller

We have already made some good progress on the core functionality of our app. However, before we move any further, we should reflect on the code we have written. Ultimately, we haven't actually written that many lines of code, but it can definitely be improved. The biggest shortcoming of our code is that we have put a lot of business logic inside our view controller. This is not a good separation of our different model, view, and controller layers. Let's take this opportunity to refactor this code into a separate type.

We will create a class called `PhotoStore` that will be responsible for storing our photos and that will implement the data source protocol. This will mean moving some of our code out of our view controller.

First, we will move the photo's property to the photo store class:

```
import UIKit

class PhotoStore: NSObject {
    var photos = [Photo]()
}
```

Note that this new photo store class inherits from `NSObject`. This is necessary for us to be able to fully satisfy the `UICollectionViewDataSource` protocol, which is our next task.

We could simply move the code from our view controller to this class, but we do not want our model to deal directly with our view layer. The current implementation creates and configures our collection view cell. Lets allow the view controller to still handle that by providing our own callback for when we need a cell for a given photo. To do that, we will first need to add a callback property:

```
class PhotoStore: NSObject {
    var photos = [Photo]()
    var cellForPhoto:
        (Photo, NSIndexPath) -> UICollectionViewCell

    init(
        cellForPhoto: (Photo,NSIndexPath) -> UICollectionViewCell
        )
```

```
    {
        self.cellForPhoto = cellForPhoto

        super.init()
    }
}
```

We need to provide an initializer now so that we can get the callback function. Next, we have to tweak our data source implementations and put them in this new class:

```
extension PhotoStore: UICollectionViewDataSource {
    func collectionView(
        collectionView: UICollectionView,
        numberOfItemsInSection section: Int
        ) -> Int
    {
        return self.photos.count
    }

    func collectionView(
        collectionView: UICollectionView,
        cellForItemAtIndexPath indexPath: NSIndexPath
        ) -> UICollectionViewCell
    {
        let photo = self.photos[indexPath.item]
        return self.cellForPhoto(photo, indexPath)
    }
}
```

The `collectionView:numberOfItemsInSection:` method can still just return the number of photos in our array, but `collectionView:cellForItemAtIndexPath:` is implemented to use the callback instead of creating a cell itself.

The second thing we need to add to this class is the ability to save a photo. Let's add a method to take a new image and label that returns the index path that should be added:

```
func saveNewPhotoWithImage(
    image: UIImage,
    labeled label: String
    ) -> NSIndexPath
{
    let photo = Photo(image: image, label: label)
    self.photos.append(photo)
    return NSIndexPath(
```

```
        forItem: self.photos.count - 1,
        inSection: 0
    )
}
```

This looks identical to the code we wrote in the view controller to do this, but it is better separated.

Now our photo store is complete and we just have to update our view controller to use it instead of our old implementation. First, lets add a photo store property that is an implicitly unwrapped optional in `ViewController` so we can create it after the view is loaded:

```
var photoStore: PhotoStore!
```

To create our photo store in `viewDidLoad`, we will call the photo store initializer and pass it a closure that can create the cell. For clarity, we will define that closure as a separate method:

```
func createCellForPhoto(
    photo: Photo,
    indexPath: NSIndexPath
    ) -> UICollectionViewCell
{
    let cell = self.collectionView
        .dequeueReusableCellWithReuseIdentifier(
        "DefaultCell",
        forIndexPath: indexPath
        ) as! PhotoCollectionViewCell

    cell.imageView.image = photo.image
    cell.label.text = photo.label

    return cell
}
```

This method looks almost identical to our old `collectionView:cellForItemAtIndexPath:` implementation; the only difference is that we already have a reference to the correct photo.

This method allows our `viewDidLoad` implementation to be very simple. All we need to do is initialize the photo store with a reference to this method and make it the data source for the collection view:

```
override func viewDidLoad() {
    super.viewDidLoad()
    self.photoStore = PhotoStore(
        cellForPhoto: self.createCellForPhoto
    )
    self.collectionView.dataSource = self.photoStore
}
```

Lastly, we just have to update the save action to use the photo store:

```
let saveAction = UIAlertAction(
    title: "Save",
    style: .Default
) { action in
    let label = textField.text ?? ""
    let indexPath = self.photoStore.saveNewPhotoWithImage(
        image,
        labeled: label
    )
    self.collectionView.insertItemsAtIndexPaths([indexPath])
}
```

You can run the app again and it will operate as before, but now our code is modular, which will make any future changes much easier.

Permanently saving a photo

Our app works pretty well for saving pictures, but as soon as the app quits, all of the photos are lost. We need to add a way to save the photos permanently. Our refactoring of the code allows us to work primarily within the model layer now.

Before we write any code, we have to decide how we are going to store the photos permanently. There are many ways in which we can choose to save the photos, but one of the easiest is to save it to the file system, which is what we conceived of in our conception phase. Every app is provided a documents directory that is automatically backed up by the operating system as a part of normal backups. We can store our photos in there as files named after the label the user gives them. To avoid any problems with duplicate labels, where we would have multiple files named the same thing, we can nest every file inside a subdirectory named after the time the photos is saved. The time stamp will always be unique because we will never save two photos at the exact same time.

Now that we have that decided, we can start to update our photo store code. First, we will want to have an easy way to use a consistent directory for saving. We can create that by adding a method called `getSaveDirectory`. This method can be private and, as a convention, I like to group private code in a private extension:

```
private extension PhotoStore {
    func getSaveDirectory() throws -> NSURL {
        let fileManager = NSFileManager.defaultManager()
        return try fileManager.URLForDirectory(
            .DocumentDirectory,
            inDomain: .UserDomainMask,
            appropriateForURL: nil,
            create: true
        )
    }
}
```

This code first gets a URL representing the documents directory from an Apple-provided class called `NSFileManager`. You may notice that `NSFileManager` has a shared instance that can be accessed through the `defaultManager` class method. We then call the `URLForDirectory` method, give it information indicating that we want the documents directory for the current user, and return the result. Note that this method can throw an error, so we marked our own method as throwing and did not allow any errors to propagate.

Now we can move on to saving all added images to disk. There are a number of things that we will need to be done. First, we need to get the current time stamp. We can do this by creating an `NSDate` instance, asking that for the time stamp and using string interpolation to turn it into a string:

```
let timeStamp = "\(NSDate().timeIntervalSince1970)"
```

`NSDate` instances can represent any sort of time on any date. By default, all `NSDate` instances are created to represent the current time.

Next, we are going to want to append that onto our save directory to get the path where we are going to save the file. For that, we can use the `URLByAppendingPathComponent:` method of `NSURL`:

```
let fullDirectory = directory.URLByAppendingPathComponent(
    timestamp
)
```

This will ensure that the proper path slash is added, if it is not already there. Now we need to make sure that this directory exists before we try to save a file to it. This is done using a method on NSFileManager:

```
NSFileManager.defaultManager().createDirectoryAtURL(
    fullDirectory,
    withIntermediateDirectories: true,
    attributes: nil
)
```

This method can throw if there is an error, which we will need to handle later. It is still considered a success if the directory already exists. Once we are sure that the directory has been created, we will want to create the path to the specific file using the label text:

```
let fileName = "\(self.label).jpg"
let filePath = fullDirectory
    .URLByAppendingPathComponent(fileName)
```

Here we used string interpolation to add a .jpg extension to the file name.

Most importantly, we will need to convert our image to data that can be saved to a file. For that, UIKit provides a function called UIImageJPEGRepresentation that takes the UIImage and returns an NSData instance:

```
let data = UIImageJPEGRepresentation(self.image, 1)
```

The second parameter is a value between zero and one representing the compression quality we want. In this case, we want to save the file at full quality, so we use 1. It then returns an optional data instance, so we will need to handle the scenario where it returns nil.

Finally, we need to save that data to the file path we created:

```
data.writeToURL(filePath, atomically: true)
```

This method on NSData simply takes the file path and a Boolean indicating if we want it to write to a temporary location before it overwrites any existing file. It also returns true or false depending on if it is successful. Unlike directory creation, this will fail if the file already exists. However, since we are using the current time stamp that should never be a problem.

Lets combine all of this logic into a method on our photo structure that we can use later to save it to disk, which throws an error in case of an error:

```
struct Photo {
    // ...

    enum Error: String, ErrorType {
        case CouldntGetImageData = "Couldn't get data from image"
        case CouldntWriteImageData = "Couldn't write image data"
    }

    func saveToDirectory(directory: NSURL) throws {
        let timeStamp = "\(NSDate().timeIntervalSince1970)"
        let fullDirectory = directory
            .URLByAppendingPathComponent(timeStamp)
        try NSFileManager.defaultManager().createDirectoryAtURL(
            fullDirectory,
            withIntermediateDirectories: true,
            attributes: nil
        )
        let fileName = "\(self.label).jpg"
        let filePath = fullDirectory
            .URLByAppendingPathComponent(fileName)
        if let data = UIImageJPEGRepresentation(self.image, 1) {
            if !data.writeToURL(filePath, atomically: true) {
                throw Error.CouldntWriteImageData
            }
        }
        else {
            throw Error.CouldntGetImageData
        }
    }
}
```

First, we define a nested enumeration for our possible errors. Then we define the method to take the root level directory where it should be saved. We allow any errors from the directory creation to propagate. We also need to throw our errors if the data comes back nil or if the `writeToURL:automatically:` method fails.

Now we need to update our `saveNewPhotoWithImage:labeled:` to use the `saveToDirectory:` method. Ultimately, if an error is thrown while saving the photo, we will want to display something to the user. That means that this method will need to just propagate the error, because the model should not be the one to display something to the user. That results in the following code:

```
func saveNewPhotoWithImage(
    image: UIImage,
    labeled label: String
    ) throws -> NSIndexPath
{
    let photo = Photo(image: image, label: label)
    try photo.saveToDirectory(self.getSaveDirectory())
    self.photos.append(photo)
    return NSIndexPath(
        forItem: self.photos.count - 1,
        inSection: 0
    )
}
```

If the saving to directory fails, we will skip the rest of the method so we won't add it to our photos list. That means we need to update the view controller code that calls it to handle the error. First, let's add a method to make it easy to display an error with a given title and message:

```
func displayErrorWithTitle(title: String?, message: String) {
    let alert = UIAlertController(
        title: title,
        message: message,
        preferredStyle: .Alert
    )
    alert.addAction(UIAlertAction(
        title: "OK",
        style: .Default,
        handler: nil
    ))
    self.presentViewController(
        alert,
        animated: true,
        completion: nil
    )
}
```

This method is simple. It just creates an alert with an OK button and then presents it. Next, we can add a function to display any kind of error we will expect. It will take a title for the alert that will pop-up, so we can customize the error we are displaying for the scenario that produced it:

```
func displayError(error: ErrorType, withTitle: String) {
    switch error {
    case let error as NSError:
        self.displayErrorWithTitle(
            title,
            message: error.localizedDescription
        )
    case let error as Photo.Error:
        self.displayErrorWithTitle(
            title,
            message: error.rawValue
        )
    default:
        self.displayErrorWithTitle(
            title,
            message: "Unknown Error"
        )
    }
}
```

We expect either the built-in error type of NSError that will come from Apple's APIs or the error type we defined in our photo type. The localized description property of Apple's errors just creates a description in the locale the device is currently configured for. We also handle any other error scenarios by just reporting it as an unknown error.

I would also extract our save action creation to a separate method so we don't overcomplicate things when we add in our do-catch blocks. This will be very similar to our previous code but we will wrap the call to saveNewPhotoWithImage:labeled: in a do-catch block and call our error handling method on any thrown errors:

```
func createSaveActionWithTextField(
    textField: UITextField,
    andImage image: UIImage
    ) -> UIAlertAction
{
    return UIAlertAction(
        title: "Save",
        style: .Default
```

```
    ) { action in
    do {
        let indexPath = try self.photoStore
            .saveNewPhotoWithImage(
            image,
            labeled: textField.text ?? ""
            )
        self.collectionView.insertItemsAtIndexPaths(
            [indexPath]
        )
    }
    catch let error {
        self.displayError(
            error,
            withTitle: "Error Saving Photo"
        )
    }
    }
}
```

That leaves us with just needing to update the `imagePickerController:didFinish
PickingImage:editingInfo:` method to use our new save action creating method:

```
// ..

alertController.addTextFieldWithConfigurationHandler()
{
    textField in
    let saveAction = self.createSaveActionWithTextField(
        textField,
        andImage: image
    )
    alertController.addAction(saveAction)
}

// ..
```

That completes the first half of permanently storing our photos. We are now saving
the images to disk but that is useless if we don't load them from disk at all.

To load an image from disk, we can use the `contentsOfFile:` initializer of `UIImage`
that returns an optional image:

```
let image = UIImage(contentsOfFile: filePath.relativePath!)
```

To convert our file path URL to a string, which is what the initializer requires, we can use the relative path property.

We can get the label for the photo by removing the file extension and getting the last component of the path:

```
let label = filePath.URLByDeletingPathExtension?
    .lastPathComponent ?? ""
```

Now we can combine this logic into an initializer on our `Photo` struct. To do this, we will also have to create a simple initializer that takes the image and label so that our other code that uses the default initializer still works:

```
init(image: UIImage, label: String) {
    self.image = image
    self.label = label
}

init?(filePath: NSURL) {
    if let image = UIImage(
        contentsOfFile: filePath.relativePath!
        )
    {
        let label = filePath.URLByDeletingPathExtension?
            .lastPathComponent ?? ""
        self.init(image: image, label: label)
    }
    else {
        return nil
    }
}
```

Lastly, we need to have the image store enumerate through the files in the documents directory calling this initializer for each one. To enumerate through a directory, `NSFileManager` has an `enumeratorAtFilePath:` method. It returns an enumerator instance that has a `nextObject` method. Each time it is called, it returns the next file or directory inside the original directory. Note that this will enumerate all children of each subdirectory it finds. This is a great example of the iterator pattern we saw in *Chapter 9, Writing Code the Swift Way – Design Patterns and Techniques*. We can determine if the current object is a file using the `fileAttributes` property. All of that lets us write a `loadPhotos` method like this:

```
func loadPhotos() throws {
    self.photos.removeAll(keepCapacity: true)

    let fileManager = NSFileManager.defaultManager()
```

```
        let saveDirectory = try self.getSaveDirectory()
        let enumerator = fileManager.enumeratorAtPath(
            saveDirectory.relativePath!
        )
        while let file = enumerator?.nextObject() as? String {
            let fileType = enumerator!.fileAttributes![NSFileType]
                as! String
            if fileType == NSFileTypeRegular {
                let fullPath = saveDirectory
                    .URLByAppendingPathComponent(file)
                if let photo = Photo(filePath: fullPath) {
                    self.photos.append(photo)
                }
            }
        }
    }
}
```

The first thing we do in this method is remove all existing photos. This is to protect against calling this method when there are already photos in it. Next, we create an enumerator from our save directory. Then, we use a while loop to continue to get each next object until there are none left. Inside the loop we check if the object we just got is actually a file. If it is and we create the photo successfully with the full path, we add the photo to our photos array.

Finally, all we have to do is make sure this method is called at the appropriate time to load the photos. A great time to do this, considering we want to be able to show errors to the user, is right before the view will be displayed. As the view controllers have a method for right after the view has been loaded, there is also a method called viewWillAppear: that is called every time the view is about to appear. In here we can load the photos and also display any errors to the user with our displayError:withTitle: method:

```
override func viewWillAppear(animated: Bool) {
    super.viewWillAppear(animated)

    do {
        try self.photoStore.loadPhotos()
        self.collectionView.reloadData()
    }
    catch let error {
        self.displayError(
            error,
            withTitle: "Error Loading Photos"
        )
    }
}
```

Now if you run the app, save some photos, and quit it, your previously saved photos will be there when you run it again. We have completed the saving photos functionality!

Summary

This app is far from being something that we could put on the store, but it gives you a good first dive into what it is like to build an iOS app. We have covered how to conceptualize an app and then how to go about making it a reality. We know how to configure an interface in a storyboard, how to run it, and we got into the practical details of saving photos both temporarily and permanently to disk and displaying those in our own custom interface. We even got some practice writing high quality code by ensuring our code sticks with the model-view-controller design pattern as best we can.

Even though we have covered a lot, this clearly isn't enough information to immediately write any other iOS app. The key is to get an insight into what the app development process looks like and to start to feel more comfortable in an iOS app project. All developers spend lots of time searching the documentation and the Internet for how to do specific things on any given platform. The key is being able to take solutions you find on the Internet or in books, determine the best one for your use case, and integrate them effectively into your own code. Over time, you will be able to do more and more on your own without looking it up, but with ever-changing frameworks and platforms, that will always be a part of your development cycle.

With that in mind, I now challenge you to complete the feature list we conceptualized. Figure out how to delete a picture and add whatever other features, usability tweaks, or visual tweaks you want. As I said before, app development is a completely new world to explore. There are so many things that you can tweak, even with this simple app; all of it will help you learn tons.

Coming up in our final chapter, we will look at where you can go from here to become the best Swift developer you possibly can.

12
What's Next? – Resources, Advice, and the Next Steps

At this point, we have covered a lot in the book. Swift is not a small topic and app development itself is orders of magnitude bigger than that. We learned most of Swift but it would not have been practical to cover every little feature of the language and Swift is still a new and evolving language. You are never going to be able to keep everything you've learned in your memory without being able to refer to it later. You can always refer back to this book but Apple's documentation can be a great reference too. Beyond that, if you truly want to become a proficient Swift developer, you can ensure your success by always learning and evolving. It is extremely hard to do that in a vacuum. The best way to ensure that you are keeping up with the times is to follow and participate in the community around whatever topics interest you the most. In this chapter, we will go over how to use Apple's documentation and some suggestions on where you can find and participate in the Swift, iOS, and OS X developer community. More specifically, in this chapter we will cover:

- Apple's documentation
- Forums and blogs
- Prominent figures
- Podcasts

Apple's documentation

Apple puts a lot of time and effort into maintaining its documentation. This documentation can often be a very valuable tool to determine how you are expected to interact with their frameworks.

Xcode actually integrates with the documentation quite well. One of the main ways you can look at the documentation is within the **Quick Help** inspector. You can display it by navigating to **View | Utilities | Show Quick Help Inspector** from the main menu. This inspector shows you the documentation of whatever piece of code you currently have your cursor on. If that particular class, method, or function is a part of Apple's frameworks, you will get some quick help with regards to it, as shown in the following screenshot:

Here the cursor is on UICollectionView, so the **Quick Help** inspector gives us the high-level information about it.

You can also look at the documentation in its own window if you need more information or want to do more exploring. You can open up this window at any time by navigating to **Help | Documentation and API Reference** and you can search for any topic you want. However, you can also jump right to a specific piece of code's documentation by holding the *Option* key and double-clicking on it. For example, if you were to hold the *Option* key and double-click on isSourceTypeAvailable, you would get the following full documentation window:

This window acts very similar to the Web. You can navigate through the documentation by clicking on any of the links or searching for a completely unrelated topic. You can also jump to specific parts of a documentation page using the outline view on the left-hand side of the screen.

This documentation is particularly useful when you already have a sense of what parts of the framework you need to use for a particular task. You can then use this documentation to figure out the specifics of how to properly use that part of the framework. As you get better acquainted with Apple's frameworks, this will become more useful, because it is relatively easy to remember what parts of the framework you use for all of the common tasks, but it is far more difficult and often impractical to remember exactly how they work. However, sometimes the documentation is not enough. The next place you should look for answers is online.

Forums and blogs

Whenever you have a problem or question while programming, odds are almost guaranteed that someone else has already run into it and the odds are also very good that someone has already written about it somewhere. Before you jump right to asking a question on a forum, I strongly recommend that you do your own searching. First of all, you want to save the valuable time of the community members. If they are constantly answering the same questions over and over again, they are dedicating a lot less time to truly new questions. Second, you will often find that you discover the answer for yourself in the process of formulating your thoughts, on how to search for it. Lastly, you will become much better at searching for programming related problems as you practice it more. Forums are usually going to be very slow compared to finding your own answer and obviously time is money.

Most of the time when you use a search engine to look up a problem; you will find two main types of resources with answers: blog posts and forums.

Blog posts

Similar to books, blog posts are fantastic for larger, higher-level considerations. You may search for something, such as: "ways to permanently store information," and you will probably find many blog posts talking about the different ways you can do that. Blog posts are generally better for this because they can discuss the nuances of different solutions and they aren't restricted to target a small problem.

Blog posts can also be great for extremely in-depth and nuanced problems. For example, there are some major and complicated repercussions of our move from 32-bit to 64-bit processors. Truly understanding the underlying problem will be far more valuable for you in moving forward than finding a quick solution for your immediate problem; if you can't find a book, blog posts are ideal to give you that kind of understanding.

Forums

Forms are incredible at giving you very quick solutions to very specific problems. The most common forums are probably `http://stackoverflow.com/` and `forums.developer.apple.com`. On sites like these, there are very dedicated communities of people answering and asking questions. The Apple developer forum even has Apple employees answering questions. Asking good questions is just as important as answering questions well. These sites act not only as a way to get an answer to a new question but as living documentation for people searching for an answer in the future. A well-framed question is going to be more easily answered and more easily found by a search engine.

Stack Overflow has a great documentation on what makes good questions and answers, but generally they should have the following characteristics:

- Be specific and clear about what you are asking for.

- Make it easy for other people to reproduce the problem on their own systems.

- Be respectful of any answerer's time by putting as much effort as you can into the question up front.

The last point is the most important one. You want to phrase your questions to allow someone with more knowledge than you to hone in on the exact problem instead of wasting time on things you could figure out on your own. This will often mean describing all of the things you have tried already and what roadblocks you hit. The clearer you make it that you have put real effort into solving the problem yourself, the better reception you will get from the community and also better answers. I cannot even count all the times that I have figured out the solution to a problem while I was writing up a question on a forum. This type of solution is going to be far more memorable and long lasting than a solution that someone else gives you.

Prominent figures

The more experienced you get at programming with a specific language and/or framework, the more likely you are to get stuck in a pattern of solving problems the same ways over and over again. Odds are that other people have figured out better ways to solve the same problem and someone, somewhere, is talking about it. You have to at least observe the community, even if you are not participating in it yourself.

One of the best ways to follow the community is to follow the prominent figures in it. For example, for Swift, it is a great idea to follow Chris Lattner, the original creator of Swift. While numerous people now develop Swift, he spent more than a year as the sole developer and continues to run the Developer Tools department at Apple. You can follow him on Twitter `@clattner_llvm` and it can also be useful to follow his activity on Apple's Developer forums at `https://devforums.apple.com/people/ChrisLattner`. You can click on the **Email Updates** button to get emails about his activity.

Other than Chris Lattner, there are many other valuable people to pay attention to but only you can decide who is valuable to you. Pay attention to the names you are seeing a lot within the community and find out if they have blogs, podcasts, or any other places you can keep up with what they are saying.

Podcasts

If you are not familiar with podcasts, they are an incredibly valuable way of keeping up with virtually any topic in a relatively passive manner. They are essentially on-demand radio shows that you can subscribe to. You can listen to them whenever you want like when driving, doing housework, or working out. That is why they are particularly valuable: they can turn relatively dull situations into fantastic learning opportunities.

Apple has a podcast app built right into iOS that you can use or there are also numerous other podcast apps on the app store that I recommend you check out. Most of these apps include discovery mechanisms that make it easier to find new podcasts and many podcasts will also talk about other podcasts they recommend.

It is hard to recommend specific podcasts because most development podcasts do not last particularly long. It takes a lot of time and energy to produce a podcast, so many people do it for a while and take long breaks or decide to stop after a while. However, because of the on-demand nature of podcasts, it can still be very valuable to go back and listen to old episodes of podcasts. Three podcasts that are great to get you started are:

- **Core intuition**: Great podcast from prominent developers Daniel Jalkut and Manton Reece about general development topics.

- **Accidental tech podcast**: General, Apple oriented tech discussion from big names in the industry including Marco Arment: a very inspirational developer for me.

- **Under the radar**: A nice and concise podcast that is always 30 minutes or less but often contains valuable nuggets of information centered around independent Apple development. It is hosted by Marco Arment and David Smith, another inspirational developer.

Some podcasts are so valuable and entertaining that you will want to listen to every episode. Others are great for picking and choosing episodes that seem interesting and relevant to you. Whatever you do, I recommend you don't miss out on this free and easy opportunity to keep up with the development community.

Summary

The short length of this chapter is in stark contrast to its importance. If there is one thing I could leave you with after reading this book, it is that the best developers know how to seek out and find solutions for themselves from the many sources available to us. Sometimes those solutions are in books like this one; other times they are in documentation, blog posts, forums, podcasts, or even conversations with other people. The developer that can not only find these solutions, but also integrate and truly understand them is going to be incredibly valuable for the rest of their career. However, if you feel overwhelmed at the beginning, do not fret because we all started there. Focus your energy on one problem at a time and don't settle for a solution that just seems to work. Make sure that you understand every solution you put in place and you will quickly, without even realizing it, become an incredibly proficient developer.

Index

L

lazy evaluation 108, 109
lazy properties
  about 198
  logic to concerned property, localizing 199
  unnecessary memory usage, avoiding 198
  unnecessary processing, avoiding 199
Leaks 152
leaky abstraction 78
loops
  about 22, 23
  while loop 22
lost objects
  about 158
  between objects 158
  with closures 159

M

Mac App Store
  reference 3
member and static functions 42
member constants 41
member variables 41
memory management 137
methods
  overriding 57, 58
model view controller pattern 188-190
mutating method 43

N

named parameters 29
navigation bar 239
nil coalescing operator 87

O

Objective-C
  background 202
  constants 203
  containers 205
  control flow 208
  functions 212, 213
  functions, using 228
  projects 225
  reference types 203, 204

  Swift's relationship 202
  type system 213
  value types 203
  variables 203
Objective-C code
  bridging header 228
  calling, from Swift 227
object-oriented programming
  about 39, 97
  example 109-111
object relationships
  about 147
  strong 147-149
  unowned 150
  weak 149, 150
objects 39
observer pattern
  about 180
  callback 181
  notification center 182
optional
  about 47, 81
  debugging 91-94
  defining 82
  forced unwrapping 85, 86
  nil coalescing operator 87
  optional binding 83-85
  unwrapping 83
optional chaining 87, 88
overriding initializer 54

P

parameterized functions 26, 27
photo
  saving permanently 263-271
  saving temporarily 250-253
photo grid
  populating 254-259
picture taking
  allowing 247-250
playgrounds 7, 8
podcasts
  about 278
  accidental tech podcast 278
  core intuition 278
  under the radar 278